I0199408

Voices

VOICES

TRIBUTES IN MEMORY OF
SHAMAR RINPOCHE,
THE LATE 14TH SHAMARPA

*Tributes, memories, essays, poetry, photographs, and
thoughts in memory of the 14th Shamarpa,
Shamar Rinpoche (1952-2014)
from students, teachers, and friends of
Bodhi Path Buddhist Centers.*

Bird of Paradise Press
Lexington, Virginia

2016, 2017 © Bird of Paradise Press

All rights reserved. No part of this book may be reproduced, stored in or introduced in a retrieval system, or transmitted in any form or by any means (electronic, mechanical, photocopying, recording or otherwise) without the prior written permission from the publisher or author, except for the inclusion of brief quotations in a review or for the private use of readers.

Individual contributors all retain copyright on their individual writings and images.

ISBN: 978-0-9965059-3-2
Library of Congress Control Number: 2016905289

Bird of Paradise Press
1223 N. Lee Highway, #250
Lexington, Virginia, USA

birdofparadisepress.org

Editor: Sharon Gambsy
Designer: Carol Gerhardt

Cover photographs: Kunzig Shamar Rinpoche on both the cover and page 49, courtesy of Peter Simon.
Photographs of cloud formations taken at Shamar Rinpoche's cremation ceremonies on cover, page 53 and 175, courtesy of Yvonne Wong.

Note on photographs in this collection: Centers and students around the world have shared photographs with one another over the years, often without individual photographer attribution. We would like to express gratitude to all those who shared images and also invite any community members to notify the press by writing to office@birdofparadisepress.org whenever a photographer would like to be identified or have their name privately recorded for historical purposes.

TABLE OF CONTENTS

◆ From the Editor

It is my honor and privilege to be a member of the worldwide Bodhi Path family; my life is meaningful beyond measure because of having known and received the blessings of Shamar Rinpoche, and because of the relationships I've developed within our large and colorful community. These relationships have a preciousness that is beyond ordinary; they are deeply meaningful—truly deep and unusually full of meaning.

One by-product of my commitment to our organization has resulted in the development of my role as editor of Bodhi Path's North American magazine, *The Path*. Bodhi Path is a volunteer organization, and I volunteered to shepherd articles into fruition before passing them along to a cadre of proofreaders, co-editors, and our wonderful graphics professional, Carol Gerhardt. I am editor not because I am a trained editor, but rather because things have simply evolved that way.

When Shamar Rinpoche passed away in June 2014, *The Path* team immediately decided to compile a special tribute to our beloved teacher, rather than print the 2014 issue of the magazine we had prepared to go to press. Therefore, this book, *Voices*, is an offshoot of our yearly magazine. This tribute volume represents our compilation of homage, praise, stories, reflections, and memories, although we know that endeavoring to capture Rinpoche's essence is yet another lesson in emptiness. However, moved to pay tribute, we gathered many voices, accruing as many testimonials and photographs as circumstances and time allowed. In August 2014, we began collecting stories and interviews at the Bodhi Path North America annual program. Over the next eighteen months we invited more participation, widening the circle organically through word of mouth, recognizing that for some friends it was too soon or too painful to express the depth of loss and gratitude. We sincerely apologize to anyone whose words weren't included. We acknowledge that we can't comprehend the scope of Shamar Rinpoche's myriad friends and disciples. We deeply regret any omissions.

This project started as an internal newsletter, and some articles originated from audio recordings. The diversity of our voices is reflected in the book. I want to add my personal apology for any mistakes in the transcription or editing of the voices in this book. Additionally, in order to help this collection read cohesively, I made certain grammar and spelling editorial choices, especially in regard to Sanskrit and Tibetan terms, which were often presented differently by different authors from around the globe.

Please accept this attempt to evoke a meager collage of our devotion, our joy, and the tremendous gratitude we share because we have known a true Dharma King, the 14th Kunzig Shamar Rinpoche. Rejoice!

Sharon Gamsby

◆ Introduction

The Sanskrit word *vajra* is often translated as "diamond," and thus, in Tibetan Buddhism, Vajrayana is referred to as the "Diamond Vehicle." A polished cut diamond is luminous, hard, multi-faceted, indestructible, precious, and pure. Metaphorically, it is a means to cut through illusion and reach enlightenment.

Each of the 65 poems, vignettes, essays, prayers, anecdotes, and reminiscences in *Voices* represents a different facet of a truly rare and priceless diamond—the 14th Shamar Rinpoche. This diamond was so brilliant and multi-dimensional that ordinary beings could understand only a few particular aspects of him. Even this volume's evocative photographic montage depicting Rinpoche fails to capture the totality of such a great Bodhisattva.

The contributors to *Voices* include the 17th Karmapa Trinley Thaye Dorje, Shamar Rinpoche's relatives, lamas, khenpos, former assistants, and many disciples from the Americas, Europe, and, to a lesser extent, Asia. Most authors tell of their encounters with Rinpoche and explain the effect he had on them.

The very personal stories in *Voices* reveal how Rinpoche engaged people and transmitted the Dharma to them. Bodhisattvas manifest themselves in myriad ways. So too with Rinpoche: he had the ability and insight to connect with each person in a way that would uniquely reach that individual.

In their efforts to capture the essence of Rinpoche, *Voices* contributors have drawn on a surprisingly wide range of adjectives: *radical … forthright … unimpeachable … exuberant … authentic … kind … unpretentious … impatient … powerful … natural … avuncular … compassionate … genuine … simple … unique … profound … unassuming … joyful … spontaneous … selfless … astute … accessible … playful … skillful … unorthodox … fearless … inspiring … tireless.*

Each of these descriptors is like a single facet of a diamond. Collectively they suggest how extraordinary Rinpoche was, yet they do not fully reveal the perfect fullness of his being. Many more facets to his diamond remain hidden to all but a few who have achieved a high degree of realization.

The 65 "voices" in this tribute volume all respond in one way or another to the compelling, crystal clear voice of Shamar Rinpoche that contributors heard in their lives. How fitting it is, then, that *Voices* includes two of Rinpoche's own teachings. The first is a talk he gave promoting his book *The Path to Awakening*. The second is adapted from his forthcoming magnum opus *Boundless Wisdom* about *mahamudra*.

Among Shamar Rinpoche's many contributions to the Karma Kagyu lineage, his most enduring legacy is as a mahamudra master. Shamar Rinpoche's adamantine voice will echo through the ages!

Edmund H. Worthy

Amitabha, the Buddha
of Infinite Light

Official Address,
June 30, 2014
Karmapa International
Buddhist Institute,
New Delhi, India

◆ The Passing of Kunzig Shamar Rinpoche

Dear Friends,

The Buddhist world has been cast into darkness. Tibetan Buddhism has lost in this life one of its greatest torch-bearers and masters, Kunzig Shamar Rinpoche. The Karma Kagyu tradition has lost a supreme leader and one of our lineage holders—and I have lost my teacher, my spiritual father. I have practiced the Buddha Dharma all of my life, and learned about what death means and how we can use that understanding to do more in life. However, the actual experience of losing Shamar Rinpoche has affected me deeply and personally. I need, and we all need, time to grieve, to focus on our practice, and to move together in peace.

There is great wisdom and compassion in the Buddha Dharma. The mourning period of forty-nine days is just one example of this. It is natural and understandable that everyone is deeply affected by the passing of Shamar Rinpoche. There is a lot of emotion. Many will be asking what now, what next, and have fear for the future. I am speaking to you today to say that there is no need to fear for the future.

In Shamar Rinpoche's final teaching, he said: "You don't need to be afraid of death if you know how to practice in death," and so it is in life. As long as we focus on our practice, stay true to our core, our inner wealth, and our inner values of compassion and wisdom, there is no need to be afraid. There is great teaching in Shamar Rinpoche's passing: the teaching of impermanence, the lesson that all beings—even the Buddha himself—must pass.

Friends, it is very important that as practitioners we are not led by emotion. The forty-nine day period is a time for grieving, for practice, and for processing what has happened. This must be the focus for all of us, including myself. During this time and beyond, we must guard ourselves against thoughts, words, and actions that are led by emotion, cause any harm, or lead to any unnecessary karma. Therefore, this is a time for wisdom. This is a time for responsibility. Right now our focus must be on practice, mourning the loss in this life of our great teacher, to learn from his wisdom and compassion, and to cool our emotions and move together in peace.

On the 31st of July, His Holiness Shamar Rinpoche's physical manifestation (the *kudung*) will be cremated in Kathmandu. As Karmapa, I have the duty, obligation, and honor to preside over the ceremony, along with many great masters of our time. We anticipate that there will be tens of thousands of practitioners in Nepal, and many thousands more of you who would like to be present but are unable to do so. For you, I would like to assure you that focusing on your practice and staying true to yourself will have great, great benefit. In this way, by meditating together on the life, the teaching, and the swift return of His Holiness Shamar Rinpoche, we will all be connected in ways that transcend boundaries of space and time.

As a superior Bodhisattva, Shamar Rinpoche will be reborn due to the power of his compassion for all sentient beings and his prayers to benefit others. May we all pray together for the benefit of all beings, bound together by loving kindness and compassion.

FRIEND
Vesuvius, Virginia

◆ SHAMARPA'S FAREWELL

Listen carefully, you people of my community,
Lend your ear and mind to the sound.
There is no need to despond,
    Take heart!

Since life is just a conditioned state,
    It is transitory;
Since the objective world is light-form,
    It is insubstantial;
Since the path is delusive,
    It has no validity;
Since samsara is emptiness,
    It is unreal;
Since the mind is its conflicting thoughts,
    It has no foundation.
I have seen nothing whatsoever that is ultimately real.

You faithful brothers and sisters assembled here,
There can never be any meeting or parting.
Those forming karmic connection with the guru automatically have his guidance,
And others will be saved by his impartial compassionate emanations.

So there is no reason for sadness, brothers and sisters.

*Composed by
Thaye Dorje, His Holiness the
17th Gyalwa Karmapa
on the full moon day
of June 13th, 2014.*

*Translation by
Trinlay Rinpoche.
Edited by
Lara Braitstein.*

◆ Prayer for the Swift Rebirth of Kunzig Shamar Mipham Chokyi Lodro

Om svasti

Masters of the authentic lineage who unify the wisdom and compassion
Of the Buddhas and Bodhisattvas of countless worlds,
To these infallible objects of refuge, to the Three Jewels and the protectors,
We pray with reverence, one pointedly, with body, speech and mind.

Lord of Sukhavati, the embodiment of all the Buddhas,
You who manifest countless, boundless emanations everywhere,
Venerable Dharmamati (Chokyi Lodro), union of the three families,
May you reign upon the crown of all fortunate beings!

The power of your compassion comes from the expanse of your wisdom,
vast and profound.
Kindness to sentient beings is the sublime display of your emanations.
Inseparable from the three mysteries, in the manner of the lords
of the three families,
Dharmamati, may your sublime emanation manifest soon!

For the benefit of infinite sentient beings throughout infinite aeons
Having perfectly accomplished the bodhisattva's conduct and having attained
The sublime level of unity, you who manifest the activity of emanations
In infinite worlds, may you manifest soon!

Having especially upheld the tradition of Gampopa's lineage,
You were peerless in revealing the sunlight of the Buddha's doctrine.
Dharmamati, root and limbs of the practice lineage,
May your sublime emanation manifest soon!

By the blessing of the truth of the infallible Three Jewels and
By the might of the unhindered activities of
Mahakala and his lordly consort and retinue,
May these aspirations be fulfilled exactly as they were made.

LAMA JIGME RINPOCHE
(Brother of the late Shamar Rinpoche)
Renchen-Ulm, Germany

◆ His Holiness the 14th Shamar Rinpoche passed away on June 11, 2014 at the Bodhi Path Buddhist Center in Renchen-Ulm, Germany.

At the end of May, Shamar Rinpoche visited Dhagpo Kagyu Ling in France for a one-week teaching course. During this time, he told me that everything was now done from his side and he would go on holiday for some time, but before going on holiday, he would spend time in his Bodhi Path Center in Renchen-Ulm, Germany. After visiting Dhagpo, Shamar Rinpoche went to Manchester and London, England to teach, and then arrived in Renchen-Ulm, where he gave his last course. On the evening of June 9, after the course was finished, Shamar Rinpoche announced that he would have his last dinner then. The next day, he had only a light lunch and skipped dinner. On the morning of June 11, just before breakfast, about 7:30 a.m., he passed away.

It was a very clear, calm, and hot day, over 32° Celsius, and this heat wave continued until June 14. Shamar Rinpoche remained in *tukdam* meditation for two days and two nights. In Buddhist tantric teachings, specifically in the cycle of teachings known as *mahamudra*, it is taught that at the time of death the Buddhist tantric practitioner rests the mind in its enlightened knowledge, on the basis of which the practitioner is able to realize the *dharmakaya* (the all-pervasive wisdom of Buddha, the enlightened state, which is wisdom beyond reference). Accordingly, great Buddhist masters who possess such a quality of practice rest their mind in this kind of meditation at the time of death. This is referred to as *tukdam* in the Tibetan language. During this period, his body showed no signs of deterioration at all, remaining continuously seated in the meditation posture. Shamar Rinpoche left his meditation at daybreak on June 13, an auspicious day according to our Buddhist calendar, the full moon day of Saga Dawa.

The significance of this day and time is that the historic Buddha of our era, Buddha Shakyamuni, was born at daybreak more than 2500 years ago on this day. Later in his life, he attained enlightenment under the Bodhi tree in Bodh Gaya, India at daybreak on the very same day; and he also passed into *parinirvana* at daybreak on this same day at the end of his life. Wondrously, the late Shamar Rinpoche ended his tukdam on the same day, and at daybreak. After the *kudung* (Shamar Rinpoche's body) was prepared, he was brought to the chapel of the cemetery in Renchen. Thaye Dorje, His Holiness the 17th Gyalwa Karmapa, came immediately from India and performed pujas all day long with other Dharma masters and monks. Condolences and support were received from state officials such as His Majesty the 4th King of Bhutan, Druk Gyalpo Jigme Singye Wangchuck, and also

Amida Buddha (wood)
Japanese School (17th century)
San Diego Museum of Art
Bequest of Mrs. Cora
Timken Burnett
Bridgeman Images
Used with permission

from masters related to all lineages of Buddhism. Thousands of people from all over the world came to pay their last respects to Shamar Rinpoche.

One outer sign for high-level meditative attainment is a clear and cloudless sky devoid of wind during the tukdam period; this phenomenon indicates the resting of one's mind in the dharmakaya. Another outer sign is a cool breeze that passes through the area; indicating one's manifestation of the two forms, or *kayas*. Yet another outer sign is the clouds gathering at some distance in the sky; this indicates that disciples will come together at the feet of his or her manifested form or kaya.

These were exactly the outer conditions during Shamar Rinpoche's tukdam period. As mentioned earlier, June 11 and 12 were very clear, with calm weather; then from the morning of June 13, when the tukdam period ended, a cool breeze was felt passing through the area, and distant clouds clearly gathered in the sky. Many rainbows appeared, including round ones around the sun, and birds flew directly above the area in special formations, and so on. During the final procession, many people received a red rose, and still today, nearly a year later, they are talking about how these roses are not showing normal signs of withering.

Karmapa invited Shamar Rinpoche's kudung to New Delhi, India, where he stayed about one week, during which time many different masters led meditative practices according to the tradition, day and night, and many lamas came to pay their respects. After this, on July 1, the kudung was brought to Shri Diwakar Vihara Institute in Kalimpong, where practices were again continuously performed, during which thousands of people came every day to pay their last respects.

On July 27, the kudung was transported to the Kingdom of Bhutan and welcomed for two days at the Royal Palace in Paro. The Prime Minister himself carried the kudung into the palace. The senior-most Bhutanese monks performed two days of practices during which His Majesty the 5th King, Druk Gyalpo Jigme Khesar Namgyel Wangchuck, together with members of the royal family and many practitioners, visited to pay their personal last respects according to Bhutanese tradition.

On July 29, the kudung was brought to Kathmandu, Nepal. Many thousands of people lined the streets, waiting all day to have a chance to pray during the passing of the convoy. For three days, different Buddhist groups and Nepalese clans came to receive the blessing of the final presence of Shamar Rinpoche in their country.

The cremation of Shamar Rinpoche was performed on July 31, on the most auspicious day of Chokhor Duchen, when Buddha Shakyamuni gave his first sermon after having attained enlightenment. Shamar Rinpoche was born on this same auspicious date of the Tibetan calendar in 1952.

The kudung was prepared on the previous night, according to all the traditional requirements. During the early morning of July 31, the kudung was placed in the cremation stupa on the highest rooftop of Sharminub Institute. The principle

Dharma holders and teachers of different lineages conducted his last rites. Karmapa led Gyalwa Gyamtso practice, Lektso Lopon Rinpoche led the Akshobhya practice, Luding Khen Rinpoche led the Hevajra practice, Tulku Ugyen Rinpoche led the Dzokchen Kunzang Thuktik practice, Trungram Gyaltrul Rinpoche led the Khorlo Demchog practice, and Beru Khyentse Rinpoche led the Dorje Pamo practice, all accompanied by many other Karma Kagyu lineage holders.

The highest lineage holders positioned themselves around the kudung in all four directions and performed the lighting of fire. Everyone present witnessed a very light rain, like flower petals falling from the sky. In the course of all the simultaneous rituals, the strength of the fire increased and the thick smoke arose in the windless sky, going in turn in each of the four directions and then rising straight up in the sky for a period of time.

Thousands of people from Nepal, the surrounding countries, and all over the world gathered and joined in prayer on this occasion. They all witnessed the unusual glory of the sun shining behind an immense cloud at the end of the ceremony. Subsequently, a clear rainbow appeared in the opposite direction.

A few days before his passing, Shamar Rinpoche gave his last interview and reminded us never to forget: "Everything, everything is impermanent. Therefore, we should not be surprised when we see that something has changed."

SONAM RINCHEN
Hong Kong

◆ MY PERFECT GURU

Buddhism means Enlightenment: nothing more.
It is not a narrative or formula of sorts.
Words don't give you enlightenment;
Practice will.

If Buddha exists: it is about how but not what.
Therefore, knowledge is superfluous—
like sitting for an exam, to be rewarded if you pass.

Honesty instead is essential in this enterprise.
For that, perfect Self-Knowledge is needed:
You are your own judge in your own practice!

Therefore not only proffer no judgment,
but invite none also.
The Perfect Guru: He does not judge,
nor will he give answers. Buddha knows!

KARMA TRINLAY RINPOCHE
Paris, France

✦ IN LOVING MEMORY OF THE 14TH SHAMARPA MIPHAM CHOKYI LODRO

The quick and unexpected passing of our root teacher, protector, and friend causes us all great sorrow. I feel a greater sadness than if I had lost the most precious and magical wish-fulfilling gem itself. In our grief, if we reflect with loving appreciation on Rinpoche's lasting accomplishments and example, I believe we may see the infinite blessings he has bestowed upon us, and we will realize how fortunate we were to have known him and been his disciples. This may bring us a degree of consolation and help give meaning to our own lives.

Shamar Rinpoche was an extraordinary and marvelous being. Whether followers or not, everyone who was in his presence would agree that he was special. He was genuine, unpretentious, and simple, yet regal and graceful, always joyful and spontaneous, and at the same time profoundly wise. Above all, he was truly selfless, the embodiment of pure kindness itself. One might consider him a marvel of nature, but actually he was a marvel of Awakening, a Buddha, or, according to tradition, one of the manifestations of the Buddha of Infinite Light—Amitabha.

In this tribute to him, I offer my understanding of who he was and what he achieved in his 62 years of mortal life. A tribute such as this can only examine him in broad brushstrokes. It would take a lengthy book to even begin to do him justice.

To understand Rinpoche, it is important for us to learn the spiritual and historical background of his life, see how he lived in accordance with the principles of the bodhisattva's altruistic ideal, and how he fulfilled the great responsibilities that were passed on to him.

The 14th Shamarpa was, from 1981 to 2014, the head and principal lineage holder of the Karma Kagyu, also known as Kamtsang, order[1] of Buddhism, which is predominant in the Himalayas and is now quite well-established internationally. As the Shamarpa, he was regarded by tradition as a buddha's emanation in the form of a bodhisattva—in other words, an awakened being who chooses to carry the burdens of ordinary life so as to benefit others directly. Such altruistic motivation deeply characterized all of Shamar Rinpoche's activities. He had an inexhaustible capacity and desire to help sentient beings without discrimination and, above all, to inspire them.

---

1. I'm using the word *order* to translate two terms: ཆོས་ལུགས་ (spiritual tradition) and, within the historical context, བསྟན་པ་ (dispensation or presentation). I understand the term *order* to designate a particular system of spiritual practice and all those who are devoted and engaged in its practices. The lineage (བརྒྱུད་པ་) is the unbroken line of successive gurus (རྡོ་རྗེ་འཛིན་པ་) who each have mastered the teachings and gained realization. The 14th Shamarpa is the 42nd master in the unbroken succession of realized gurus of the Karma Kagyu lineage originating from the Buddha.

According to Mahayana teachings, an awakened being is considered, through his or her realization, to have the ability to manifest simultaneously an infinite number of emanations in various places to help other beings. The Shamarpas are believed to be a series or line of such emanations, manifesting to serve the historical Buddha's activity and to benefit the world. As recorded in a prophecy within the Bhadrakalpita sutra, the Shamarpa's coming was said to have been foretold by the historical Buddha Shakyamuni himself.

The Karmapa (founder of the Karma Kagyu order) and the Shamarpa are regarded as two different manifestations of the same awakened being. The second Karmapa, Karma Pakshi (1204-1283), foretold that he would take rebirth in the future as two different emanations. The third Karmapa, Rangjung Dorje (1284-1339), declared his principal disciple Drakpa Sengge (1283-1349) to be his equal in realization, and offered him a red replica of his own black crown. Then the 4th Karmapa, Rolpe Dorje (1340–1383) reaffirmed in Khacho Wangpo (1350-1405) the continuation of the second emanation of Karma Pashi.[2] Thereafter, the two incarnation lines were always known in Tibetan as the "Karmapa Shanagpa" and the "Karmapa Shamarpa," literally the black-crowned Karmapa and the red-crowned Karmapa.

The Karmapas are the first to have institutionalized the unique form of succession through rebirths or reincarnations known as the *tulku* system. This method of succession was later adopted by other Buddhist orders of Tibet, notably with the Dalai Lamas of the Gelug order, which emerged much later, in the 15th century.

As the two main figures of the Karma Kagyu lineage, the Karmapas and Shamarpas have alternatively recognized each other in their respective positions—thus producing two of the most famous lines of reincarnates in history. Incarnations within this line have never failed to prove themselves worthy of their illustrious predecessors in erudition and spiritual attainment, as well as in accomplishments for the welfare of sentient beings.

It is mainly to the deeds of the Karmapas and Shamarpas that we owe the conservation of the historical Buddha Shakyamuni's legacy in all its aspects. Within the Karma Kagyu institutions, they emphasized both the instructions of the great accomplished masters (*mahasiddhas*) of India brought to Tibet by Marpa (1012-1097), and the Mahayana approach stressed by the great Bengali master Atisha (980-1054), for nearly a thousand years. In particular, they maintained the ultimate legacy of the Buddha as transmitted through the very special and unique teachings known as *mahamudra*. The practices of the Karma Kagyu order are, therefore, renowned for focusing directly on contemplative experience, beyond the ritualistic or dialectical approaches more common within other orders of Buddhism.

2. The Shamarpa, as the second incarnation line of Karma Pakshi, is also associated with previous Indian and Tibetan masters, regarded as his earlier incarnations. In particular, Dasananda ཚིལ་པོ་དགའ་ (11th century), a disciple of Tilopa (c. 988–1069); Sarvavid གུན་རིག (11th century), the pupil of Naropa (c. 1016–1100); Tsultrim Pal (1098–1132), a disciple of Gampopa (1079–1153) and Rechungpa (1110–1193); and the masters Namkha O (1133–1199) and Tashi Drakpa (1200–1282) two eminent students of the 1st and 2nd Karmapa, respectively. More generally the Shamarpas are considered to be the emanations of the Buddha Ratnanga དཀོན་མཆོག་ཡན་ལག as well as the Buddha Amitabha.

The activity of the Karmapas and Shamarpas brought the Karma Kagyu order great renown in the regions of Tibetan culture as well as in their neighboring countries. Particularly during the 15th, 16th, and the first half of the 17th century, they were preeminent within Tibet. Because of this, some early Shamarpas also had to bear important responsibilities of state. The most notable example is the 4th Shamarpa, Chodrak Yeshe (1453-1524), who was asked to fulfill the religious responsibilities of the throne of Tibet during the Phagmodrupa dynasty at the turn of the 16th century. His spiritual accomplishment and erudition led many of the great Buddhist scholars of that time, even from different orders, to consider him as their principal spiritual master.

Later, the fame and prestige of the Shamarpas remained undiminished, despite the general decline of the Karma Kagyu institutions and forced conversion of almost all their monasteries to the Gelug order in the aftermath of the Mongol invasion of Tibet in 1640. Because of his prestige, foreign language skills, and presence in Nepal, the 10th Shamarpa, Mipham Chodrup Gyatso (1741-1792), was solicited by both Tibetan and Nepalese authorities to mediate the Tibetan currency's minting rights and valuation issue. This ultimately led to what is now known as the Sino-Nepalese War (1788-1792). However, the 10th Shamarpa's cooperation was used against him by influential Tibetan aristocrats who sought to mitigate their losses in this war; falsely accusing the 10th Shamarpa of instigating the war, they confiscated all of his assets, coercing his seat monastery Yangpachen to convert to the state's Gelug order, and succeeded in convincing the Tibetan government to enforce a prohibition against the enthronement of any future Shamarpas.

Recognized by the Karmapas, the line of Shamarpa incarnations nonetheless continued, secretly and unofficially. According to a prophesy of the 5th Shamarpa Konchog Yenlag (1526-1583), he would take rebirth several times as the Karmapa's relative. Thus, the 11th Shamarpa was Chokyi Wangpo (c.1805–1880),[3] the brother of the 14th Karmapa; and the 12th Shamarpa was Jamyang Chokyi Nyima (c.1892–1947), the son of the 15th Karmapa (1871–1922). They were both great masters in their own right. The 13th incarnation, Trinlay Kunchap (1948–1950), passed away in infancy.

After the ban imposed by the Tibetan state on the Shamarpa for political purposes, other rinpoches of the Karma Kagyu order, most notably the Tai Situpas, fulfilled some of the main functions normally exercised by the Shamarpas, such as finding and recognizing the Karmapa. When the 14th Shamarpa was recognized privately soon after birth by the 16th Karmapa (1924-1981), it remained uncertain whether the ban imposed upon his predecessors could be lifted, and if the incarnation would be allowed to fully exercise his spiritual functions in Tibet.

Shamar Rinpoche was born in 1952 amongst auspicious signs into the Athup family, which was quite prominent in the kingdom of Derge, located in what is now the Tibetan autonomous prefecture within China's Sichuan Province. His family produced a number of political and religious leaders. His father, who died when

3. Precise dates of the three previous Shamarpas are unknown. The 14th Shamarpa is sometimes counted as the 11th when considering the official throne holders, or the 12th Shamarpa when considering only the ones who had been enthroned (including privately), or also as the 13th because Trinlay Kunchap may be excluded, as he passed away at the age of two before, in fact, being properly recognized.

Rinpoche was a year old, was active politically, and several uncles were respected rinpoches. Most notable among them was the 16th Karmapa.

In 1956, their mother sent Rinpoche and his older brother Jigme Rinpoche to the Karmapa's main seat, Tsurphu Monastery, in central Tibet. For the next three years, they lived there with their uncle, but were not considered part of the monastic community—they led a carefree existence and did not receive any formal training or schooling.

A few months after his arrival in Tsurphu, Rinpoche first revealed his identity as the Shamarpa. During a major ceremony attended by people from different parts of Tibet, Rinpoche pointed to a group of pilgrims who appeared to be nomads. He told them they were his monks. As it happened, they actually were monks from the monastery of Yangpachen, the historical seat of the Shamarpas. Astounded, they immediately asked for his blessing.

The following day, properly dressed in their monk's robes, they requested an audience with the Karmapa and expressed their eagerness to have Rinpoche return to Yangpachen with them. The Karmapa refused, explaining that he couldn't publicly proclaim Rinpoche as the Shamarpa because of the ban the Tibetan government still held in effect against the recognition of the Shamarpa.

In 1957, Rinpoche joined the 16th Karmapa for an extended trip to Sikkim, India, and Nepal, and on their way back to Tsurphu, they stopped at Yangpachen. Although the monastery was administered by the Gelug order, the statues of the previous Shamarpas had not been removed from the shrines, though the red crowns of the figures had been replaced with the distinctive yellow hats of the Gelug hierarchs. The original crowns were left on the laps of the seated images. As Rinpoche was carried around into the different chapels, he pointed—without error—to the different statues of previous Shamarpas and said each time, "This is me," and pointing to the red crowns, "That is my hat." When he saw certain objects belonging to his previous incarnations, he exclaimed, "This is mine!"

His Holiness the 14th Dalai Lama—the head of state of Tibet—paid a rare formal visit to Tsurphu in 1956, at the invitation of the 16th Karmapa. The Karmapa took this occasion to request his honored guest to lift the sanction imposed on the incarnation line of the Shamarpas. The Dalai Lama agreed in principle to have his government do so, but said the time was not yet appropriate to formally rescind the ban because of the ongoing turmoil in Tibet. The Karmapa took advantage of the Dalai Lama's tacit agreement, privately enthroning Rinpoche as the 14th Shamarpa during an internal ceremony at Tsurphu. From then on he was known as Dorje Rinpoche.

The Chinese Communist invasion in 1959 forced the 16th Karmapa and many of his countrymen to leave Tibet. The Karmapa's party traveled to Bhutan, where Rinpoche and his brother remained with a few others. At the invitation of the King of Sikkim, the Karmapa established his new seat at the old Karma Kagyu monastery of Rumtek, and Shamar Rinpoche soon joined him. Most of the important Karma Kagyu rinpoches, as well as many important masters from other orders, such as Dilgo Khyentse Rinpoche, had regrouped there around the Karmapa. Rinpoche undertook the traditional monastic curriculum, memorizing the Karma Kagyu liturgy and studying Buddhist scriptures. He proved to be particularly gifted in learning, thanks to his exceptional intelligence, his ability to master subtle and complex notions, his innovative mind, and his uncommon photographic memory.

In 1960, the 16th Karmapa bestowed upon him the Kagyu Ngag Dzo and the Dam Ngag Dzo, two of the most important collections of empowerments, transmissions, and key instructions that respectively gather the heart and source of the spiritual legacy of all of the Kagyu orders and the eight great practice lineages of Buddhism that were brought from India to Tibet.

In 1964, Rinpoche was officially enthroned as the Shamarpa. The 16th Karmapa elevated him publicly to the highest position beyond himself, within the Karma Kagyu order, and appointed him as his main heir and as the next lineage holder. On this occasion, the 16th Karmapa addressed a prayer of long life to the Shamarpa, in which he wrote:

The most exalted, the lord of the lands of snow is Avalokiteshvara.
The coalescence of his essence is the glorious Karmapa.
Inseparable from his three mysteries, in the manner of the three lords,
Is his manifestation, the great emanation; the majestic sun,
Whom I invest now as sovereign of the practice lineage's order.
By the power of scattering auspicious flowers of excellent virtue
Combined with the true words of the rishi's truthfulness
May he successfully and everlastingly be the sovereign of the order.[4]

The Dalai Lama's approval was not necessary, as he no longer held political authority. Nevertheless, out of courtesy the Karmapa sought to secure his consent. Since the Dalai Lama and his government were in exile and had lost their dominion, the reinstatement of the Shamarpa was no longer an issue for them. The 14th Dalai Lama personally performed the traditional "hair cutting" ceremony for the 14th Shamarpa at his seat in Dharamsala, India.

In the following years at Rumtek, Shamar Rinpoche dedicated himself fully to the study of the Buddhist classics—Abhidharma, Vinaya, Pramana, Madhyamaka, and Prajnaparamita—and to putting the essence of the numerous transmissions he received from the Karmapa and other masters into practice. Rinpoche demonstrated his prodigious nature in many ways. To the great amazement of his teachers and fellow students, Rinpoche would raise questions no one had thought of and propose original solutions to complex problems.

For example, at one point Rinpoche found that the arguments he had heard explaining how rebirth was possible were unconvincing. Knowing that it was an important point of the teaching that needed an irrefutable explanation, Rinpoche thought about it carefully. One morning, as he was struggling to resolve this, the great Buddhist master Vasubandhu (c. 4th century) appeared to him in a vision and gave him a simple yet pertinent solution in verse.[5]

---

4. ཞུ་དག་ཚོང་པར་འཛིན་པ་འཛིང་སྐུ་འཕྲེང་བཅུ་གཉིས་པ་ཆེན་པོ་མཆོག་གི་ཞབས་བརྟན་སྐྱོན་ཆགས་རྡོ་རྗེའི་ལུང་ཚོ་རྒལ་བའི་སྐུ་སྤྲུངས་ལས། འཕགས་མཆོག་གངས་ཅན་མགོན་པོ་སྤྱན་རས་གཟིགས། ཌོ་གཅིག་བསྲོན་དཔལ་ལྡན་ཀརྨ་པའི། གསང་བ་གསུམ་དབྱེར་མེད་རིགས་གསུམ་མགོན་པོའི་ཚུལ། གང་དེའི་རྣམ་འཕྲུལ་མཆོག་སྤྲུལ་ཉིན་བྱེད་དབང་། སྒྲུབ་བརྒྱུད་བསྟན་པའི་བདག་པོར་མངའ་གསོལ་ཞིང་། ཨེ་ལེགས་ཤིས་པའི་མེ་ཏོག་འཕྲོར་བ་དང་། ཌྲང་སྲོང་བདེན་པའི་བདེན་ཚིག་རྩང་འཕྲེལ་བསྒྲུབས། བསྲུབ་པའི་བདག་པོར་ཏག་བརྟན་རབ་རྒྱས་ཤོག །

5. Rinpoche kindly repeated the verse to me. I provide a translation of it at the conclusion of this tribute.

During this period, Rinpoche received transmissions such as the Gya Chen Ka Dzo, the collected teachings of Jamgon Kongtrul the great, and the collection of Sadhanas assembled by the 9th Karmapa known as the Chig She Kun Drol. Most importantly, the Karmapa imparted the instructions of mahamudra, including the 9th Karmapa's "Three Cycles of Mahamudra;" the Indian sources of mahamudra teaching gathered by the 7th Karmapa known as the Chag Chen Gya Zhung; and all of Gampopa's teachings, as well as oral instructions that had never been put into writing.

As he was destined to be his sole successor, in 1976 the Karmapa for the second time bestowed the Kagyu Ngag Dzo upon Shamar Rinpoche in much greater detail. In 1980, the year before his passing, the Karmapa gave to the Shamarpa alone the lineage's very special and unique transmission of "Ultimate Realization," which had been passed—without interruption—from lineage holder to lineage holder, from the Buddha Vajradhara and Tilopa up to the 16th Karmapa himself.

Besides transmissions from the Karmapa, Shamar Rinpoche also received many important and rare transmissions from several other accomplished masters. For example, he received from Dilgo Khyentse Rinpoche (1910-1991) the Nyingthig cycle and the teachings of Longchen Rabjam; from Kalu Rinpoche (1905-1989), the Six Dharmas of Naropa and the complete transmission of the Shangpa lineage teachings; and from Ugyen Rinpoche (1920-1996), the Rinchen Terdzo and the Chokling Tersar.

In 1985, following the Karmapa's advice, Shamar Rinpoche had the distinction of obtaining hidden key mahamudra instructions never committed to writing from Nenang Pawo Rinpoche (1912-1991), the last main living disciple of the 15th Karmapa. Later, Rinpoche also received a unique oral transmission that the Karmapa had given to Lama Gendun Rinpoche (1918-1997) alone; with instructions to later transmit it to the Shamarpa and the next Karmapa. This transmission related to the practices of transforming and mastering the process of life and death, which empowered the practitioner with the ability to communicate directly with Buddhas in their respective realms. No other practitioner or teacher of Rinpoche's generation was able to receive—let alone master—these particular transmissions.

In this way, Rinpoche was—in addition to being a great Buddhist scholar and holder of the triple ordination of pratimoksha, bodhisattva and vidyadhara vows—the true guardian of the Buddha's ultimate legacy. He had an unparalleled knowledge of the Buddha's teachings, and through practice he gained not only experience, but also the actual realization of awakening, as the extraordinary example of his actions confirms.

This was, to my understanding, Rinpoche's greatest quality. He did not just hold a historical title and position. He actually embodied, through his spiritual realization, its true meaning and function. He was in this way truly equal to all his predecessors: the Shamarpa, a Mahasiddha, and an unsurpassable lineage holder. Thus, he was able to unerringly guide disciples towards their well-being and awakening.

The 14th Shamarpa's activity was curtailed by several circumstances that were not of his making. First, he had to re-establish a highly responsible position that had been dormant for nearly two centuries. Stepping into the position, he did not have a pre-existing administration to help him; as an exile in India, he could not rely on the normal support system he would have benefited from in Tibet. Furthermore, although he had not received a formal Western education, he nonetheless had to deal with the modern world in which the teachings of the Karma Kagyu lineage had started to spread for the very first time as the result of the 16th Karmapa's wishes and activity. In spite of these challenges, Rinpoche's great capacities and eagerness to benefit sentient beings were manifest from an early age.

As the Karmapa's destined heir and regent, Rinpoche represented him in numerous functions, traveling to teach in different Karma Kagyu centers and monasteries. In the late 1970s, he restored the historical Karma Raja Mahavihara temple founded by his predecessors next to the Swayambhunath stupa in Kathmandu, Nepal.

After the parinirvana of the 16th Karmapa in 1981, Rinpoche fully assumed the responsibilities of leading the Karma Kagyu order. He oversaw Rumtek Monastery and guided the Karma Kagyu institutions—numbering over nine hundred—founded across the world under the blessing of the 16th Karmapa. Fulfilling the Karmapa's wish, Rinpoche published a new edition of the Buddhist canon's Tengyur corpus—240 volumes primarily containing Sanskrit exegesis in Tibetan translation—printing hundreds of copies and offering them to monasteries and temples throughout India and Tibet. Rinpoche also saw to the completion of projects the Karmapa had left unfinished. One notable example was the Karmapa International Buddhist Institute built in New Delhi, India, which was inaugurated in 1990.

In the late 1980s, the Chinese government granted the request of the monks of Yangpachen to revert to their original denomination and rejoin the Karma Kagyu order. The monastery had been completely destroyed after the communist takeover and the Cultural Revolution. The reconstruction of the monastery and retreat center, and more recently the Buddhist Academy, were all completed thanks to Shamar Rinpoche's support and guidance.

On August 2, 1993, the Karmapa's main seat of Rumtek in Sikkim was unlawfully taken over by certain Tibetan factions, namely the present 12th Tai Situpa and his followers, who supported the Chinese Communist Party's recognition of a 17th Karmapa. With the backing of the then Chief Minister of Sikkim Mr. Bhandari, whom they had bribed, these people violently evicted all the monks, as well as all of the monastery's rightful caretakers, who had been chosen by the 16th Karmapa. This act violated both Buddhist ethics and Indian law, and damaged all that the previous Karmapa had set up. Daily practices and ceremonies that had been perpetuated for almost a millennium were interrupted for the first time. The Karmapa's monks of Rumtek were subsequently left homeless and without support. Shamar Rinpoche assisted them in all material and spiritual matters. He ensured, even in these difficult times, that their needs would be fulfilled and that the thousand-year-old Karma Kagyu order's intangible cultural heritage would be perpetuated and preserved intact.

In 2002, Rinpoche founded the Shri Diwakar Institute for higher Buddhist studies in Kalimpong, a primary school for young monks near Darjeeling in India, and a three-year retreat center in Pharping, Nepal. He thereby perpetuated the historical ties of his predecessors with the Buddhist communities of Nepal and the Himalayan regions. One of Rinpoche's main aims was education and the preservation of the Buddha's legacy for future generations in the modern world. For that purpose, one of his more ambitious projects is the Sharminub Institute on the outskirts of Kathmandu, Nepal. Construction of this large complex began in 2003 and is now nearing completion. As Shamar Rinpoche considered that the perpetuation of the purity of monastic discipline is crucial, a special monastery was built on the higher grounds of Sharminub. It is designed to accommodate elder monks who are committed to practicing mahamudra meditation and strictly following the 253 rules of the Vinaya—the Buddhist monastic code. Not only did Rinpoche provide the monks and disciples in all these different institutions and monasteries with education, but he also cared for most of their basic needs—food, clothing, and medical support.

The 14th Shamarpa's activity was, however, mostly international. He traveled constantly, sometimes going around the world several times in a year. Rinpoche had a great number of disciples across the world, the majority being from the Himalayan region, but he also had many close and devoted disciples in the Far East and in the West.

To committed disciples in the setting of the traditional retreat centers, he imparted the Vajrayana empowerments and instructions for their practice. For example, from 1984 onwards Rinpoche guided the Dhagpo Kundreul Ling retreat centers in France, as well as their affiliate retreat centers elsewhere in Europe, where he transmitted all the necessary transmissions to many hundreds of disciples committed to practicing in retreat. Rinpoche also cared for the monastic institutions in the West, and encouraged the establishment of full ordination for women within the Karma Kagyu order for the first time.

To the greater number of his disciples, Rinpoche gave the precious Mahayana teachings on cultivating loving kindness, meditation, and especially the practice leading to Buddha Amitabha's Pure Land of Bliss, Sukhavati. Rinpoche particularly emphasized the teachings of mind training known as *lojong* and the unsurpassable teachings of mahamudra.

In this regard, starting in 1996, Rinpoche founded a new international network of meditation centers called Bodhi Path. He developed these for lay practitioners, wishing them to be places where anyone from any cultural background could study and practice, in their own language, the genuine teachings of the Buddha. He designed them as places perfectly integrated into the secular modern world, free of the Tibetan cultural framework or any sectarian bias. He didn't want these places to be, or even appear to be, religious or cultural, but rather to be places where anyone would be comfortable to pursue the understanding and experience of the natural reality of their mind, rationally and without bias, in order to gain greater well-being in their own lives as well as benefit others. Rinpoche delineated precise guidelines for study and practice, drawing on the most profound Buddhist teachings he deemed suitable for our present day.

Rinpoche considered the Buddha's true message to be more than a set of beliefs and a faith. Rather, at the core of the Buddha's message is a genuine science of the true reality of mind's nature that can greatly benefit people. Rinpoche believed that if a point of Buddhist doctrine did not correspond to reality, it should be abandoned. Rinpoche successfully convened several symposia called "Sciences of Mind," gathering Buddhist thinkers and highly trained scientists. They discussed and compared Buddhist and scientific understanding of the mind and its nature. Many interesting parallels were found, and the basis for further collaboration was established.

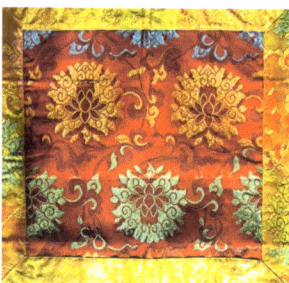

The limited space of this tribute does not allow a complete and precise description of all of Rinpoche's various altruistic activities, but a few important deeds may be briefly mentioned. For example, Rinpoche, in his constant concern for the well-being of the world, established the foundation Shanti Path for the purpose of helping and educating underprivileged women and orphans in India and Nepal; and the Infinite Compassion Foundation for the care and humane treatment of animals around the world, especially in China, where animals are commonly handled with much cruelty. In addition to his dedication to the Karma Kagyu lineage, whenever he could, Rinpoche also helped and supported many other charitable projects started by others.

There is also Rinpoche's prolific writing. As a scholar and talented poet in Tibetan, Rinpoche wrote a number of books on diverse subjects—ranging from traditional commentaries on Buddhist classics to practice manuals, biographies, historical studies, original philosophical treatises, and political theory in pursuit of describing the most ideal and transparent democratic system. Rinpoche thought that his concept for a democratic system could become especially useful for Nepal in the future.

However, above all, one of the most important accomplishments of the 14th Shamarpa—towards which he dedicated his greatest efforts—was the installation of the genuine 17th Karmapa Thaye Dorje.

The Shamarpa's position naturally carries many responsibilities, the most important of which is unquestionably the pure continuation of the Karmapa's spiritual legacy and, for that sake, the finding of the genuine emanation of the Karmapa.

The 17th Karmapa Trinley Thaye Dorje was born as Tenzin Khyentse in Lhasa, Tibet, on May 6, 1983 to the 3rd Mipham Rinpoche and his wife Dechen Wangmo. At a very young age, when usually an infant is still unable to speak, he clearly declared on several occasions, notably in the presence of an old disciple of the 16th Karmapa, that he was the Karmapa.

Early in 1986, the most senior master of the Sakya order, Chogye Trichen Rinpoche (1920-2007), had a very vivid vision of the Karmapa, and the same day a pilgrim offered him a picture of the infant Tenzin Khyentse. This was clear evidence to him that this child was the actual rebirth of the 16th Karmapa. Changing his schedule, he immediately went from Kathmandu to New Delhi to see Shamar Rinpoche to convey his vision and the coincidence.

Prior to this, an older and spiritually accomplished practitioner, who had received a detailed prophecy from the 16th Karmapa regarding his next incarnation, confidentially informed Shamar Rinpoche of this prophecy. Its indications coincided perfectly in designating the same child, born in 1983.[6] Furthermore, Rinpoche later learned that the 1st Mipham, Jamyang Namgyal Gyamtso (1846–1912), prophesized that his future incarnation would father a Karmapa.

6. The 16th Karmapa had also given indications to other close disciples and friends which all confirm Thaye Dorje as the unmistakable Karmapa. As an example, I shall disclose what I personally witnessed from the 16th Karmapa, which I have never previously mentioned to anyone, including Shamar Rinpoche, until Karmapa Thaye Dorje finally arrived in New Delhi. Although I was only a six-year-old boy, I clearly remember that when accompanied by my father, I saw at Queen Mary's Hospital in Hong Kong the 16th Karmapa for the last time. He told us then not to be sad, we would meet him again in the future, and he said specifically not to forget that he would come back after a year and a half and before two years. This time frame he gave to my father and me corresponds precisely to when Karmapa Thaye Dorje's birth took place.

In addition, Shamar Rinpoche performed special divinations in front of several sacred shrines in Nepal, and without exception, each time the signs corroborated, affirming beyond any possible doubt that this child was the genuine 17th Karmapa. Nevertheless, as the unmistakable recognition of the Karmapa was of the utmost importance, during a contemplative retreat Shamar Rinpoche undertook special examinations, which led to clear visions that revealed to him, with absolute certainty, that this child was the genuine emanation of the 16th Karmapa.

Subsequently, Shamar Rinpoche discreetly sent people on three occasions to assess the child, starting in 1987 with Lopon Tsechu Rinpoche (1918-2003), who was traveling to Lhasa for an official event. When one of these search parties, without revealing their purpose, approached the boy, he displayed his clairvoyance, saying: "Have you not come here to find me?"

Shamar Rinpoche undertook all of this in absolute secrecy. He didn't inform any other rinpoche or even his closest relatives, as he feared external and political interference. If the 17th Karmapa were to get trapped in politics, he would lose the freedom to fulfill his spiritual activity. Later Rinpoche even traveled incognito to Tibet in an attempt to meet with the reincarnation and bring him personally to freedom in India. However, Chinese surveillance did not allow him to go anywhere near the young boy or his parents.

Starting in the early 1990s, Rinpoche was faced with a great number of obstacles set up by formidable parties outside of and within the Karma Kagyu order, such as the Chinese government, which sought to take control of the Karmapa; and Tai Situpa, who openly collaborated with them. Because of this situation, Shamar Rinpoche couldn't, for the child's security, immediately reveal to the public the identity of the genuine 17th Karmapa.

Since the start of the Karma Kagyu order, temporal political powers, such as China or Tibet, never had claimed any legitimate authority or right to intervene in the recognition of a Karmapa, which was not the case for the Dalai Lamas. The principal lineage holder of the Karma Kagyu order, with the support of the Karmapa's administration, always recognized the Karmapa. It was through the lineage holder's clairvoyant ability and, in many instances, also with the help of precise written or oral prophecies left by the previous Karmapa, that his successor was found. The Shamarpas were the highest spiritual authority in the Karma Kagyu order after the Karmapa, and, when alive, they were the principal lineage holders, taking precedence over all other rinpoches in the recognition of the Karmapa.

Regardless of the above-mentioned historical and Buddhist considerations, or for that matter even communism's own physicalist beliefs,[7] the Chinese government passed legislation proclaiming their right to recognize Buddhist reincarnates, or "living Buddhas" as they call them. Only those officially recognized by the government would be allowed to teach in China. In this way, the government could control Buddhist orders in Tibet. In 1992, they officially inaugurated this new policy with the enthronement of their "17th Karmapa." The Chinese government decided their first official recognition of a reincarnate was going to be from the first and oldest line of reincarnated Buddhist masters in history: the Karmapa.

---

7. The belief that rebirth is impossible because the mind is thought to be a by-product of the body.

All of this was done with the support of Tai Situpa, the third highest-ranking rinpoche in the Karma Kagyu order. He and other influential rinpoches such as Akong (1939-2013), for example, had developed close ties and interests in China starting in the mid-1980s. During one of his trips to eastern Tibet in the late 1980s, Tai Situpa picked the boy Apogaga, later named Ogyen Trinley, as his candidate for the 17th Karmapa because of the boy's physical resemblance to the 16th Karmapa. Subsequently, Tai Situpa also forged a corresponding prophecy letter, which he presented as being written by the 16th Karmapa, to the Shamarpa, the late Jamgon Kongtrul (1954-1992), and Gyaltsap. He claimed that the letter had been in an amulet pouch presented to him by the 16th Karmapa and that he had only recently discovered it.

Shamar Rinpoche, Jamgon Kongtrul, and Topga Yugyal were all very familiar with the 16th Karmapa's handwriting and style, and expressed their strong doubts about the authenticity of the letter. Shamar Rinpoche naturally demanded an independent forensic analysis and refused to give his consent unless the letter was authenticated. However, Tai Situpa, joined by Gyaltsap, did not comply. Tai Situpa and his followers, who instigated false rumors and confusion, also managed to rally support within the exiled Tibetan community and with people in Sikkim.

Eventually, His Holiness the Dalai Lama and his government in exile got involved. Instead of remaining neutral, they publicly took the side of Tai Situpa, and thus indirectly the Chinese government. Most astonishingly, they honored Tai Situpa, who had associated himself with the very tyranny they claim to stand against, while Shamar Rinpoche, who endeavored only to continue, in perfect conformity, a tradition almost a thousand years old, was shunned—to say the least.

This situation was probably effected by China, which appeared to be leaning toward a rapprochement with the Dalai Lama's administration at the time, or at least to be more understanding. At the same time, for the Dalai Lama's administration, aside from trying to compromise with China, an endorsement of China's 17th Karmapa candidate was also an opportunity to impose, beyond the Dalai Lama's accepted temporal authority, his unprecedented supreme spiritual authority over all Tibetan Buddhist orders, which his administration in exile had started to claim for him in the early 1960s. Joining the different orders under a single leadership associated with the Tibetan political movement was undoubtedly an important policy, implemented in the hope of creating the needed unity in their feud against China within the dispersed and very diverse Tibetan community.

At first, this union of religion and politics might seem irrelevant and anodyne, but looking closely, it has far-reaching implications. It means, for example, that all Buddhist organizations and centers around the world founded by Buddhist masters of Tibetan origin would be subjected to the authority of the spiritual and temporal king of Tibet, the Dalai Lama, and compelled, or at the least encouraged, to follow his political agenda. It would also destine the different Buddhist orders to slowly lose their specific identity and heritage. This would reduce them to being only an aspect of Tibetan culture, in contradiction with the universal, philosophical, and spiritual nature of Buddhism. Most importantly, the pursuit of political power and hegemony is completely antithetical to the Buddhist path.

Many leaders of independent Buddhist orders of Tibet, including the 16th Karmapa, Dudjom Rinpoche (1904-1987), Chatral Rinpoche, and others, voiced firm opposition to this proposed policy to mix and submit their independent orders to the temporal rule of the Tibetan government. The 16th Karmapa warned his disciples about the danger of mingling religion and politics and told many people, my parents included, that his disciples who engaged in Tibetan politics would not meet his next incarnation.

In any event, after the Chinese government officially nominated Ogyen Trinley as the 17th Karmapa, the Dalai Lama endorsed him as such. By doing so, he implicitly acknowledged the Chinese government's authority to recognize Buddhist reincarnates, unquestionably setting an unfortunate precedent for the future. Regardless, Shamar Rinpoche managed to save the institutions of the Karma Kagyu order that have remained faithful to Buddhist ethics and the genuine lineage.

Unsolicited, through the unlikely yet actual conjecture of their respective politics, the different parties mentioned above invited themselves into the Karmapa's recognition process—illegitimately and deceptively proclaiming themselves to be authorities in this matter. The general public was confused by false arguments, and particularly by the forged prophecy letter. Because of financial and political powers and international media coverage, which Tai Situpa managed to harness through his connections, it became impossible for Shamar Rinpoche to prevent the usurpation of the Karmapa's name by Ogyen Trinley.

Even when Shamar Rinpoche was treated unjustly and suffered from efforts to undermine his authority, he nevertheless continuously sought to maintain harmonious relationships with the different parties. He tried, by all peaceful and honest means, to find a compromise that would keep the genuine Karmapa free from politics and able to pursue his spiritual activity.

Shamar Rinpoche never sought to harm the Dalai Lama in any way. Avoiding any association with groups such as the Shugden followers, who oppose the Dalai Lama, Rinpoche remained very respectful towards him, and repeatedly told his own disciples never to denigrate the internationally esteemed Buddhist teacher. It is worth recalling that some members of Rinpoche's family had given their lives for the Dalai Lama during the resistance against the Chinese occupation of Tibet.

The recognition of the Karmapa put Shamar Rinpoche under tremendous political pressure. Rinpoche received multiple overtures soliciting his approval of the Chinese government's candidate. It would have been easy, and certainly profitable for him in a worldly sense, to go along with this. However, he couldn't forsake finding the real Karmapa, nor let the Karma Kagyu order serve a political agenda and lose its spiritual integrity. Rinpoche knowingly bore all the burdens entailed in securing the freedom of the Karmapa and the purity of the lineage.

The position of the Karmapa, like that of the Shamarpa, is neither political nor cultural, but solely spiritual and charitable—an institution dedicated to preserving the Buddha's legacy, which Shamar Rinpoche endeavored to perpetuate at great cost and hardship. In accordance with the Buddhist principle of non-violence, Rinpoche stood firm. Facing the powerful financial and political forces opposing him, he peacefully employed his one and only weapon—the truth of legitimacy.

Historical precedent clearly confirms that there is no person or institution above and beyond Shamar Rinpoche who can legitimately recognize the Karmapa. More importantly, without receiving the ultimate transmissions of the Karma Kagyu lineage from the 14th Shamar Rinpoche, who was its sole guardian, even if a person were to be designated as the Karmapa, he wouldn't be able to accomplish the Karmapa's actual function of being the lineage holder of the Karma Kagyu order, which is the Karmapa's primary raison d'être. Tai Situpa and all the rinpoches following him never received the ultimate transmission. Furthermore, Tai Situpa personally led the violent takeover of Rumtek monastery in 1993. Because this act violated the three degrees of Buddhist ordinations—shravaka, bodhisattva, and vidyadhara—Tai Situpa and his active followers have forfeited, according to Buddhist scriptures, the necessary qualification to give transmissions and ordinations. Having the title of rinpoche or being a genuine reincarnate tulku doesn't mean that one is infallible. A rinpoche can still be hindered by personal afflictive states of mind and engage in negative or criminal actions.

The many complex and troubling events of what has come to be known as the "Karmapa controversy," are too many and too long to recount here. Over time, Shamar Rinpoche almost single-handedly managed to overcome all obstacles and install, free of political control and in pure accordance with tradition, the legitimate 17th Karmapa, Trinley Thaye Dorje, who had been confirmed with absolute certainty in myriad ways to be the sole and genuine emanation of the Karmapa.

The 16th Karmapa wrote a prophecy in verse in Tsurphu, Tibet as early as 1944, which was widely disseminated during his lifetime, where he clearly foretold obstacles surrounding the recognition of his rebirth, and also very precisely the date when he would come together again with his disciples:

In the start of Pausa [the 12th month]
of the bird's year
I have the wish that we may,
in joy, come together.[8]

Without anyone being aware of the prophecy at the time, the 17th Karmapa miraculously escaped the grips of Communist China and arrived unexpectedly in New Delhi, India on January 15, 1994—in the Tibetan Buddhist calendar, the 4th day of the 12th month in the year of the bird, a date in accordance with the 16th Karmapa's prediction. He was then reunited with the Shamarpa and his faithful disciples at last.

Soon after, on March 17, Shamar Rinpoche held a public recognition ceremony in New Delhi. In 1996, Shamar Rinpoche conducted the first monastic ordination and the official enthronement of the 17th Karmapa under the Bodhi tree at Vajrāsana, Bodhgaya, the site of the Buddha's enlightenment. The Kagyu Monlam, a great prayer congregation attended by many thousands of monks and lay practioners, accompanied the ceremony. The Kagyu Monlam has taken place regularly once every year ever since 2007, thanks to the blessings of the 14th Shamarpa and the 17th Karmapa.

As lineage holder, Shamar Rinpoche carefully transmitted all the most important transmissions he had himself received from the 16th Karmapa to the 17th Karmapa, as well as a number of transmissions he had received from other great

8. སྣབས་སུ་བབ་པའི་སྟྲང་གྲུ་ཀངྫུག་བྱུང་བའི་སྟེང་དྲུངས་ལས། །ཁོ་བདག་པོ་ྀུ་ྒྱལ་འརྫིན་ྒུས་སུ། །དྲུག་སྟྲེད་དོ་འརྫོམས་པའི་སྨོན་ལམ་ྠེད།

23

masters throughout the following years. In 2003, Shamarpa offered the 17th Karmapa, upon the completion of his formation, the title of Vidyadhara, Wisdom Holder, confirming him as the supreme lineage holder of the Karma Kagyu order.

Shamar Rinpoche also facilitated the Karmapa receiving other important transmissions of the Karma Kagyu lineage, as well as transmissions from all the different practice lineages of Buddhism preserved by various masters, many of whom are from other orders. These masters include the late Chogye Trichen Rinpoche, the elder Luding Khen Rinpoche and Pewar Rinpoche from the Sakya order; Kyabje Tsikey Chokling Rinpoche, a living manifestation of the great Padmasambhava from the Nyingma order; and Beru Khyentse Rinpoche and Khenchen Trinley Paljor Rinpoche from the Karma Kagyu order.

Everything Shamar Rinpoche ever did was for the benefit of others and for the conservation of the Buddha's genuine legacy. As we may see by examining them, his actions were never motivated by self-interest or even hope of recognition, gratitude, or gain. Dedicating himself fully for others, he was the true and living example of all the Buddha's teachings, the unparalleled Bodhisattva.

Shamar Rinpoche's numerous accomplishments for Buddhism, and the Karma Kagyu lineage in particular, are of great historical significance and are truly remarkable. However, they denote merely a faint reflection of his virtues. It is impossible to describe his myriad extraordinary qualities, let alone his great realization. However, through recollections and anecdotes I will briefly endeavor to describe his unique characteristics and share aspects of what he has meant to me, in order to illustrate glimpses of the great being that he was.

I had the privilege of knowing Rinpoche throughout my entire life, as far back as I can remember. I was always impressed by the marvelous and extraordinary ways he embodied all the ideals of a Bodhisattva, of a Tulku, as well as those of a perfect teacher. The epitome of the nine occupations[9] of the Buddhist master, he was a symbol of perfection.

From my childhood years, I remember Shamar Rinpoche still in his youth. Except for the ushnisha protuberance and the long earlobes, he looked like the most magnificent and beautiful statue of the Buddha come to life. Simply catching sight of him or being in his presence one felt blessed. Afflictions of mind dissipated, clarity arose, and at times ineffable understanding was experienced. His speech was clear, articulate, and naturally melodious. Rinpoche would read out the scriptures during transmissions so fluently and with such clarity that the listener's attention was naturally and effortlessly captured. Even throughout long sessions, one would remain focused and undistracted; and although he read at a fast pace, the meaning of the text resonated so clearly in one's mind that comprehension was far more lucid than when reading it oneself. I myself have received transmissions from many of the greatest masters of our time, but never experienced this with any of them.

When Rinpoche spoke in Tibetan, he was very refined and eloquent in a kind manner, polite yet very straightforward. In whatever language, his speech was very

ANONYMOUS

in the sun
everything
ever wanted
needed
dissipates

9. Being engaged in the study, examination, and cultivation of the Buddha's legacy, being knowledgeable, full of moral integrity, benevolent, and, for the benefit of others, always teaching, writing, and reasoning.

pleasant, spontaneous, candid, and often playful, and he would skillfully adapt his presentation or explanation to his audience. This would make his point immediately clear, or trigger listeners to question their assumptions. Shamar Rinpoche knew how to shatter our illusions and fixed ideas. He was an extraordinary teacher. One felt he was gracious, yet uncompromising with truth and reality. He conveyed a sense of uplifting joy in all circumstances. It seemed as if he faced all situations with both the purity of a child, who is without prejudgment, attachment, expectation, or fear—and the ageless wisdom of a great sage.

Rinpoche's precise knowledge and faithful memory were extraordinary. For instance, he noticed things and found relationships among them that most of us failed to grasp. When I accompanied him to a new place, he often seemed to know it already. I was told that once he went to a research center that had a text he was looking for, but the staff didn't know quite where to find it, telling Rinpoche they would search for it. He then just pointed to a shelf and said, "Couldn't it be there?" They looked, and discovered he was right! I personally remember numerous times that he mentioned a passage in a book, and if we had a copy available, he would randomly open it to the exact page with the passage in question. Sometimes he would say, "How lucky!" as if this feat were perfectly serendipitous.

There was something marvelous about Rinpoche, as if he transcended the limits of our world at will. On numerous occasions when the weather was bad, I recall he would blow into the sky, and within the next minute the rain would stop. He would then wink at me and say with a smile, "Don't tell anybody!" Seemingly nothing escaped Rinpoche's mind. Many times I had a question, or had thought of one prior to seeing Rinpoche. Inevitably, before I could ask or even hint at it he would look at me with his usual discretion during our general conversation and skillfully give me the answer. Or sometimes he would casually talk about a subject that would lead to clarifying my understanding and answer my question. It was really as if he saw right through one's mind and knew everything about the person.

Rinpoche had such warm kindness that one felt cared for and appreciated, as with no one else. Being in his company seemed particularly meaningful and the only worthwhile place to be. Although most people seemed to be captivated by some aspect of his unique character, in his presence I felt truly blessed to realize that I faced a manifest emanation of Awakening, whose infinite radiant qualities were only dimmed by the veils of my mind. The grace, marked with dignity, joy, and wisdom that Rinpoche exuded gave him a natural, regal charm. He never acted artificially, nor did he stand on ceremony or display superior airs.

Within the Tibetan cultural sphere throughout the ages, many high-ranking Buddhist hierarchs, partly due to the influence of the Chinese imperial court, came to exercise or be associated with temporal authority and its trappings, resulting in a demeanor that was similar to a prince surrounded by an array of assistants. Even today, some rinpoches are very attached to their rank and stature, inherited from a bygone legal structure. In striking contrast, Shamar Rinpoche couldn't have cared less about his lofty position. Although the Shamarpas are historically one of the highest-ranking Buddhist masters, Rinpoche disdained the hierarchical system. He also made no pretense about being a reincarnate. When asked about previous lifetimes, he would say, "I can't recall any memories of the previous Shamarpas."

Rinpoche did not choose his position and its responsibilities; they were imposed upon him. Nevertheless, he selflessly accepted them and resolutely carried the burden of his primary function to serve Buddhism and benefit others. Rinpoche was always very simple, genuine, easygoing, and equally accessible to everyone. He never had a big entourage, and dispensed with pomp and circumstance whenever he could. He preferred taking care of himself and traveling alone with a single set of ordinary cotton robes, a pair of shorts, the sandals on his feet that he wore both in summer or bleak winter alike, and a large t-shirt or two. At times he had to use a traditional throne and ceremonial clothes for public events, but this appeared to make no difference to him; he could be seated on the floor or on a throne, it was all the same to him. Rinpoche never demanded respect; he asked not to be addressed as "His Holiness;" he instructed people not to prostrate to him before his teachings, which is the traditional practice, instead requesting that they join him in prostrating towards the Buddha.

Rinpoche once playfully told us that he was a revolutionary. In the best possible sense, I believe he really was. Rinpoche didn't submit to political, cultural, ritualistic, or other worldly goals, as many religious, spiritual, and even Buddhist teachers appear to do. Rinpoche was absolutely committed to the truth of the Buddha's teachings. Thus, he led us on the path to overthrow the suffering in our lives, and like a great helmsman he steered us through the fog of cultural and ritualistic jumble, beyond the contrary winds of our afflictive states of mind, to the free shores of the Buddha's ultimate legacy: the simple innate nature of our mind.

Shamar Rinpoche endeavored to keep the Karma Kagyu order away from serving political or financial interests, criticizing the use of Buddhist teachings for personal gain. He particularly cautioned people to be wary of some lamas' or masters' abuses that were perpetrated through using the "guru" position, and the misuse of "samaya" commitments for worldly purposes. Today, many self-proclaimed masters, unqualified to teach the Dharma, abuse their followers. Unfortunately, even certain legitimate rinpoches, both in Tibet and in exile, take advantage of their followers and use their position to extend their personal influence and power. Some, for example, have taken to recognizing hundreds of reincarnates (tulkus), often from influential backgrounds, in order to create large support bases for themselves.

Shamar Rinpoche's commitment to truth extended to all aspects of his life and activity. Identifying and installing Trinley Thaye Dorje as the 17th Karmapa, one of Rinpoche's greatest achievements, was met by widespread resistance and outright attacks, yet whatever the threat, he relied solely on truth and peace to counter it. He never tried to gain support by any means other than claiming the validity of his legitimacy.

As a person of unimpeachable principles, Rinpoche never contravened Buddhist ethics or human law. He always responded truthfully and with kindness, constantly reminding his disciples of the natural law of karma. What counted for him above all was spiritual practice and genuine altruistic action. The pursuit of power did not appeal to him. The very few tulkus he recognized were recognized because they are genuine, not because of an ulterior motive.

Through his unwavering devotion to the 16th Karmapa and the Karma Kagyu lineage, Shamar Rinpoche's main concern was to preserve its purity, protecting it from political influence; this was his responsibility as the principal lineage holder. However,

Rinpoche's wholehearted commitment to the Karma Kagyu lineage notwithstanding, he was truly a non-sectarian master. In fact, he upheld the teachings of all the different practice lineages of Buddhism that had been introduced to Tibet. He never engaged in glorifying his personal lineage by belittling others, or other religions or philosophies, and he sincerely and profoundly respected genuine teachers of all Buddhist orders, as well as people of science, integrity, and altruism. Making the Buddha's teachings accessible to everyone beyond any cultural and linguistic frame, bridging cultures, bringing people together in harmony, and contributing to peace and the well-being of humans and animals were among Rinpoche's main wishes.

Rinpoche was not attached to the cultural or ritualistic aspects of Buddhism, such as the tantric ritual choreography, arts, chants, etc., even though he was steeped in these subjects and completely knew how to appreciate them. He considered them external, however, as secondary expressions of the ultimate essence of Buddhism; manifestations of latter developments of Buddhism as influenced by Indian and Tibetan culture and historical contexts. The most important thing for Rinpoche, and what he tried his best to convey, was the actual meaning behind these aspects, the original, genuine teachings of the Buddha. Shamar Rinpoche not only sought to perpetuate a true intellectual understanding of Buddhism, but also emphasized the importance of actual experience of contemplative practice. "Students, most scholars even, when explaining the progression on the spiritual path to awakening, only list the different levels and instances and are unable to explain the actual experiences. They should be called enumerators, since they have almost more to enumerate than the Samkhya,"[10] Rinpoche quipped.

One of the last wishes Rinpoche conveyed to me was to gather both Mahayana and Theravada practitioners and experts in a conference at Sharminub, on the topic of the twenty kinds of sangha. He was always open to discussing and questioning all points of the teachings as well as his own views. He wished only to dispel confusion and benefit sentient beings. Amidst the surrounding darkness of confusion that fuels the perpetuation of samsara, Shamar Rinpoche was the beacon of truth illuminating the path to awakening for sentient beings.

Shamar Rinpoche treated everyone with equal kindness and without preference; he didn't make distinctions. He was comfortable with people of all origins and cultures; whether they were rich or poor, powerful or weak, it made no difference to him. He was always the same and benevolent with everyone, even those who tried to hurt him.

On March 17, 1994, at the Karmapa International Buddhist Institute in New Delhi, as the official recognition ceremony for the 17th Karmapa was concluding, a violent mob, mostly Tibetans gathered by Tai Situpa's administration, physically attacked the building with stones, sticks and small weapons, shattering many windows. Luckily participants inside managed to shut the gates to the main hall in time to save most people from harm and injury. Considering the life of the Karmapa to be in danger, some of the monks and laymen attending the ceremony were infuriated and wanted to fight back to repel the attackers. Shamar Rinpoche forbade them from doing so, telling them that if they wanted to use violence, they were no longer his disciples. Throughout the 38 years that I knew Rinpoche, I can't ever remember seeing him get truly angry. At times he would show wrathfulness

10. Samkhya སྒྲ་ཅན་པ: A non-Buddhist philosophical school in India.

to disciples; never through self-concern, always through compassion. He was like a parent who scolds his children in order to protect them.

When Rinpoche was attacked or had to defend his position, mostly in regard to his recognition of the 17th Karmapa, he would reason calmly, using perfect logic backed up with examples. He often gave an amusing twist to his arguments. Where others would get upset, Rinpoche remained serene. At times he even seemed amused by the pointlessness of those who were against him. He was deeply saddened by the harm human beings cause each other. When they harmed him, he was not moved by resentment, only by compassion. He tried to benefit even those who wished him harm, or had done so. He actually repaid all those who opposed him with benevolence.

For example, even though Tai Situpa and his supporters contravened history and tradition by enthroning a Karmapa of external political choice, for the sake of peace Shamar Rinpoche went so far as to concede that the boy who isn't the rebirth of the Karmapa could nonetheless use the name of Karmapa. To cite another example, in 2008, prior to giving permission to Ogyen Trinley to leave India for his first tour in the West, the Indian government approached Shamar Rinpoche and assured him that if he had reason to oppose the decision, they would not authorize the trip. Though he easily could have blocked Ogyen Trinley's travel, Rinpoche did not. It has occurred to me that not only did Rinpoche try to benefit those who harmed him, but he also tried to take their negative karma upon himself.

Shamar Rinpoche supported and protected his disciples according to their needs. In addition to guiding them on the spiritual path, whenever he could he also provided those in difficulty with material assistance. He was accessible to everyone and always made himself available; he was like the great bodhisattva Avalokiteshvara, who in his clairvoyance watches over and cares for us. I remember him reaching out to me, with startling synchronicity, at crucial moments in my life. For example, without having informed him, I would receive a reassuring phone call minutes before a family member's surgery or before an important decision I had to make. He was always there in times of need.

Of particular importance, Shamar Rinpoche has imparted the entirety of the profound and priceless teachings of the lineage to us. We couldn't be more fortunate, we can't benefit from any greater gift than this, as there is nothing more precious. The great master Saraha (c. 8th century) said:

If while living
you do not change,
then there is nothing but to grow old and die;

through the guru's teaching,
awareness is purified—
that's wealth, what's worthy besides that?[11]

Shamar Rinpoche embodied benevolence. His deeds and accomplishments are a lasting witness and testament to his great kindness. His life is an incomparable, inspiring example for all of us to follow. In everything Rinpoche did, he manifested

---

11. དྲན་མཛོད་ཀྱི་སྒྲུ་ལས། གསོན་པ་གང་ཞིག་རྣམ་པར་མ་གྱུར་པ། །དེ་ནི་རྒས་ཤིང་འཆི་བར་འགྱུར་རམ་ཅེ། །བླ་མས་བསྟན་པ་དེ་མེད་སྦྱོས་ཤེ། །དེ་ཉིད་ནོར་ཡིན་གཞན་པ་ གང་ཞིག་སོ།

genuine kindness, simplicity, and truth. Looking back at the events surrounding Rinpoche's death, one can see clearly that he was awakened, having mastery over his lifespan. It appears that not only was he aware of his imminent death, but that he actually chose the precise moment as well.

Long before his death, Shamar Rinpoche told many of his disciples that he would not live very long, and that he would pass away at the age of sixty. Chogyam Trungpa (1939-1987) performed a mirror divination and foresaw that Shamar Rinpoche's life span would not exceed five cycles of twelve years. However, like a Buddha who has control over the length of his own life, Rinpoche extended it by over two years in response to his disciples', and especially the 17th Karmapa's, repeated requests for him to live longer. In the months and weeks preceding his passing, Rinpoche gave many indications. He told me he would not be teaching much more in his Bodhi Path centers and that he counted on me. At the last dinner we had together, an older couple in their late sixties was sitting at another table. Rinpoche looked over at them and told us, "I will not be that old. I don't want to live to be that old."

In similar and even more direct ways, Rinpoche indicated to some of his disciples that he was going to leave us soon. He insisted on speaking about impermanence, the meaninglessness of samsara, and the pointlessness of fearing death if one knows how to practice at that moment. He mentioned he was going to take a vacation and that he had basically finished his work. At other times he told us we should not wish him to live too long, for this would be wishing him to be old and diminished.

These hints about his impending death notwithstanding, Rinpoche simultaneously spoke about many projects, more it seemed than at any other time. In retrospect, this appears to me to be his final will, his last instructions on what he wanted us to accomplish. This was his way of skillfully associating his disciples to the great merit of his vast awakened activity.

As if to clarify the teachings on impermanence and the inevitability of death, on the morning of June 11, 2014, in the presence of his brother and a few disciples, Shamar Rinpoche suddenly but peacefully withdrew his manifestation from this world and entered into parinirvana, the pristine awakened state. Over the following two days, his body remained in the seated meditative posture and appeared as if alive, with none of the usual signs following death. During this period, disciples felt Rinpoche's strong blessing in their practice. At dawn on June 13, on the very auspicious day of the anniversary of the historical Buddha's awakening, signs that Rinpoche's meditation was completed appeared. Subsequently, silence in the sacred body's presence was broken with solemn requests beseeching Rinpoche to emanate his benevolent manifestation in this world again. A tulku, or emanation, is the manifest expression of an awakened being's compassion. Tulkus do not appear in the world through attachment to an identity, but because they are truly selfless. Their activity is thus limitless.

It is true that we have lost the most marvelous and incomparable teacher. It is sadder still because such a genuinely realized master is extremely rare, like a rare bee in winter, or a visible star at noon. We are extremely fortunate to have met Rinpoche, and now it is more important than ever that we put his precious teachings into practice, as death awaits us all. If we do not make progress in this life,

it is uncertain whether such fortune will be ours again. The mind in its nature is immortal, as the following verse that appeared in Shamar Rinpoche's vision of Vasubandhu proves:

[The mind's] arising continuously being without hindrance
Is the evidence that proves its start is in infinity,
All the causal conditions [for its arising] being present without hindrance
Is the evidence that proves its end is in infinity.[12]

The great Milarepa (c.1052 – c.1135) said he did not fear death, just rebirth. Considering this, we should all strive, through discipline and meditation, to become masters of our own mind, and thus of our destiny. Shamar Rinpoche, because of his great affection for us and for all sentient beings, will never forsake us. We can be confident that his blessing will perpetually accompany us, until we are able to reach his high ground of complete and true freedom. I remember someone asking Shamar Rinpoche if there was a formulation or prayer specific to the Shamarpa, like the well-known "Karmapa khyeno" (Karmapa know of me). Rinpoche just looked out into space, as he sometimes did, and replied in English, "Shamarpa knows." He added nothing else, which I interpreted to mean: you don't need to say anything special, because I will always know your situation and care for you.

Shamar Rinpoche has shown us how the meaning of life is found through cultivating bodhicitta, and his practice of this should inspire us to emulate his example. It is time for us to renew our vows, steadfastly practice, and follow the steps Rinpoche has laid out before us. Although he is no longer physically with us, his blessings and legacy are forever present. Nothing can hinder Rinpoche's activity; he will continuously manifest infinite emanations until samsara completely ends. However, for us to always be in his blessing and have the privilege to meet his future emanations, it is important that we join our prayers in harmony for his swift return. It is said that without the ring of devotion, the hook of blessing can't pull us out of the ocean of samsara.

May Shamar Rinpoche, the Buddha Amitabha, soon manifest his presence again in this world for the benefit of all sentient beings!

---

12. སྐྱེ་ལ་རྟག་ཏུ་གེགས་མེད་པས། །རྒྱས་ཀྱི་སྔ་མཐའ་རྒྱག་མེད་གྲུབ། །རྒྱུ་ཚོགས་ཆང་ཞིང་གེགས་མེད་པས། །རྒྱས་ཀྱི་ཕྱི་མཐའ་རྒྱག་མེད་གྲུབ།

SHAMAR RINPOCHE
A PHOTO ALBUM

Kunzig Shamar Rinpoche was photographed throughout his life, throughout the world. What follows is an eclectic grouping of intimate, formal, and informal photos of the man we all loved deeply, quite frankly chosen just because we continue to love to look at him. Some are oldies-but-goodies, others not as well known. They cannot encompass the countless facets of Rinpoche's vast life and activity; they are simply a sample of photos we had.

The photos in this book were taken from diverse sources, many in the public domain with the photographer unknown. Of the photographers we do know, we would like to thank: Karine LePajolec, Shahin Parhami, Topka Korlo, Peter Kiar, Yvonne Wong, Peter Simon, Manfred Hornung, Thule Jug, Tsony Devroux, and Carol Gerhardt. And many thanks to those photographers whose names are lost to us.

李克勤居士攝於1980年

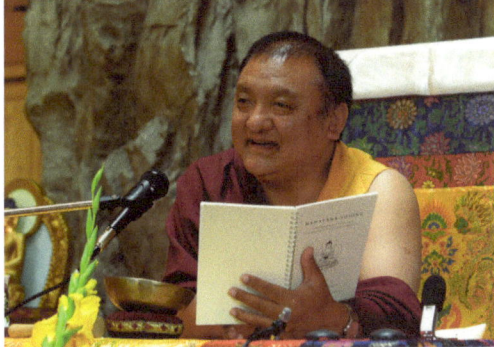

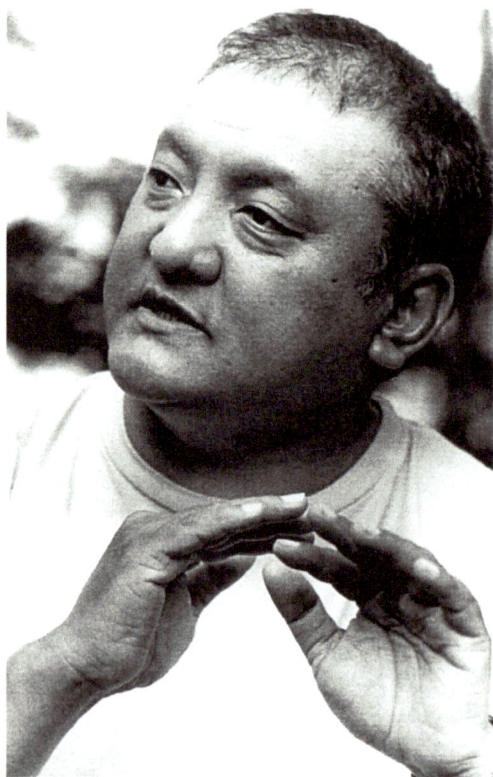

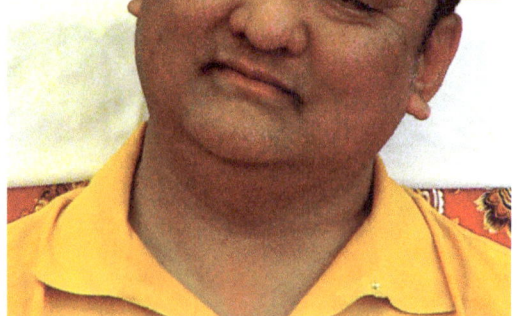

SANDY YEN (HO-TZU CHUANG YEN)
Menlo Park, California

◆ REMEMBERING RINPOCHE WITH DEVOTION

In 1991, I took a pilgrimage trip to India led by Mr. Xia, a long-time disciple of Karmapa and Shamarpa. This was before I met either of these great lineage holders. Our guide was Shamarpa's close attendant Lama Danding, and at one point during the trip he mentioned that he wanted to come back as Shamarpa's attendant again in his next life. I was so surprised to hear this, because life in India can be so difficult. Why would he want to come back for such a difficult existence, I wondered? I realized the reason for this wish was his strong devotion to his guru.

Lama Danding's devotion touched me so deeply that I eagerly wanted to meet his guru, Shamarpa. A friend of mine told me that his older brother, Lama Tashi, also served as Shamarpa's attendant, so I asked my friend to introduce me to Shamarpa. Not long after I returned to California, Lama Tashi called me to say that Shamarpa was giving refuge and Bodhisattva vows in Bodhgaya. He invited me to go, and without hesitation, I jumped on a plane so that I could take vows from Shamarpa under the Bodhi Tree. That was February 29, 1992. The rest is history.

During all the years I was privileged to be Rinpoche's disciple, I always felt he was very humble and approachable, even though he was a high lama and a lineage holder. A simple, but for me, very revealing proof of this occurred when I asked Rinpoche how to do my prostrations, and Rinpoche immediately prostrated on the floor to show me. Another incident I remember so vividly happened when I was riding with Rinpoche in a car along a mountain road somewhere in India. Lama Danding was driving, Rinpoche sat in the front seat with him, and I was in the back seat. At one point Lama Danding parked the car on the roadside in order to buy something. While Rinpoche and I waited in the car, it started to roll down the hill. I was very alarmed, however Rinpoche quietly got out of the car, walked behind it, climbed into the driver's seat and stopped the moving car. To this day I clearly remember his swift but very calm reaction.

Rinpoche was so compassionate toward all beings. He always granted my requests, as a Bodhisattva does for sentient beings. Some time after I took refuge from him, I told Rinpoche my wish to provide provisions for as many monks as I could. He understood that on our path we need merit; therefore, in early 2000 he allowed me to support three Kagyu Monlams. Later he also allowed me to participate in some projects at the Bodhi Path center in Virginia.

Rinpoche was able to sense his disciples' needs even when they did not express them to him. A case in point was my depression after the passing of both of my parents in 2001. In 2003 Rinpoche asked me to invite Karmapa to California in order for Karmapa to receive a series of empowerments from various highly respected Rinpoches of different lineages. In July 2003 Karmapa came to our Bodhi Path center in Menlo Park for these empowerments. Shamarpa had also arranged for Karmapa to stay in my house. These events lasted three months. With all these major activities going on, I forgot my own sorrow of losing loved ones.

Rinpoche never forgot to protect his disciples from harmful situations. Six months before his passing, which we believe he knew ahead of time, he visited my husband and me during Christmas, 2013. He brought Delphine with him, and gave us some poinsettias. Before he left, without any explanation, he told us to move out of our house within the next 18 months. My husband was very reluctant to do so. However, from past experience, we realized Rinpoche had always been right whenever he advised us what to do. After considerable effort, we managed to move out of our house in May 2015, almost at the end of the 18-month time period. We hadn't yet sold our old house, and so we kept returning to pick up more things. Some months after we moved out, the roof started to leak. When the repairman came to fix it, he found our attic was full of mold and other cancer-causing substances, such as rat and other animal deposits. The roofing company told us that if we had continued to live there our health would have been greatly harmed.

How can I repay Rinpoche's kindness to us for so many years! I can't stop my tears whenever I think of him. I pray that we will meet the 15th Shamarpa very soon.

TERRY MORRIS
Lexington, Virginia

◆ POEM FOR SHAMARPA

My dear teacher
how to thank you

silly, naïve, devoted, still you taught me

When you first came to live in your new house in Virginia,
I remember sitting with you and another student at the dining room table.
The other student was saying how he had learned to meditate some years
ago, and I remember thinking, "Great. I can't meditate."
As my thought completed, you turned your face to me and said,
"I can teach you. Come with me."

oh my dear teacher
simple, profound
so many pearls I missed
every lesson different
so much more I wish I had done

thank you

teaching me to love the dharma,
not just you

Like a child without her father,
Endless gratitude

Sadness still

May you come again soon
and may I find you then

◆ Shamar Rinpoche, the Bodhisattva I Served and Loved

"There is nothing in this world that is permanent except impermanence itself. The only thing permanent you will find in this world in your lifetime is impermanence." These are the words of an extraordinary individual who was unconventional in all senses of the word—and genuinely unique in the strict sense of that word.

During our countless conversations long past midnight, Shamar Rinpoche often passed along to me many words of wisdom, such as those about impermanence. Who knew that insomnia would play a major role in our bonding and lead to innumerable serious conversations, many of which I have yet to fully fathom?

Without a doubt, those conversations were the best teachings about spirituality and life that I will ever receive in this lifetime. It has been more than a year since he left us, and not a day goes by without my thinking of him and reflecting on what he told me. I try to recall and understand what he really meant.

Rinpoche was a great teacher. He spread the Dharma to massive crowds of Buddhist devotees—and in his infinite wisdom and compassion, he also could look into an individual's heart and offer that person just the right insights and guidance he or she needed.

Although Shamar Rinpoche made himself available to anyone who needed him and treated everyone equally, his disciples perceived him through their own individual lenses. Consequently, no one has a complete understanding of him. Each of us saw only a tiny part of him and how he manifested himself to the world.

I find it a great irony that in Rinpoche's death, or more accurately at his funeral services, the different ways people perceived him came face-to-face. Most Westerners in attendance had never experienced how he seemed god-like and distant to Himalayan disciples. Conversely, these disciples had not seen how many of the Westerners had strong personal attachments to him. Each of us treasures our particular memories of him. My own memories are very special to me. I saw him from the eyes of both a Himalayan and a Westernized person.

When I was growing up, I never imagined that one day I would work closely for a very high-ranking lama—and certainly not the Karma Kagyu Lineage Holder. Some time during the summer of 1995, my uncle, who was a close friend and disciple of Rinpoche, took me to have an audience with him. Before that day I had seen Rinpoche on many occasions from afar, but had not met him personally in a private setting. I still remember that morning very clearly. He and Hannah Nydahl were sitting on the balcony of the house where the Karmapa presently lives in Kalimpong (at that time, the Karmapa had not yet traveled to Kalimpong).

The first part of our meeting was filled with the usual courtesies. But about half an hour into our conversation, I began to realize that unbeknownst to me, my uncle had, some time previously, volunteered me to study at the Karmapa International Buddhist Institute (KIBI). Apparently, he did this based on a long ago conversation he and I had had, when I had shown an inclination to study Buddhism.

I was one of five Himalayan boys with a normal school education to be enrolled in the semester starting that autumn. During my meeting with Rinpoche, I would not have known any of this, had Rinpoche not asked me, "So. When are you going to Delhi?" Thus began my "path to awakening." Though I walked behind Rinpoche for nearly two decades, I have finally just realized that I am indeed still asleep—and have a very long way to go before I wake up.

Assisting Rinpoche all those years did not involve a clearly defined, fixed set of job responsibilities. Rather, I had to be flexible and learn to adapt. What I learned was not to be fixated on one task, but to be able to let go and move on to another—at a moment's notice, just like his travel plans. This was a valuable lesson in impermanence and non-attachment.

Rinpoche was a teacher whose thinking was quite advanced, and whose ideas, in many respects, were ahead of his time; consequently, some people misunderstood him. However, the people who understood even a fraction of what he communicated were in awe of him. He was, indeed, one of the most extraordinary Buddhist teachers of our time. And perhaps because of his unconventional, non-traditional way of doing things, he attracted a lot of young people to him. He was someone who wanted to start new things—especially in the sense of being previously untried.

Rinpoche did not want people to change or abandon their own culture in order to follow Buddhism, nor did he encourage them to stick too rigidly to their existing ways. He was very forthright and straightforward, calling things as he saw them— he taught in much the same way. It wasn't always easy for everyone to digest his teachings or what he said during conversations because he never really told you what you wanted to hear. Maybe that is one of the reasons some people did not approve of him.

Shamar Rinpoche consciously decided not to set up his own administration (*labrang*) in the way many other high lamas have, both historically and in the present day. Among other reasons, he did not want an administration to survive him and cause the same kinds of problems he experienced with the 16th Karmapa's administration before and after Karmapa's passing. The absence of an administration was one of the main reasons he personally involved a close circle of people who supported him in all his projects. He set up and ran his different organizations in such a way that they would survive intact without him. He said, "When I come back everything will be in one piece." Accordingly, he specifically instructed different individuals about how he wanted things handled.

To my knowledge, Rinpoche never named a specific place as his main seat in the traditional sense. However, I know he considered the center in Natural Bridge, Virginia his main home, where he was constantly creating and carrying out different plans to develop the facilities there according to his ideal vision.

On many occasions Rinpoche expressed his deep satisfaction in being able to establish a network of Bodhi Path Buddhist centers that were non-sectarian and would draw in everyone. Therefore, he did not want Bodhi Path to be bound by the rituals and traditions of Tibetan Buddhism; rather he hoped Bodhi Path centers would be open to and accommodate individuals with different motivations and at different levels—those simply wanting to learn about and practice meditation, people with a curiosity about Buddhism, plus more serious Buddhists who wanted to deepen their understanding of the Dharma.

He wanted the doors of Bodhi Path to be open also to people who were not Buddhist, but simply wanted to have a better life and a peaceful mind. Indicative of this is the fact that he always stressed mastering the basics rather than diving into advanced and esoteric practices. This is why he advised people to just try to master the simple meditation practice of following the breath. He did not feel people necessarily needed to don monk's robes, become celibates, or go into retreat.

Rinpoche chose the US to start Bodhi Path because he felt the geographic expansiveness of America offered two advantages. First, he believed that in America, Bodhi Path centers could be established without the scrutiny of tradition-bound individuals or organizations. Second, he felt that because of the freedom and openness he found in America, the Bodhi Path centers would not interfere with other existing centers.

People have their own views about Rinpoche's sudden departure from this world. I for certain don't understand why he chose to leave samsara when he did, and I have not yet been able to come to peace with this wrenching event. I fervently await his return and hope his reincarnation will continue to be more than just a teacher to me.

LAMA JAMPA THAYE
London, United Kingdom

◆ SHAMAR RINPOCHE: RADICAL ORTHODOXY

Every great master both stands in a line of succession and extends it—his thoughts and teachings echo those of his lineage, but a master presents them afresh for a new age. So it was with Kunzig Shamar Rinpoche, our precious Mipham Chokyi Lodro. Of course in this respect, we naturally look back to Rinpoche's thirteen predecessors in the line of Red Hat Karmapas. However, I want to suggest that—in important ways—the fourteenth Shamarpa's vision of Dharma recalls Gampopa, the great patriarch of the Kagyu school, who more than anyone else endowed the tradition with its distinctive characteristics and ensured its survival.

In articulating his sense of what Karma Kagyu should be in these modern times, Shamar Rinpoche seems to me very reminiscent of Gampopa. Back in the twelfth century when Gampopa appeared on the scene, the nascent Kagyu School was little more than two generations of yogins who had gathered around his predecessors in the lineage—Marpa and Milarepa. At that time, the early Kagyu were merely one among a number of groups, each with their own preferred cycles of tantric instructions; whether it was mahamudra, as with Marpa and Milarepa's disciples; or *chod*, with the disciples of Machik Labdron. So how then did Gampopa come to make such a difference to the subsequent history of the Kagyu tradition?

What Gampopa did was to fuse together the tantric teachings obtained from Milarepa with the teachings he had received in his several years training as a Kadampa monk. Thus, he ensured that from then on, Kagyu doctrine and practice would encompass both the graduated Mahayana path teachings (subsequently elucidated by Gampopa himself in the *Jewel Ornament of Liberation*, which is itself largely a reiteration of Atisha's *Lamp of the Path*), and the esoteric teachings of the tantras, brought to Tibet by Milarepa's master Marpa, heir to the Indian yogins Naropa and Maitripa. Gampopa's achievement became known as "The blending of the two streams of *Ka* (Kadam) and *Chak* (mahamudra)." In terms of meditation practice, the most vital part of this synthesis would be the dual emphasis upon *lojong* (mind training) and mahamudra.

A second contribution made by Gampopa was his introduction of monasticism into what had hitherto been exclusively non-monastic. This undoubtedly helped to make the Dagpo Kagyu a "total" form of Buddhism, in that unlike many of its rivals it possessed all the major expressions of Buddhist doctrine and practice. Again, as with the doctrinal and contemplative developments ushered in by Gampopa, one can easily argue that this feature aided the long-term survival of the Kagyu tradition.

Perhaps the most radical aspect of Gampopa's vision was his insistence that mahamudra, which had until then been seen as the apex of Anuttarayogatantra and therefore realizable only by major initiation and the practice of the development and completion stages, was also to be found in the sutra teachings, such as the Prajnaparamita, the Samadhi Raja Sutra; and very importantly, the Mahayana Uttaratantra treatise of Maitreya. Gampopa said to his disciple Phakmo Drupa: "The root text of our doctrine of mahamudra is the Mahayana Uttara Tantra treatise, composed by Lord Maitreya."

The practical effect of Gampopa's understanding of mahamudra was that it would now be accessible to many more than just a restricted group of tantric yogins. The great historian Go Lotsawa's comment is apposite: "Dakpo Rinpoche (Gampopa) produced an understanding of mahamudra in those beginners who had not obtained initiations." This method of teaching became known as "sutra tradition mahamudra." One should note, however, that alongside this tradition Gampopa continued to transmit "mantra tradition mahamudra" and tantric initiations on to his innermost disciples, such as Karmapa Dusum Khyenpa. So Gampopa's synthesis was "roomy" enough for these different emphases to be maintained side by side.

From this brief account, it should not be too difficult to see that Shamar Rinpoche's activity, not least in the curriculum he developed and taught in Bodhi Path, reflects some features of Gampopa's vision. I would even suggest that at this crucial time Shamar Rinpoche's work allows us to renew our tradition, by reaching back to its broad roots in Gampopa's creative synthesis. Indeed, Rinpoche told me privately that one of his motivations in founding Bodhi Path had been to counter somewhat deficient presentations of Kagyu Dharma.

Thus, what Shamar Rinpoche chose to emphasize in his teaching is of the highest significance. In this respect, Rinpoche bestowed many Vajrayana initiations, such as the cycle of "Knowing One Liberated in All," upon H.H. the 17th Karmapa, as well as initiations for such deities as Amitabha and Gyalwa Gyamtso recently in Europe. However, the core of his teaching was surely lojong and mahamudra, and this is an obvious echo of Gampopa's earlier fusion of Kadam Dharma and the tantric teachings of Milarepa.

In addition, like Gampopa, Shamar Rinpoche identified a "sutra tradition mahamudra" in texts like the Samadhiraja sutra. For him, such Mahayana works were the source of mahamudra, alongside tantric material like the Sri Anabila Tantra and the songs of the Indian siddhas, such as Maitripa and Naropa.

There are other aspects of Shamar Rinpoche's work that echo those of Gampopa. One of these was his concern to preserve an authentic monasticism, evidenced in his establishment of Sharminub Institute in Nepal as a monastic setting for the revival for the full maintenance of the Vinaya vows.

Furthermore, just as Gampopa, following the early Kadam style, introduced Mahayana scholarship to the tradition, so Shamar Rinpoche labored at Diwakar and at KIBI to ensure the continuation of our Kagyu intellectual legacy. Of course, this aspect of Shamar Rinpoche's contribution was also reflected in his own brilliant exposition of scholarly texts, ranging from Mipham Rinpoche's *Gateway to Knowledge* to Mikyo Dorje's commentary on Candrakirti's *Introduction to Madhyamaka*.

Based on this brief survey of his activities, it occurs to me that one might characterize Shamar Rinpoche as an example of "radical orthodoxy," akin to Gampopa. By this apparently contradictory term I want to reflect the fact that Rinpoche had a sublime confidence in the Kagyu tradition, combined with a fearlessness, curiosity, and generosity of mind, and that these very features made him entirely at ease teaching Dharma in modern times without need for compromise, dissembling, or manipulation. Furthermore, what might appear to be innovation was never a fabricated "improvement" but in reality, something always utterly consistent with the wisdom of the lineage.

In other words, Rinpoche always drew his teachings from the actual heart of the Kagyu tradition. He had no need to resort either to the populism of those who would seduce the crowd, nor to the cultivated air of inscrutable superiority affected by those who have much about which to be inscrutable. As all of us who knew him can attest, he was a master for our time and all times—a man for all seasons.

Although my own connection with Shamar Rinpoche began in 1981, when I had a private meeting with him at a Kagyu conference in Germany, due to the vagaries of subsequent politics I was not able to study with him as extensively as I would have wished. However, I consider myself fortunate to have received from Rinpoche some parts, at least, of his Dharma legacy—ranging from the Gyalwa Gyamtso initiation to Karmapa Rangjung Dorje's "Aspiration Prayer of Mahamudra," and Shamar Konchok Yenlak's commentary on *The Seven Points of Mind Training*.

In fact, it seemed to me that when he gave this last teaching during his stay in Manchester, he actually bestowed upon us the full transmission of the heart of the Kagyu. To receive the teaching was to have the courageous path of the bodhisattva unfolded for us by one who breathed these very qualities. Although the subject was ostensibly lojong, it seemed radically different from the five or six other transmissions of Geshe Chekhawa's teaching I had received. Rinpoche opened his vast mind to us and allowed us to see the utter spaciousness of Buddha nature.

However, as everyone knows, it was not merely in formal teaching that Rinpoche embodied and transmitted the Dharma. Rinpoche's alertness to the world and concern for everyone shone through even in the most casual conversations. I felt that with him, unlike with so many who have such fearsome responsibilities, the playful spaciousness of his mind and the openness of his heart had never diminished. At the same time, his every word was reliable wisdom because he had no need to feign the externalities of a "spiritual person." He was the same utterly authentic person, whether he was talking of his love for English gardens or the recent difficulties in our tradition, or discussing mutual friends, acquaintances, and others.

Shamar Rinpoche left Manchester on June 2. We saw him off the next day from London en route to Germany. All the plans we had discussed together were blazing in my head.

It was early Wednesday morning the following week when the telephone rang.

DELPHINE FORGET
France

◆ TRIBUTE TO KUNZIG SHAMAR RINPOCHE

I had the great privilege to work for Shamar Rinpoche as one of his assistants for many years, and directly witnessed his vast, constant, and multi-faceted activity. His activity was so immense that it is not easy to recount or retrace.

From what I could see of even just one day of his life, it's impossible to put a number or estimate on his capacity; Rinpoche could do so many things in one day. And I was only seeing the tip of the iceberg.

As impressive and diverse as his activity was, what is clear to me is that Shamar Rinpoche was working non-stop from morning to evening, or even through the night, in order to help beings in so many different ways.

Not only through his spiritual mind, with prayers, writing, and advice, but also through his substantial and tangible efforts focusing on myriad projects worldwide—helping everyone he could in order to make the world a better place.

I would say that he was a visionary, an entrepreneur of his time. By reading his books, one can clearly see this aspect of him.

In my personal experience, I realize now that all these years working for his activity has made my spirit so stable—it was a profound training which is a concrete gift for this life.

I dearly miss his humor and unique personality.

I am just so thankful to Shamar Rinpoche—his boundless realization clearly helped so many of us.

SABINE TEUBER
Bodhi Path Renchen-Ulm,
Germany

◆ THE GREATEST GIFT

In 1997, my daughter Nina and I met Shamar Rinpoche for the first time. We had the wonderful opportunity of being introduced to him personally by Lama Yeshe Drolma in the presence of Jigme Rinpoche. How powerful Rinpoche's appearance was! He left a deep impression on us, and we knew we didn't have to search any further on our spiritual path. During the following years, we didn't miss a single opportunity to meet Shamar Rinpoche when he came to Europe, wherever he was. In the meantime, my other daughter, Julia, took refuge, and felt a close bond to Shamar Rinpoche as well. She then did a 4-year program of study in the Karmapa International Buddhist Institute (KIBI) in New Delhi.

It didn't take long before all my wishes to be of help for the activity of both Rinpoches came true: I was asked to find a house in Germany, which could serve as the first European Bodhi Path center. Along with my friend Barbara Lutz, we started looking for a suitable house, and finally found a place in Remetschwiel, a village in the very south of Germany, close to the Swiss border. This property was purchased by a foundation, and the first EU Bodhi Path center started its activity there in April of 2004.

After two years, though, we moved to a more suitably accessible place in Renchen-Ulm, near Strasbourg and close to the French border—very easy to reach from all sides. This in itself is a very nice story about Rinpoche's capacities: Shamar Rinpoche called me on September 22, 2005, requesting that I find a house near Strasbourg on the German side, in a hilly area, but not too high up in the mountains. So again Barbara and I started our search, and exactly one month later, on October 22, the most suitable place was found—a former guesthouse with a big room that served as a bowling alley. All the facilities we needed came together here; it was like a miracle. When I called Rinpoche to tell him about this house, he just said: "Good. Then buy it." … ;-) We did our best to find a financial solution and with all the blessing we were able to buy the house in January of 2006. Actually, we moved in on the 22nd of that month, which means that it took exactly 4 months to move here after Rinpoche had asked us to find a house. What proof of Rinpoche's qualities!

The house is built like a combination of three or four houses, so one part of it was transformed into Rinpoche's private house, with a beautiful garden full of apple trees and flowers. Rinpoche really loved this place and spent a lot of time here whenever he was in Europe. Not only during courses, but also privately, in between his journeys from Asia to America, or vice versa.

When I met Shamar Rinpoche for the first time, it never entered my mind that I would be able to get to know him so closely, or to really support his activity. But that had been my wish, and Rinpoche gave me so much more than just fulfilling this wish of mine. He was like the perfect spiritual father, the perfect guide and teacher. Rinpoche helped us all so much, in any kind of trouble, and he always showed us the right way to deal with difficulties. It was amazing to see how many projects Rinpoche was active in, for how many people all over the world he was this wonderful guide, never rejecting anyone.

It's very difficult to describe Rinpoche's vast activity. He was constantly working and meeting people in order to help all beings and create helpful projects all over the world. There wasn't a single moment one would see him without his incredible love and compassion for everyone. Even when he was pointing to something in a more serious way, his compassion was always present and one could always feel it (even in difficult moments). For his disciples, Rinpoche was the most precious guide one can think of, and he was caring for every single being, even for the tiniest animal. At the same time, Rinpoche was like a warrior when it came to injustice or lies or situations that would lead to suffering, or when it came to the big challenge of keeping up the lineage in a proper way.

How can I, a most simple human, ever be able to describe a Buddha such as Shamar Rinpoche suitably? I can only describe my own humble experience of Rinpoche's incredible capacities. There is no way to talk about Rinpoche other than with my deepest love and devotion—and Rinpoche himself gave us his greatest gift at the end, even if it was the most shocking moment: passing away amidst us, in a family-like situation, during breakfast.

What happened in his last two days? On the last day of Rinpoche's final course here, June 9, 2014, Rinpoche was suddenly very quiet for several seconds—it's not easy to say for how many. We were wondering what happened, whether Rinpoche was meditating, or something else. When we started to really get worried, Rinpoche suddenly "came back." He was very present again and said, "Now it almost happened." After some refreshments, he continued his teaching in his unique way, finishing *A Concise Lojong Manual* by the 5th Shamarpa, as he had promised.

Afterwards, during lunch, Rinpoche suddenly said, "I will die soon." Only a few of us were present, and we hurried to protest, telling Rinpoche that we needed him and that he should stay many more years. But Rinpoche kept silent. That evening Rinpoche went out for dinner, announcing, "This is my last dinner," but for the few people present it was hard to believe while seeing Rinpoche so lively. Rinpoche didn't have dinner the next day, though.

On June 11, Rinpoche said he would have breakfast together with all of us (Jigme Rinpoche, the center residents, and a few other people). Breakfast was scheduled for 7:30 a.m., but at 7 o'clock Rinpoche called me and announced that he would come "now." We hurried to set the table; Rinpoche had already arrived. The hastily served breakfast had just started when Rinpoche suddenly passed away—leaving us all with an incredible shock. None of us could say one word except to organize what had to be done, like calling the emergency doctor. We had to control our emotions as much as we could because immediate action was required. Only after the doctor confirmed Rinpoche's passing were we able to grasp this unbelievable fact.

Rinpoche was then brought into his house and set in an upright position, and after only one or two minutes it seemed as if Rinpoche had come back to life. This was another incredible moment, to see Rinpoche in total peace, sitting there as if he was meditating—he had passed into *tukdam*, the post-mortal meditative state of highly realized masters. During this state Rinpoche still looked alive, having a warm glow around him and not showing any signs of decay. The blessing around his room was immense and could be perceived by everybody coming to the center. Rinpoche stayed in tukdam for two days, and was then brought to the cemetery hall in Renchen, which had much better facilities to host Rinpoche's kudung— making it possible for thousands of people to pay their last respects.

Soon after Rinpoche's passing, more and more people started to arrive; first of all many other rinpoches, lamas, monks, and nuns—along with thousands of his disciples. His Holiness the 17th Karmapa Thaye Dorje came as soon as his visa was granted, and was brought to the cemetery hall right after he arrived. Everyone was in deep grief, and at the same time everybody was very touched by the incredible, profound atmosphere. Most of the inhabitants of Renchen and Renchen-Ulm are Catholics, but nevertheless many of them came to the cemetery hall and passed Rinpoche's body, surprised by the peaceful and blessed atmosphere. Many of our neighbors started to search online for Shamar Rinpoche—who he was and what he stood for.

We had such amazing support from the community, the mayors, and the guests who swarmed in from around the globe. Everything was made possible in a very short time. Even the Bhutanese ambassador from Switzerland came, assuring us that any support we needed would be provided by him, as he had been advised to offer by the Royal Bhutanese family and their government in Bhutan. Thanks to the help of many friends, hundreds of people visiting the center and attending the huge daily pujas in the shrine room were provided with food and drinks. Everyone spontaneously helped with what was needed. Receiving this huge support from all sides was an incredible experience for all of us.

It's still a shock somehow that Rinpoche left his *nirmanakaya* form, and from time to time tears run down our cheeks when thinking of some of the special situations each of us had with Rinpoche. We can only have confidence in Rinpoche's enlightened state, trusting that he knew exactly when it was the right moment to leave. For us here in the Bodhi Path center in Renchen-Ulm, the greatest gift Rinpoche ever gave to us was that he passed away in our midst, making us witnesses of the first time a Buddha entered parinirvana in Germany, and thus creating a holy atmosphere right here. We now have the task to follow Rinpoche's advice, his teachings, and his curriculum—to keep everything in the best way until Rinpoche fulfills our strongest wish for his swift rebirth.

Thank You, dearest Rinpoche, forever!

PAMELA GAYLE WHITE
Virginia

This piece originally appeared on Tricycle Magazine*'s website just after Shamar Rinpoche's death.*

◆ TRIBUTE TO SHAMAR RINPOCHE UPON HIS PASSING

Shamar Rinpoche passed away suddenly on June 11, 2014, at his center in Renchen-Ulm, Germany, at the age of 61. The 14th Shamarpa, Mipham Chokyi Lodro, was born in Tibet and recognized and enthroned there by his uncle, the 16th Gyalwa Karmapa, supreme head of the Karma Kagyu lineage of Tibetan Buddhism.

Beyond the traditional education reserved for tulkus, Shamar Rinpoche simply loved learning for learning's sake. He was keenly interested in a far-ranging variety of subjects, including neuroscience, literature, physics, music, and animal welfare. An unparalleled mahamudra teacher, he focused on making Dharma accessible to practitioners of all levels. His vision of Buddhism was vast and nonsectarian; he chose to make lojong, calm-abiding meditation, and classical Buddhist philosophy the main focus of his Bodhi Path centers the world over.

Rinpoche was a maverick: he never shied away from blazing a new path if he felt that it would be of benefit to others. His enthusiasm, originality, and spontaneous nature earned him both respect and criticism. Those of us who worked closely with him rarely knew what to expect, but we always learned and benefited from his luminous mind and boundless heart.

I first saw Shamar Rinpoche in the 1980s in Dordogne, France. I watched him arrive at Dhagpo Kagyu Ling, where a traditional welcome awaited him: incense, Tibetan trumpets, many Tibetan lamas, and an assembly of mostly European monastic disciples. I was a fledgling Buddhist; it was my first visit to Dhagpo.

I remember observing Rinpoche as he stepped out of the car and walked along the auspicious symbols toward the main house, smiling at the crowd. I thought, "We are in the presence of royalty." He was so naturally, so comfortably regal. I immediately felt that I belonged to whatever mandala he was the center of; that near or far, my life would somehow orbit around him.

My heart teachers, Gendun Rinpoche and Sherab Gyaltsen Rinpoche, reinforced this certainty through their deep connection with and utter confidence in Shamar Rinpoche. I can't say it was easy for me. Part of me yearned for more security, more predictability, more ease. I've always had a deep rebellious streak, and my difficult relationship with my father left me with an unreasonable mistrust of authority. Rinpoche unfailingly pushed buttons both salient and subterranean. Sometimes, often, I doubted that I had what it takes to stay close; every single time I was inches from my limit, he would reach out to me and let me know that I was where I should be, and that I mattered.

He called me "Pemala" in private, but always referred to me as "Pamela White" in public. He teased me about my weight until the day I told him I could take it from him, but I wouldn't take it from someone who was slim. He delighted in music and liked my songs. He complained about the smell of my well-worn sandals; my floral soap made him sneeze. With a gaze, he would transform the space around a crowd of people into vibrant emptiness. He once asked me if I was a vegetarian because I was a nun and therefore rigid; I said I'd never been a nun. He was the king of the karmic curve ball. He could darken the world with a frown … and then laugh like a sunburst. He told me to behave.

He loved roses. He delighted in English and enjoyed inventing terms like "pushy crowdy karma." He was born for mahamudra—to live it, to teach it—but spent many years doing his utmost to protect his lineage instead. One moment he would lack tact, utterly; the next he would be as subtle as a seasoned diplomat. Backstabbing bewildered him. He was versatile and readily adapted his course to the current situation; it wasn't always easy to keep up. His integrity was bulletproof: he always championed ethics even when a wee dose of "arranging" may have led to more expedient results.

In the West, Shamarpa asked us not to prostrate, not to stand on circumstance, not to nurture traditions foreign to our mores. Instead, he said, we should meditate, study, and learn why principles are important. He would talk about pure realms and other dimensions as if he'd just been there. Though emptiness was his milieu, he built and organized incessantly in fields as diverse as religion, education, human rights, animal rights, and interdisciplinary dialogue.

I last saw him three weeks ago, again in Dhagpo: a circle closed. He was wrapping up a weekend teaching on the four applications of mindfulness. Before giving refuge to a long line of people, he came down from his elevated seat and sat directly on the dais facing relics of the Buddha that were on loan at Dhagpo. His presence was so direct, so simple and respectful that it took my breath away. After he prayed and gave refuge we lined up, group by group, for his blessing. I was at the tail end of the "lama" group. He took my offering scarf, bopped me firmly on the head with his palm, wrapped the khata around my neck and gifted me a generous smile.

As much as I'll miss having him here—acutely, ardently—my gratitude for his presence among us will carry me through. All of the friends I speak with here and afar, from his closest disciples to new practitioners, voice just this blend of sorrow and confidence. May we continue to honor him with our dedication to his vision, in quiet strength and harmony.

JOURDIE ROSS
St. Léon-sur-Vézère, France

◆ WE LOST A GOOD ONE TODAY.
ONE OF THE BEST ONES.

Exactly two weeks ago today I was having tea with Shamar Rinpoche, talking about the future of Buddhism in the West, the future of his centers in Europe and the States, and my own future—as a practitioner, disciple, aspiring teacher, and dutiful minion in the operation of Dharma centers in the Karma Kagyu lineage. For nearly the first time in my life, I had had the courage to ask for something I wanted; to nudge and persist and dare because it felt important. And I got it—an interview with my teacher! The guide I had been following, but from afar, for the last eight years of my life.

When I discovered the Dharma as a wayward seventeen-year-old in New Zealand, the woman who introduced me to meditation and the teachings of the Buddha was a student of Shamar Rinpoche. When I chose to pursue the spark of recognition I felt with Buddhist practice and philosophy, I did so at a Bodhi Path, the network of centers set up by Shamar Rinpoche around the world. When I chose to leave California in search of a life rooted in the Dharma, the teachers who directed me on my way were under the guidance of the very same. When I arrived in India, I had the incredible fortune to meet Shamar Rinpoche's primary disciple, the Kar-mapa—the young successor in the Karma Kagyu lineage. I even crossed paths with Shamarpa himself, but I didn't dare say hello, so intimidated was I by this figure who had so deeply influenced my life, without ever even knowing who I was.

And then, a month ago, I picked up the phone at the Lama House with my usual, "Maison des Lamas. It's Jourdie," only to hear an imperious, "Hello! Where is Jigme Rinpoche?" It only took me a few sentences of Tibetan-inflected English to realize that the voice on the other line was none other than the holder of the lineage, my guide from afar, the one-and-only Kunzig Shamar Rinpoche. Made ever more clear when, while I was scrambling to find someone who could answer his question more precisely than I could, he said, "You are the American girl. I am Shamar Rinpoche." Not only did I know who he was, but, rather more surprising-ly, he knew who I was. While I ascertained that Jigme Rinpoche was not in France, was in Spain, was in Malaga, was gone for the next five days, Shamarpa asked me questions about my life. "So, you are well in Dhagpo? You have not yet visited the center in Germany? You are too busy eating French salami and baguette!" When I mentioned I had been baking my own bread he said, "Ah, and when will you come to bake bread in Virginia? We are beginning to set up the dining hall. We will talk when I come."

He left me in a swirling frenzy, wondering if I would be plucked by fate and neces-sity from a life I love to some other calling, useful but unexpected. Shamarpa is famous for this, turning your whole life on its head to teach you to be flexible and lighten up with your attachments. He's famous for not showing up for teachings or showing up in countries other than those pre-decided. He's famous for bringing storms and wrecking plans—I can testify to this as I lived through the most perilous rain and power outages that I've yet seen in the Dordogne, plus a wind that shattered half the Lama House's fancy dinner service two days before a major event. He is famous for dispensing with ceremonial procedure in one context, and demanding it with vehemence in another. He's famous for being unpredictable, blunt to the point of harshness, and utterly unwilling to bend to norms designed to make people feel comfortable—especially if it doesn't also make them more aware.

He's not famous for being gentle, cajoling, and avuncular. He's not famous for being patient, direct, and reassuring. And yet, I never felt as cared for in my life as when speaking with him. As if my every uncertainty was acceptable, worthwhile even. As if I could lay all my hopes and fears on the table before him, and together we might find the sense in them. It was for this that I asked to meet with him while he was here. Knowing he's busy aiding all beings all the time, knowing he's looking after dozens of centers and projects and teachers, knowing I'm small and recent and have other people to look after me. He made me sure that I have something to offer and that it's worth taking the time to figure out how best to do so.

And so we had tea. I brought a basket of offerings from a ceremony at the center and a white silk prayer scarf; traditional ceremonial things that I felt slightly uncomfortable about. And then I brought things from me: artisanal salami from the nearby town, a letter to tell him the things I feared I would not be able to say out loud. I set the basket of offerings on the table, where it stayed until probably ten minutes after I left, when someone brought it back to Dhagpo to be eaten by the voracious, worldly beings that are me and my cohort of volunteers. The prayer scarf I kept in my pocket.

I gave him the salami right away, and he tapped it on his head, as one would with a sacred text in blessing. I gave him the letter, which he read on the spot. I swallowed hard, smiled at my nervousness, and reminded myself of my commitment. The letter said, "I'm all in." I'm here for you, for the activity of the lineage, for the benefit of beings, from now until enlightenment. Understood: I'm terrified and limited and even though I doubt my own capacity to reach this thing called enlightenment, I know that you don't, and I am confident that this is the thing absolutely most worth doing with this life. So here is my life; my heart and my mind and my hands and all of my wishes. Help me find the way.

He read it and laughed, folded it up, and offered it back to me. I told him to keep it, not because I thought he'd do anything with it, but because I needed that, to give my commitment in a concrete way. Then we talked about France and Virginia and California and long retreats and teaching English and maybe one day teaching Dharma. We talked about tradition and culture and the Western mind. He told me some people don't accept philosophy because they want their teachers to be deities. "They don't believe we are quite human," he said. "We are one hundred percent human." I realized I didn't quite believe it myself.

He told me to stay at Dhagpo, to study, to train myself enough to teach, if I can. He told me things in an hour that will help

me decide my life for as long as I live it. And when I ran out of questions to ask, he closed his eyes and fell half asleep. Part of me wanted to stay, just a little while, to keep feeling cared for. And part of me realized it was time to go, to start to live the wish that his care will carry me and I will learn to take care of myself.

I said, "Thank you Rinpoche," and he opened his eyes. He pushed back his chair, stood up, and lifted his arms. I walked over and tucked my head toward my chin, hands together at my heart. He touched his hands to both sides of my head, and in the space of the blessing I said grace for all beings. I remembered the prayer scarf in my pocket, unrolled it into my hands and said, "A little tradition, not too much," as he had said to me earlier. He touched my temples again, and placed the scarf over my neck. I grinned. He smiled at my gleefulness and nodded his head. I walked out the door and back to the car and went to do groceries, to carry out my commitments, to train in benefiting beings.

I woke up this morning like usual. Took my vitamins, filled my offering bowls, sat down to meditate. Partway through the practice, I felt a touch of pain in my eye, and when I stood up, the white was completely bloodshot. I googled "emotional significance conjunctivitis" to no sensible result, then shook my head at my superstitiousness, put on my glasses, and went to breakfast. Nybou saw me walking up the stairs and stopped still, staring. I wondered if the veins in my eye were that visible, or if it was a new way to say good morning.

When I got close, he blinked twice, put his hand on my shoulder and said, "I have bad news. Shamar Rinpoche had a heart attack in Germany this morning. He's dead. It happened about half an hour ago."

I closed my eyes over the glaring veins and cursed Google, and impermanence, and everything I have left to learn. I ate breakfast and trained a volunteer and turned in circles around the stupa with my stupefied family. Then I walked into an empty room and fell to my knees and cried. Not for him, but for me and for us. I feel small and recent and uncertain. I feel like so many of us are. I feel like I found my family, and now a crucial part of it is gone.

People keep telling me that he's not gone. His wisdom abides. Body changes, but the nature of mind remains. And it's true, I know; I suppose; I guess I'll accept. The lineage is intact. Thank goodness for Karmapa and Jigme Rinpoche and all the teachers who remain to guide us. And reincarnation is a thing the masters know how to handle, and probably he'll come back. I'm making wishes; we all are. And his activity continues, and the centers carry on. I'm making wishes for that too; we all are.

But you know what? Screw rationality and stoicism, just a little. I need them and I get it and I'm grateful that things are clear—support each other, support the Dharma, develop wisdom and be devoted. But at the same time, I'm in mourning and I'm mortal and we all are and this just really sucks. So the tears come and I let them.

And I hope you come back soon and that I'm stronger than I think I am. And I love you and I'm grateful and I'll follow your instructions, even if I don't find this final lesson very funny.

Safe travels, teacher. Shamarpa Chenno (heed me).

DENNIS SIEG
Dusseldorf, Germany

This poem was written on June 11th, 2014.

Drawing of Shamar Rinpoche by Dennis Sieg.

Oh precious teacher,

Countless eons ago,
you cut all suffering at the root
and realized that
whatever is dependently arisen
is unceasing, unborn,
unannihilated, not permanent,
not coming, not going,
without distinction, without identity,
and free from conceptual construction.

Yet I, for whom these are but words,
am struck with grief on this sad day
that you, Shamarpa Mipham Chokyi Lodro,
stopped manifesting in this world.

Due to a small break in my bad karma,
accumulated through beginningless wandering, due to a flicker of merit in this life,
I met you Rinpoche and received your precious teachings.

The wish-fulfilling instructions on bodhichitta, you put into my hand and heart.
If now I fail to put them into practice, when could such a chance be mine again?

Therefore, kind teacher, grant your blessing, that I never fail or falter on
the bodhi path.
Through your continuous inspiration may I persevere in practice, and
diligently train my mind.

And all the merit gained thereby
I will dedicate wholeheartedly
to the fulfillment of your wishes,
so that all obstacles may be dispelled
which would hinder
your swift return.

OM AMI DEWA HRIH

LARA BRAITSTEIN

Interviewed by
Edmund H. Worthy

◆ I would like to share the story of the genesis of *The Path to Awakening*, the book that I had the great honor of working on with Shamar Rinpoche. Actually, the first person who worked on it with him was Sylvia. Then, in approximately 2005 or 2006, I was in Virginia, and Rinpoche, who had been dictating a draft of a lojong text to Sylvia in English, asked me to take a look at it. I read it over, and Pamela Gayle White, who was also in Natural Bridge at that time, looked it over as well. She looked at the organization of the slogans and the order of the ultimate and conventional bodhicitta, and mentioned how this differed from lojong texts she had been exposed to in her studies. I didn't personally know much about mind training at that point; but based on her feedback, when I talked to Rinpoche I brought up her comments. He explained to me that yes, of course there are differences in the different lojong texts. Since the transmission from Atisha, different authors—while not creating something totally new—have chosen to make additions or omissions of certain slogans, and one of the biggest differences between these lojong teachings is whether to have conventional or ultimate bodhicitta explained first.

The more we discussed this topic, Rinpoche became increasingly excited about the project, and reflected on how previously published texts had been organized. Deciding to dig in and take a more extensive look, he enthusiastically read other people's commentaries—commentaries that are hundreds of years old alongside contemporary commentaries, published both in Tibetan and English. Rinpoche was brilliant and he loved research, so he was having a great time going through this material. Meanwhile, I was sort of playing with the language in the draft. It carried on like that for a while, the draft developing through this process of vibrant discussion. But then Rinpoche suddenly decided to scrap the whole thing, saying, "I have an idea, we need to start it all over!" So we did, we started again from the ground up; we did keep some things from the original draft, but completely rearranged everything. We ended up pretty much entirely rewriting it.

We continued to work on this new text for at least a year, getting it into what felt like a workable order. Then, for the second time he said, "Scrap it, I want to start again." I'm not clear whether he was doing this solely for his own work, or if he was perhaps also doing this for me as my teacher, because it was a huge lesson in attachment; not getting attached to the idea that "I" put work into this, and "I" thought this was finished, and "we" had already spent another year on this. It cut through all my ideas about what I felt my role in it was. In retrospect, I started to understand that since he ended up making the lojong teachings so much the heart of the Bodhi Path practice—he never said anything like this to me, this is just me looking back—that of course he wanted to revise it over and over and over again, until he had it exactly the way he wanted it.

Rinpoche made a number of organizational changes, and conceptually he carefully considered the implications of starting with conventional bodhicitta or ultimate bodhicitta. He put a lot of time into his own process of deciding how he was going to explain ultimate bodhicitta. This is the teaching on emptiness, so this was particularly important; he was extremely careful about what he said, how he said it, and how he explained it. Also, since Rinpoche liked using metaphors and analogies, he was thinking in terms of sample situations he thought his readership could relate to; the same way he would teach us orally. He would sometimes completely change the examples he had used, reviewing all the possible implications. Like when it came to the chapter on the afflictions, where the text tells us to start with the strongest affliction first. There he chose the analogy: if you are fighting against an army or enemy, you need to find out who's the smartest person on the other side, who the "thinking-head" is; that's the one you need to destroy and then everyone else will run away. He wondered if people would see that analogy as too violent, since in the English-speaking cultural context of Buddhism, people tend to think Buddhism is analogous to pacifism. He wondered if a military image would disturb people, or if they would understand that because it's a metaphor for the afflicted emotions, he was actually talking about rooting something out in ourselves and destroying it; he questioned if the language was too violent, too militaristic, or off-putting. We went through that process with every single analogy he used; how was it going to be received in this cultural context, how are readers going to receive this, is it too wishy-washy, or is this the type of thing to which an English-reading audience can relate. Rinpoche was committed to careful consideration on the subtlest levels because he wanted to ensure that the examples he gave would be easy to relate to, and that readers wouldn't find anything alienating.

Rinpoche decided to place ultimate bodhicitta first in the book. If you take a look at other lojong commentaries, you'll see they order the root text differently; some begin with conventional bodhicitta, some begin with ultimate. He scrapped the whole text numerous times, maybe three or four times. There are so many levels to Rinpoche's consideration to which I have no access, and I actually forget which bodhicitta came first in the initial version, but I know he definitely considered the implications of starting with one or the other. What ends up being at stake is that if you start with conventional bodhicitta, which is the extremely profound practice of cultivating compassion for sentient beings, one runs the risk of becoming depressed. When engaging in that practice deeply, if one thinks of the suffering of limitless sentient beings as very solid and real, one can get trapped in a cycle of being overwhelmed by how much suffering there is in the world; of how much "I" can commit to giving others time, activity, or material aid. So Rinpoche decided to begin with an explanation of emptiness, ultimate bodhicitta.

Writing this book took place over four years of constant work, in person whenever we could, and also often over Skype. For me it was a very enriching process of understanding: what lojong is, how different teachers have written it, how they've taught it; it was a huge process. I was also fortunate because during that time I had an extremely intelligent master's degree student who was writing on lojong as a genre, and I got to watch his process, which also really helped me think through the material. Most of what I'm sharing is my personal experience with the text.

In terms of my work with Rinpoche, learning to work closely with him was a process of letting go of all of my own expectations and my own ideas about when something starts and when it stops, because we went through the cycle of beginning, working through, coming to completion, scrapping the whole thing, starting again—a few times. It just became a simple, really beautiful process of working with him on amazing teachings.

I can comment about Rinpoche, in very broad terms, in two directions. Shamar Rinpoche, the hilarious, entertaining, warm, wonderful man that we got to hang out with, drive around town with, and go to restaurants with; and Shamar Rinpoche who is, in the history of Tibetan Buddhism, within the second oldest reincarnate lineage, someone who ranks among the very, very top tier of reincarnate lamas in Tibetan history. If he had wanted to be a political lama, he could have had the patrons, he could have had the palaces, the land, and the power; he could have had anything he wanted—but what he really wanted was simply to preserve the authentic Kagyu lineage, and to teach Dharma. The way he taught Dharma, well, look at the activity in his centers; there is so much harmony among his disciples and no factions under him. People don't divide from each other, and they are genuinely friends with each other. Bodhi Path centers are actually pleasant places to be, which, if you've been in a lot of Dharma centers, well, they're not always positive places. You know, they're little laboratories for people to work with their neuroses, so all kind of things can bubble up, right? But Bodhi Path is almost shockingly pleasant as an environment, and that is a testament to Rinpoche.

Rinpoche was always very clear that the Dharma is perfect as it is; it doesn't need him or anybody else, it just requires understanding it clearly, and putting it into practice. For me, what I find really wonderful at his centers is when you walk into the Bodhi Path centers, you're not looking at huge photographs of Shamar Rinpoche, you're not looking at huge photographs of the Karmapa—or any other lama. He taught Dharma in such a way that Dharma was the focus. We weren't distracted by, well, maybe some of us individually were distracted by our devotion for Shamar Rinpoche, but he discouraged that as much as he possibly could. He made a space where people would come to practice Dharma and focus on Dharma.

Rinpoche was such a wonderful, natural teacher; he really lived the Dharma he taught. He was very concerned that an audience could relate to what he taught and wrote; he was concerned that people not get distracted by guru devotion, by politics, by anything like that; but rather that they stay focused on the Dharma. Nor was he gimmicky in his teaching; he was very down to earth. But when I listen to his teachings, they are incredibly profound. He was teaching from a place of total insight and realization. He was always looking for new ways to share that with people, in order to best communicate—for their benefit. He was an extraordinary Dharma teacher.

In the spring of 2014, Shamar Rinpoche traveled across North America, giving talks and interviews at bookstores and other venues to introduce the beautiful new edition of The Path to Awakening, *published by Delphinium Books, distributed by Harper Collins. This is an excerpt from Rinpoche's talk at the prestigious Milken Institute in California.*

◆ I will explain the two reasons I have written this commentary on the Seven Points of Mind Training.

The first reason is that I have been teaching in the United States and European countries for close to 40 years, and have a lot of experience with the evolution of Western society as it connects to Buddhism. According to my experience of the past up until now, a lot of change has happened. For instance, in the 1980s while I was teaching in the United States, so many hippies were interested in Buddhism; they absorbed Buddhism very comfortably, and because of Buddhism sometimes they even stopped taking drugs, were deeply involved in meditation, and very successful. Later, in about the 1990s, the yuppies started, and when they accepted Buddhism, it was a little different from the hippies (audience laughter).

In Tibet, most of the Tibetan population is divided into four Buddhist schools. It was only something of a sectarian problem when one of the schools ruled the government, but then that was for political reasons only. But in the West, when the high-level yuppies—or any business-oriented people—follow one particular Buddhist school, it is like belonging to a company, and it's as if the teacher is the boss of that company, and therefore they feel like they are competitors, similar to the business world. And so the competitive feeling is projected onto that school, or onto the spiritual leaders of that school. The sectarian problem in the West is even stronger than what they used to have in Tibet. Sectarianism is not healthy; it is not healthy to develop it within a community.

The Seven Point Mind Training lineage is a very, very pure lineage. In Tibet, all practitioners of the four schools follow the Seven Points of Mind Training. I have written this commentary of the Seven Points of Mind Training mainly for non-Tibetans, though of course Tibetans can also use it. This is a totally secular practice. You only learn how to practice meditation, and you will learn the different levels of meditation, up to enlightenment. You will not be trapped in

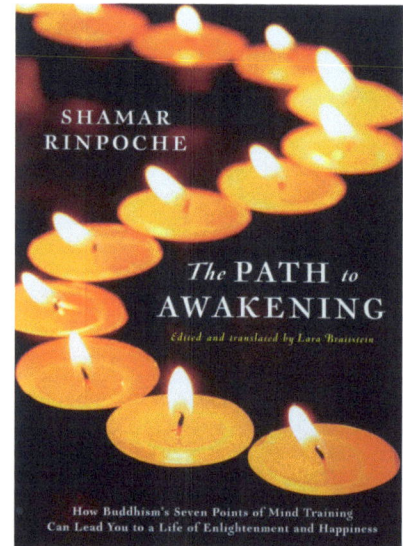

a particular commitment, such commitments as in Vajrayana practice. It is true that if a type of guru who is highly qualified in Vajrayana practice gives an empowerment to a disciple, then the disciple will follow the instructions of the guru without hesitation; they may choose not to analyze anything that the guru says. In fact, this type of dynamic practice was originally organized for the hermitage; in early times, Vajrayana practice was organized completely for the hermitage people. That's why they still go into the deep jungle, and nobody knows how the practitioners are doing practice. Until they are enlightened, you won't know what they are doing. But when Vajrayana is mixed with society, then one is required to make a lot of commitments for many reasons, and I have clearly seen that this is not very healthy. It creates sectarian problems and will not be helpful for people. Therefore, I selected the Seven Points of Mind Training, which is from the lineage of Atisha. In Tibet, also, everyone follows Atisha's teachings, and I feel it is most suitable for Western society.

Another reason I wrote this book is that so many people here are suffering from anxiety and depression. Among these seven points, the first point is very, very helpful for eliminating depression and anxiety. In the first chapter, the first practice is a very effective training. You focus your mind on your breath, and then you count: exhaling, inhaling, twenty-one times—which means five minutes—and then rest. Then you do it again and again, and accumulate a good habit with it. Then you will be able to do one hundred at one time, comfortably, with full awareness about your meditation. Once you become comfortable doing one hundred breath cycles, then you will be able to do it easily one thousand times; from that, peace of mind will develop.

Once peace of mind develops, you have no reason to have anxiety and depression, because the joy from the peace of mind has no comparison in our ordinary life. Even though this is the first step, you will have interesting and wonderful results. Then gradually, you will pass the second step, third step, even you can be enlightened! Seven Points of Mind Training doesn't mean we are trying to take away your mind. No, it means the training of your mind. The mind is like a wild horse, so

you train it, and make it peaceful, to get rid of the agitation, to get rid of the hurricane mind. To develop peace in the mind is the ultimate benefit of life.

◆ RINPOCHE WAS READY TO LEAVE

A great Buddhist master of our times, the 14th Kunzig Shamar Rinpoche manifested high levels of realization, not only during his lifetime but also at the time of his death. A number of inner and outer signs, considered auspicious according to the mahamudra tradition, were present at the time of his passing. He remained in *tukdam* (a post-death deep meditative state) for two days. His body (Tib. *kudung*) manifested signs of high realization as set forth in the Buddhist tantras. There are numerous indications, both overt and subtle, which prove that Shamar Rinpoche was aware that he would soon be leaving his physical manifestation. He prepared for his departure and took care of matters that would help continue his vast activities after his passing.

Beginning in 1996, Rinpoche started to invest a great deal of energy in the development of the Bodhi Path Buddhist Centers (BPBC) worldwide, creating a solid foundation to sustain them. After his passing, an official letter released by the BPBC assistants in September 2014 stated, "Rinpoche poured his energy into establishing our centers by developing our curriculum, training our teachers, and establishing our methods of operations. He has left Bodhi Path in a strong, stable position. In addition, it is evident to us that, through his wisdom, Rinpoche devised and cultivated Bodhi Path precisely so that it could function without him."

During his last year, Rinpoche on several occasions expressed to some of his students that he intended to retire soon, as he had already finished many things that he was supposed to accomplish. Two weeks before his passing, he told his brother Jigme Rinpoche that he had taken care of everything and he would now go on an extended holiday. However, he expressed the wish to spend some time at the Bodhi Path Center in Renchen-Ulm, Germany before leaving on holiday. Did this mean he was preparing his students to be free from dependence on his physical presence?

In 2003, Rinpoche started the construction of the Sharminub Institute in the Kathmandu valley of Nepal, a vast project dedicated to the study and practice of the Buddha Dharma. Wilfred Kroeger, the architect of this project, had a meeting with Rinpoche on June 10, 2014, the day before Rinpoche passed away. Wilfred described the meeting as being very friendly, and Rinpoche talked mostly about the future, and ways to solidify things for the long term. Rinpoche did not discuss unresolved issues during this meeting, which makes us believe that he knew he was not going to be the one handling these issues. Several members who were involved in the development of this project have stated that throughout 2013, Rinpoche fervently stressed the importance of completing the Sharminub project "on time." It is now clear to us that there was a reason for this urgency—he wanted Sharminub to be ready for his cremation to take place there, a wish that he had expressed in the past to his close students.

Due to bureaucratic reasons, the Nepalese government did not approve the plan for the cremation to take place in Nepal right away. However, Rinpoche had long before shown signs that indicated he knew the cremation would indeed take place at Sharminub. One of his closest attendants, Lama Tenam, describes how only a few months before his passing, Rinpoche gave detailed instructions for the arrival of His Holiness the 17th Karmapa Thaye Dorje to Sharminub towards the end of July of 2014, although nothing was apparently planned for such a visit. Rinpoche also gave Lama Tenam detailed instructions on how Karmapa's throne and bed should be prepared. He even gave instructions about where the guests should be placed. And when His Holiness came to Kathmandu to officiate the cremation ceremony on July 31, amazingly everything happened just as envisioned by Rinpoche.

Similarly, Rinpoche apparently also knew the route that the kudung would follow after his passing. Just a few months before he died, Rinpoche shared a very unusual plan with one of his students. He talked about organizing a pilgrimage to different places with all those who wanted to join him. His pilgrim routes included Delhi, Kalimpong, and the final stop in Kathmandu. It so happened that the kudung traveled this exact route, with thousands of people paying their respects to the kudung along the way. During Rinpoche's last visit to Bhutan, he told some of his students he would come back very soon, but just for a day. The kudung subsequently rested at the Royal Palace in Paro, Bhutan, for exactly one day before heading for its final destination, Kathmandu.

In more intimate settings, Rinpoche was forthcoming and spoke about his imminent passing. For many years, Rinpoche had repeatedly remarked to some of his closest students that he would die in his sixties. And just a few days before his passing, he called one of his close students and asked, "Will you be very sad if I die?"

In the last year before his passing, Rinpoche organized many of his personal belongings. He emptied his room at the Karmapa International Buddhist Institute (KIBI) in Delhi, and passed his home in Kalimpong over to his sister.

Two months before he died, without any apparent reason, Rinpoche deactivated his Facebook account. However, a month later he decided to reactivate his Facebook account to help spread word about the plight of Meriam Ibrahim, a Sudanese woman imprisoned for apostasy and for marrying a Christian man. Rinpoche released an official letter in which he requested everyone, including world leaders and Nobel peace prize winners, to join him in insisting on her release. He urged his students to share this letter on social media, including his reactivated Facebook account. Meriam is a free woman today and she lives in the United States!

During his last teachings at Dhagpo Kagyu Ling in France and Bodhi Path Renchen-Ulm in Germany, Rinpoche talked at length about death and the impermanent nature of everything. He gave many details about the dying process. In his last recorded interview, Rinpoche said, "You should not be surprised when you see something is changed. You should accept it; you should understand that things are not permanent. Change is inevitable."

On June 9, 2014, at his very last teaching in Renchen-Ulm, instead of continuing from the page of his own book, where he had ended the last class, Rinpoche decided to teach the short text by the 5th Shamarpa on lojong, and told the students, "You all will be very satisfied because you can finish it." In explaining the benefits of practicing lojong, Rinpoche said, "We will not be afraid of death because we have confidence. Frankly, we never know when the death comes; now you will not be afraid of death because you know how to use death."

During this teaching, some students noticed that Rinpoche blacked out for a few seconds. When he came out of the blackout, he told his students, "I nearly got that, I nearly got coma, now I woke up." Later at lunch, when only a few people were present, he said, "I will die soon." Later the same day, Rinpoche expressed his wish to have dinner at a restaurant by the river in Strasbourg. Jigme Rinpoche and I accompanied him to dinner. During the course of the meal, he suddenly said: "This is my last dinner," and ordered a second dish. The following day he had a very light vegetarian lunch and skipped his dinner. We never imagined that what he had said the previous evening about "his last dinner" would prove to be true!

I recall another incident, which only made sense to me after Rinpoche had passed away. On Sunday, June 8, 2014, three days before he passed away, he was doing a search on Google with the keywords "Shamarpa 2014." I was curious to know what he was looking for. Among other search results, he found his "official" photo with the red crown posted in a blog administered by the London Diamond Way Center, where he had recently visited. He immediately told me to contact them and ask them to remove it, giving me the impression that he did not like the photo. For some reason, I did not contact them that night. The following day Rinpoche, with a sense of urgency, asked me again whether I had contacted them. I immediately emailed the London DWC and the picture was consequently removed from the blog. I understood later that this was one of his most recent photos with the Red Crown and would be used as the official photo for all the ceremonies during the forty-nine days. Does this mean that Rinpoche had even decided which photo he wanted to be used for his funeral services?

In summation, Shamar Rinpoche has proven to us in many different ways that he was, he is, and he always will be, a great master. Rinpoche's activities are so vast and impressive that they can certainly be compared to those of the victorious sun.

Like the Sun

Our precious and unique star,
Omnipresent even if we cannot see,
All pervading beyond what we can conceive,
Equanimity embracing all beings,
Brightness illuminating the way,
Power functioning in the world.

The basis for all to happen …

May your unceasing activity remain,
melting the beginningless ice of ignorance,
drying uncountable tears of sorrow,
shining infinite love and compassion,
showing appearances like a rainbow.

—Maria Camara

◆ THE BLESSINGS AND GUIDANCE OF KUNZIG SHAMAR RINPOCHE IN MY LIFE

I had just graduated from Nalanda Institute for Higher Buddhist Studies, where Shamar Rinpoche was the director and principal, when I first went to see Rinpoche in order to seek blessings for my future. Rinpoche was staying at his residence in Rumtek then, and he granted me an audience, although he probably had no idea who I was, except that I was a student there. I asked for Rinpoche's permission and blessing to do a three-year retreat at the Rumtek retreat center.

Rinpoche thought for a moment, turned to me and said, "Aren't you a student from the institute?" I said "Yes, Rinpoche-la." Rinpoche paused for a moment and said, "If you stay in three-year retreat you will benefit from it personally, but if you teach Dharma, then a lot of other people will benefit—so you should teach Dharma." I immediately replied, "Rinpoche-la, but I don't know how to teach and I am not at all capable of teaching. I am not even one of the best students. Please allow me to go to three-year retreat." "Let me think about it and I will let you know soon," Rinpoche said.

I don't remember exactly how many days went by, but early one morning one of Rinpoche's attendants came and said, "Shamar Rinpoche has asked you to come to the 16th Karmapa's audience room, and he requested that you come in formal dress." I was so happy to hear that, thinking that now Rinpoche was going to give me the blessings and permission for the three-year retreat. I went as asked to Karmapa's audience room, feeling very blessed and joyful. As I entered the room, Rinpoche was sitting where Karmapa used to sit, and there were a few other senior monks. I prostrated three times and offered a khatak to Rinpoche. To my surprise he officially and traditionally appointed me as Khenpo right there, and said "You are going to teach the Dharma." He offered me a beautiful khatak and other official things, as it was traditionally done during the time of the 16th Karmapa. Although I didn't really meet the 16th Karmapa, I was told by the senior monks how fortunate I was that I was appointed in the 16th Karmapa's official audience and appointment room. I felt very blessed and happy, though I wasn't sure about teaching the Dharma. I never thought I could teach and become a Dharma teacher; especially not in the West!

A few years later, at the Karmapa International Buddhist Institute (KIBI), Shamar Rinpoche said that I should go to Europe and teach at Dharma centers there. I was very excited about going to the West, but I was also really nervous and unsure of my capacity to teach the Dharma. I thought I was supposed to have a translator, but somehow the translator couldn't come, and Shamar Rinpoche said, "There's no need for a translator, you can teach by yourself in English." I hadn't exactly taught Dharma in English before; actually I hadn't even really taught Dharma or philosophy before, even in the Tibetan language. So I told Rinpoche that I couldn't teach Dharma, especially not in English—I told him my English was not at all good enough. "You're going to be just fine, don't worry," Rinpoche said. But I was really nervous. My first foreign trip was to Germany, and it was in January. I had no idea that people in Germany didn't speak English. I thought that in the West there was just one language: English. Nonetheless, my trip turned out to be quite successful, and I was told people enjoyed my teaching. Since then, I've traveled to Europe pretty often, and developed many good friendships over the years.

In 2002, Shamar Rinpoche brought me and other khenpos to Kalimpong to teach at the Shri Diwakar Vihara Buddhist Institute. This was Shamar Rinpoche's first Buddhist institute for monks. Shamar Rinpoche and Karmapa both appointed me as the headmaster of the Institute, and I served there until 2008. Rinpoche was very happy with the Institute and the students there. That was one of the best times of my life, and one that I am really proud and happy about. I wholeheartedly took care of the Institute and we lived like one big happy family.

In 2006, Shamar Rinpoche brought me to the United States to teach at the Bodhi Path Buddhist centers. He wanted me to become a permanent resident in the United States. Through the Wisdom Foundation, he helped me to obtain the proper visas, and now I am an American citizen. Now I can travel to Bodhi Path centers worldwide to be of benefit, as Rinpoche envisioned.

In 2007, in Virginia, Rinpoche gave me the responsibility of running the Karmapa International Buddhist Institute (KIBI) in New Delhi. Both Shamar Rinpoche and Karmapa appointed me as the headmaster at that time. I have been back to India every year since then to stay for three months—KIBI was only run in the winter then. I am still involved, but no longer as headmaster.

The seed was planted. Rinpoche told me about Sharminub in Kathmandu, saying he wanted me to be the main Khenpo at Sharminub Monastery—he playfully said that he'd give me the best room with the best view of the valley, and that I could enjoy my life there. I guess that is not going to happen now, but I had Rinpoche's blessings at least—several times actually.

So I feel my life is a precious gift from Shamar Rinpoche. Without his blessings and guidance, I am not sure where I would be today. Now I have Bodhi Path and KIBI in my life, and I intend to spend my life serving them. I also wish and hope to serve Shri Diwakar Vihara in Kalimpong. These are three major accomplishments in Rinpoche's life, and I truly feel very blessed to be part of all three.

MICHELLE SCHAFFNER
San Luis Obispo, California

◆ 108 START

Today is my birthday. I have several partial drafts of my tributes to Shamar Rinpoche that I started as soon as he departed the human form we recognized sixteen months ago. They are upstairs on my desk but unreachable, and actually, that writing feels a world away in my current medical state. So, I lay here flat on my back and begin again, feeling gratitude and awe that I had the privilege and opportunity to know him, learn from him, and be an arm of his vast activity. But as you know, as I hope you know, his presence, his activity, and his benefit to all beings has not stopped or slowed down. It is continuing in every moment—in limitless ways, palpable or not—as is befitting the living Buddha that he was and is.

Do you realize how incredibly amazing it is for each and every being in space and time that masters like Shamar Rinpoche exist in our world? And then bring the focus down to the incredible auspiciousness of those who recognize his mastery. Then again, focus in even further—to another layer of detail, to those of us who are part of his mandala, and somewhere down in there lies a small speck of life and potential I'll call "me."

And here no other sound or syllable really suffices besides *ah*, of the classical Tibetan or Sanskrit variety, or in colloquial contemporary American—*awe*.

While recollecting and reminiscing, I realize I must have had a very good connection with Rinpoche in my past lives. When I met him, I knew I was home. I tried to be discriminating and evaluate him thoroughly as a teacher, like he taught that we should, but I couldn't doubt him. I would even try to generate the doubts that I heard others deciphering and grappling with as they talked about differing opinions and controversies, but it was not something that I needed to work with, except maybe for patiently listening to other's doubts—what a gift.

From early on in our relationship to the last time I saw Rinpoche physically, and continuing after he departed the body until today, I felt and feel a level of reverence and deference that one might feel being around royalty; a celebrity, a statesman, or … a dharma king; and was continually amazed that he kept inviting me to come in closer. His presence naturally imbued respect, yet he was so humble and surprising—from his ever so polite phone calls, "Hello?" Always inquiring first whether it was okay that he was calling me, was it a good time to talk? As if I would ever decline a call from Rinpoche, regardless of time or place! Or moving off his raised seat to sit on the floor cross-legged next to me to talk more, or inviting me out for fabulous meals, always knowing what was best yet always satisfied with whatever came, to asking me to make and attend doctors' appointments with him and discussing his medical testing and results, to him taking a quick shower while he asked me to wait nearby in his hotel room, and so on. I was continually lifted up by his ease around me.

Really beyond lifted, you see, because for a long time, sometimes even still, he had more confidence in me than I had in myself. I had confidence in him, but honestly, not much in myself. The longer I practiced and worked with him and for him, my confidence in him continued to grow and telescope out, but for a long time, not really in myself. Through him, by his trust in me and in all the projects and requests and kindness and teachings that he requested of me or gave, he showed me so many ultimate gifts, as well as more relative ones. For Buddha's sake, if he was entrusting me with so much, then he must be seeing something in me that I was not! Or, maybe it was just his unconditional compassion.

I recall one chat between the two of us in 2010. I was having increasing health problems that were getting in the way of my accomplishing tasks. I felt I wasn't able to serve his activities to the best of my abilities, or to the level of quality his projects deserved. I was uncomfortable bringing this up with him, as I really did not want to stop or slow down—but I also felt he deserved to know, so he could make choices in order to have the strongest teams for his organizations and activities. His response was immediate. Rinpoche suggested a specific medicine, told me that I had been working very hard for him for ten years—which surprised me, that he recalled so quickly and accurately the amount of time that I had been working within the mandala—and he said if I wanted to, I could stop. I silently thought to myself, but did not say out loud, 'Well, I didn't take the bodhisattva vow for just ten years, it's for all time." He smiled, and said out loud to me, "Okay then, let's continue," and we proceeded to make more plans for the Sciences of Mind project and the Infinite Compassion Foundation.

On a different occasion, he introduced me to a Rinpoche that had come to visit him and that I had not met before, and he was going on and on with these positive compliments about me. It struck me as pretty bizarre, very atypical, and I actually interrupted Rinpoche, correcting him on some of the points he was making about me, trying to bring myself down a few notches, until he shot me a look that stopped me in my tracks. I didn't know what to make of it at the time, and in fact often found things that he would say or do, which seemed incredibly out of context with whatever else was "seemingly" happening at the moment, would at some point make perfect sense, or actually unfold as he had foretold and happen in the days, months, or years following. He had such a wide, long view, that time and again others would eventually catch up, or at least see enough of a glimpse to be able to verify that he indeed sees and knows so much more than the rest of us.

His ability to give people exactly what they needed was uncanny. What he gave was what people needed absolutely, and it could be quite startling or shocking, as well as full of ease and peace, depending on the circumstances. I loved watching him and his effect on others. Sometimes people were blissed out, other times people looked wide-eyed and awake, as if their eyelids somehow had a magical eyelift, and other times you could see, or hear, them squirming and wrestling with some internal concept or *klesha* Rinpoche was helping to unravel. In crowded teachings, his face would change like a kaleidoscope as he addressed, by mind, different people in a crowd. Sometimes he would light up as brightly as a Chrismas tree; and just as quickly his demeanor pointed to another could come across as a ferocious scowl, or to another as the softest, gentlest doe-eyed kindness. Speaking all the while what appeared to be a single teaching, one unified set of words to the crowd, while individually addressing each mind in the room, and no doubt those who were there but unseen by our eyes.

Rinpoche talked to me about other people a lot. I was often uncomfortable when he gave me his opinions of the unsavory parts—the actions, behaviors, or attitudes of people we both knew and often saw, as well as others I didn't personally know. Sometimes these were seemingly random comments, other times he wanted some follow-up action on my part, which was fairly or completely out of my comfort zone. I took these as profound lessons, these examples of what Rinpoche found distasteful and unhelpful—lessons in what not to foster or be. I often grappled with what he shared, in how I should respond to and be with these folks, while maintaining their and Rinpoche's confidentiality, working with my own discomfort with the negative aspects, and also, to somehow be of benefit. It felt difficult and confusing, but I tried to think critically, be impartial and objective, and maybe most importantly, help others to be successful—sometimes at the price of "myself." It seems to have all worked out. "Seems" is the key word here. For now, I see ever more clearly that his success is our success, our success is his success, just as your success is my success. It doesn't involve any less than, or more than, any winners, or losers. It boils down to being of benefit, of rising up, in the myriad and sometimes obscure or hidden ways that manifest. This success is, in small and large ways, the awakened heart-minds of kindness, compassion, love, benefit, wisdom, and ultimate freedom. Yep, bodhichitta sums that up in one word, but Rinpoche's blessings have shown it as it is—beyond a word or description. I know I haven't gleaned all of the pearls, all the treasures, from our interactions yet, but I'm confident more will appear in due time.

Another heartwarming memory is Rinpoche's effect on my younger son, Tashi. I took both my boys to an empowerment from Rinpoche, and enjoyed watching as they got more and more excited, returning to the blessing line repeatedly. After we returned home, Tashi, at age seven, behaved in a way he never had before or since, emphatically asking, "How can I help? I want to help, a Buddha is coming," running around the house, grabbing cleaning cloths and spontaneously cleaning and wiping down the walls. In fact we were expecting Rinpoche to arrive and stay at our home in a few days time, but the cleaning was already fairly complete. Nevertheless, for those several days, Tashi self-initiated more cleaning activity, in a more joyful manner, than I have seen in the whole of his eleven years! A favorite picture of mine is of Tashi, reunited with Rinpoche in San Luis Obispo, proudly thrusting the blessing cord still wrapped around his neck towards Rinpoche, who leaned in and—to Tashi's delight—blew on the knot. And this morning, just a moment ago, I am again elated to hear Tashi asking me, "How can I help?"

There are so many stories and experiences that I could share about Shamar Rinpoche. I could perhaps relate the intersection of his sharing his medical issues with me in the months before I suddenly became incapacitated and had to turn my attention back to my own medical situation. But in the meantime, I am continuing to work hard—or rest well—or however you prefer to characterize the Path to Awakening, and look forward to the day when he returns in a nirmanakaya form, when I will be ever better suited to continue his activity as an arm of my master.

Rinpoche's methods of keeping us on our toes, of fostering flexibility and resilience to continuous change while at rest and in motion, have been priceless. I've benefited from this training countless times and in countless ways. Lately, it's coming in pretty handy yet again. The work of a bodhisattva requires this—it requires always showing up to the present, to reality as it is, whatever it is, and making the best of it. And it turns out, just as we've been taught, that the supreme path is to be of benefit, and that the obstacles and difficulties to that end always come back to ego-clinging. Clinging to a "self" that is real, different, and separate from. Trying to make sure that your "self" somehow gets in on some of the good you're trying to accomplish really, really, dilutes the benefit, if there's any left at all. Whatever our conceived notions of what we need to do, what our work is, what our lives are for, and how to be in the world, well, don't be surprised when it's all jumbled and turns out to not be so. The bodhisattva's way reveals as the need presents, and it's not really a problem. I've learned to just rest, do the practice, rely on the refuge, lighten up, and let reality be as it is. It is the solution. He gave us all we need. Don't complicate it. Develop trust in it. Do it. Rest in the unborn nature of mind.

Rinpoche's blessings are truly like the sun dispelling the darkness of night. As I lay on my back while writing this, not able to sit up, contemplating yesterday's "big news" day from my medical team's latest findings about my continuous bodily degradations—another serious diagnosis, no one quite knowing how to advise management of my almost twenty serious, several rare, many untreatable, some imminently deadly medical diagnoses—I was reminded yet again that I'd better get the important things done, one of them being trying to complete this tribute to Rinpoche that can never truly be completed. His presence and benefit have been way too grand to contain. I'm reminded of his words to me when acknowledging my carrying on with my bodhisattva promise a few years ago. All of our lives and worlds, as we once recognized them, will disintegrate and change, and sometimes we actually get to witness it happening. It isn't the end. It's merely a call in a different tune to carry on. A bodhisattva's work is changing—requiring flexibility, calm, awareness, and wisdom to be of benefit without reference points. Let's keep working. As Rinpoche said to me, "Okay then, let's continue."

Whatever I am, whatever has been developed, whatever has let go, I bow down and offer back to you, Dear one. May your return be swift. Thank you Rinpoche, for believing in me, and for helping me to see what is.

RINCHEN ATHUP
New York, New York

◆ THE INFINITE LIGHT OF THE RISING SUN

My most recent memory of the 14th Kunzig Shamar Rinpoche was at his Bodhi Path Buddhist center in Virginia, US, less than two months before he passed away on June 11, 2014. My sister and I drove down from New York City to visit him during the Easter weekend. One afternoon, Rinpoche simply pointed at a spot and told me to sit. "New York la kyipo duway?" he asked in Tibetan, which means "Are you happy in New York?" He would always ask me this question, and my mumbled response would always be "Yes, Rinpoche." He took a deep long breath, smiled at me with raised eyebrows, and gazed outside his window after that, while I just sat quietly, not knowing whether to say anything—I dared not. Natural Bridge,

Virginia was a special place for Rinpoche, and you could tell he truly enjoyed being in the mountains, listening to the birds chirping away while flowers bloomed on the trees and blanketed the hills during springtime. My sister had mentioned to Rinpoche before our visit that I had learned how to make momos (Tibetan dumplings), and the pressure was on me to deliver. I made sure to practice on a daily basis, and it paid off when I watched Rinpoche apply his dumpling-eating technique while neatly slurping away the soup.

Even though I grew up in Sikkim, India, I seldom got the opportunity to be around Rinpoche, as I was in boarding school most of the time. But I remember clearly, even as a young boy, being aware of the obstacles that Rinpoche faced and how his monks and followers were ostracized by society. Rinpoche undoubtedly understood the ripple effects of his decisions, but he was also fully aware that if anyone was to stand firm and protect the purity and rights of the Karma Kagyu School, it had to be him.

It was during my later years, after high school, that I was able to see Rinpoche more often in the US and in Nepal. He had the ability to calm my mind in an instant, making me realize not just the aura and power of his presence, but also instilling an everlasting feeling of love, compassion, contentment, and optimism. Shamar Rinpoche truly dedicated his entire life to ensuring the flourishing of the pure Dharma, evidenced when he was faced with unimaginable obstacles during his lifetime; Rinpoche always stood firm in his beliefs and stayed true to his principles. Despite the hardships and challenges, Rinpoche left no stone unturned in his efforts to spread the teachings of the Buddha in a non-sectarian manner through his establishment of Bodhi Path centers all over the world. It was his way of opening the doors of Buddhism, as taught by Buddha Shakyamuni, lifting all societal barriers and traditional norms.

No matter how hard I try, it is extremely difficult for me to simply accept the nature of impermanence whilst maintaining a calm mind—this loss is immeasurable, and the sorrow uncontainable. Shamar Rinpoche will always be a symbol of truth, fearlessness, compassion, commitment, and unwavering willpower. I believe it is up to us, his students, to uphold those values and continue to practice his teachings—this is how we can connect with Shamar Rinpoche, even if his physical manifestation is absent. The life lived and the legacy left behind by Kunzig Shamarpa is an excellent source for learning and inspiration. We are extremely fortunate to have lived in an era where all of Shamarpa's teachings are well-documented and preserved to benefit all, for generations to come.

I shall always cherish the last evening spent with Rinpoche, during that Easter weekend in Virginia. Rinpoche walked out of his living room, sat on the porch, and gazed at the horizon while the sun emitted bursts of red, pink, and magenta rays. Melancholic, yet beautiful and promising. It was the most beautiful sunset I had ever witnessed, and beyond that, alongside the great master himself. Even though I am overwhelmed with sadness now, I try to contain my emotions by remembering that special evening, gazing at the colorful horizon with Rinpoche, knowing very well that the sun shall rise again and again, to shed light onto our paths.

◆ HOMAGE

Venerable Shamar Rinpoche,

With profound gratitude I think of you, my Root Guru, who guided me in the most skillful and compassionate ways.

Rinpoche, you always knew my needs and my wishes—you have fulfilled them and so much more.

All of my thoughts were known to you—you clearly demonstrated that.

And when I was sometimes lost in emotion, calling your name for help—you responded in so many ways.

It is impossible to write about all the great help, situations, signs, and answers you manifested—it was an amazing display.

I hope I will be worthy of all the kindness you have expressed towards me.

Your patience and generosity are so amazing, and your subtle teachings go straight into the heart—pointing out the essence and way to true freedom.

May I not waste my life, and put joyful effort and perseverance into purifying my veils and following in your footsteps—the footsteps of the Buddha.

Thank you, dear Rinpoche. You are with me still, always—when I call your name you have never stopped manifesting answers and fulfilling my wishes.

May your physical form return swiftly and demonstrate what it means to "fly above trouble."

You have perfectly displayed this in your past life—please keep showing us the way to freedom in the midst of samsara.

I bow down before you, beloved Shamar Rinpoche—please keep guiding me as your humble student.

With devotion, love, and gratitude, Silk

GREG MOCK
Seattle, Washington

◆ My name is Greg Mock. I presently live in Seattle, Washington. Previously I lived near Washington, DC and attended the DC Metro Bodhi Path Center, which I was sad to leave when I moved. I'd like to talk about my participation with Rinpoche's book *Creating a Transparent Democracy,* which I believe he originally started writing as far back as 2001; at least my introduction to his ideas in the book started in 2001 when I visited him in Kalimpong, India. I was invited to stay with Rinpoche at his residence, which for me was like a dream. When I arrived, Hannah Nydahl, who often translated for him, was also visiting. We had very in-depth, interesting dinner conversations, and one day Rinpoche pulled out a diagram of a system of governance that he proposed could be a remedy for the rampant corruption he observed in Nepal and India. This system specifically addressed what he viewed as a failure of the present political systems to support poor and disenfranchised people both in India, where he had a residence, and also Nepal, where he spent considerable time. Upon further consideration, he widened his ideas to include impoverished developing countries and countries where development had been unsuccessful.

This conversation's subject matter surprised me, as I had also been exploring ideas around democratization for my job with the World Resources Institute. I entered this job thinking about solutions for environmental issues, but it quickly became apparent that no environmental progress could be made without changes in areas such as governance. New ideas around governance had been making great strides in the previous decade, but for Rinpoche to talk about these ideas amazed me, since this is the domain of experts in governance, politics, and development. On top of that, he had a rather radical view of restructuring government. He showed it to me, saying, "Here's how a country should be formulated. You should redraw the jurisdictional boundaries so that constituents, even in as small a place as a remote village, will be empowered. They should have direct access to their representatives." He was talking about representational democracy in a third world context.

It turns out he'd been thinking about this for years, jotting thoughts down in his notebook, and as he ultimately relayed in the forward of the published edition of *Creating a Transparent Democracy,* he developed these ideas over time. This wasn't just something that he plucked out of his mind one day because of something he'd read; he'd been formulating this system as a way of alleviating a fundamental problem within the human condition. There are all kinds of suffering, and of course he was equally concerned about issues such as the basics of food and clean water; poverty and its corrosive effects in general; and ultimately, the difficulty for those who lack the means to maintain a spiritual practice.

Rinpoche understood that an essential remedy for relieving people's suffering is helping them out of poverty. These are not novel ideas; coming up with a governance system, though, while connecting this with spiritual practice, and helping people develop the ability to look at their mind in order to address suffering at its source—this was new to me. When people don't have the means to sustain themselves, they don't have real freedom, they don't have political freedom, and there is negativity and oppression: certainly not an environment that fosters spiritual freedom. Rinpoche, of course, had a very wide conception of what spiritual practice is, and living in decent basic human conditions was at its base.

Rinpoche was influenced by Gandhi, I think, and also by what happened in South Africa in previous decades. He studied the way governance systems are often formulated, because even though in name there are many democracies in the world, some don't function well due to lack of mechanisms for transparency. You can be a mayor, president, prime minister, or any person of authority and say you are obeying the law, but in fact there is nothing in place to check that. Certainly not for people at the lowest income level. His idea was to implement a way to ensure that officials would be accountable in a public forum—accountable to the people they represent. Important aspects of Rinpoche's design included allowing local people to express their budget priorities; he said, "You can say whatever you want philosophically, but really, it's what people spend the money on. Do you fix the road or don't you, or does that money go for a bribe to one of your compatriots or one of your family?" Rinpoche asserted that this is the corrosive aspect; until there are checks in place to make sure people are getting their money's worth, there won't be any real change. He said, "Look, most people in rural India live in villages. What are we going to do to empower people in the village?" His idea was to start at the very base, a bottom up structure.

In 2005, four years after staying with Rinpoche in Kalimpong, I moved to the Natural Bridge, Virginia center for what I thought was going to be a six-month retreat, but in actuality I ended up staying about eight months; most of that time I worked with Rinpoche on the initial draft of the *Transparent Democracy* book. I was impressed that during those ensuing four years Rinpoche had developed his ideas into a real draft. He proffered a manuscript that had some stray ideas and some ideas that were controversial and might detract from his message, plus it wasn't organized in a way that I thought would ultimately serve or completely express his vision. Rinpoche asked me to work on it since I am a writer, and also because I had already explored these ideas with him in Kalimpong.

Much of my time there was spent talking with him, engaged in very detailed discussions about governance. My notions about Rinpoche certainly expanded, because this was real politics, not just for the sake of discussion, but a deep exploration of the structure of political decisions and decision-making: essentially, how to empower poor people in a real life system in modern times.

Shamar Rinpoche made a point of associating his ideas about democracy with his broader ideas about humanity. For instance, he had included passages about how ultimate authority and benefits are derived from the earth, and so politicians should not conceive of themselves as powerful because they had been granted some special dispensation from "heaven" or something. He said, "The real power derives from Mother Earth, and we should acknowledge that we don't hold this power. Benefits come from the earth and nature and we need to take care of them." Rinpoche had embedded environmental responsibility and responsibility to all beings in the draft. Of course! He's a bodhisattva! Animals were also mentioned in the text, associated with humans and the governance of human systems—but not only human systems, because how people treat animals was part of his larger idea. For instance, he attributed legal rights to animals. He said they should be treated humanely and that this should be embedded in the law. Rinpoche always talked in specifics about legal rights, because legality and the formal structure of legal systems were of real interest to him. He thought this was the way that human systems take their most concrete form, and that tyranny comes through the abuse of legal systems; that if transparency is going to be real, it has to be implanted in the legal system itself.

Rinpoche asserted that citizens should be empowered at the most basic level—the power to check budgets, throw people out of office if there is corruption, and those sorts of things. He truly believed in democracy, and he didn't believe that Western democracy was the only model; in fact, he critiqued Western democracy and criticized its failings. Although he originally devised this model for Nepal, he also thought about the failings of democratic systems at large. As a matter of fact, in 2014, he and I revisited this topic, and he planned to re-issue *Creating a Transparent Democracy* with a commentary about the US government system. Rinpoche was not suggesting that the US system be thrown away, but that there are certain ways that it falls short and is corrupt, and therefore could be changed.

Rinpoche sent the book to individuals in Nepal, and also published an Indian edition, both printed in English. Additionally, he thought that the world population in general could find value in this book; that benefiting people and their spiritual life shouldn't be confined to any specific area. In all the years I knew him, his interest about how healthy governance systems could benefit beings never waned; the breadth of Rinpoche's vision was really quite extraordinary. It was remarkable to me that this wasn't a short-term interest; he'd developed it over years, and the topic was still significantly important to him fifteen years after first publishing his book. In actuality, he and I were in the process of putting together an addendum to the book, and right before Rinpoche's death I got an email from him asking me if I had worked on the manuscript; he was interested right up to the end. I feel that this will be part of his continuing work; the publishing team is still considering how it will play out.

For his part, Rinpoche was aware that writing a book like this was unusual for a person in his station, and he was hopeful that the outcome would be favorable; in other words, he didn't pose as an academic or expert in governance. Rinpoche knew his expertise was in certain areas within Buddhism, but he also looked at the world and thought deeply about these things, and thought well-being could result from this system. He said that others could take this model forward, but he wanted to illustrate how he envisioned democratic transparency and how it could be pursued. Shamar Rinpoche had great vision, and he understood how his piece could be used to promote change.

Separating politics and religion, as we all know Rinpoche endorsed, didn't mean not expressing his ideas about these broad areas of human endeavor. He made it clear that he had no special authority in this area "as a religious person," clearly stating that, "Just because I'm the Shamarpa doesn't mean you should listen to these ideas. One should evaluate them on their own merit; but I think they have merit, and I'm concerned about it because of my concern for human well-being at large." He didn't claim that we should examine this because he had some special insight, he merely stated that he had come at this from a different perspective, which could be beneficial, because these issues are central to human well-being. I think that's the way he separated it—by not claiming special authority in that area. But he didn't feel that it was a subject to avoid. He felt it was legitimate if offered from a certain perspective, encouraging people to evaluate his ideas on their own.

I think the book has been influential behind the scenes. Rinpoche didn't write it to sell a ton of copies, or expect it to be embraced in a broad public manner, but I think he would have liked it if it did get public acclaim—for instance Desmond Tutu wrote the introduction for one edition of it. I think he wanted the book to be a marker for some people, to have a subtle influence, although I don't really have the measures to know if it has. He seemed happy with its reception, but his interest in it wasn't based on the reception it received. He was happy with it, and he was interested in an updated version being re-launched, and for that edition to possibly have an even wider impact. He said many times that a bodhisattva's activity has to be very wide, and of course we know now, after his death, that his activity was much more vast than any of us suspected.

This was my introduction to his keen, astute, and detailed interest in democracy. The discussions we had were very comprehensive, and occasionally I would challenge his ideas. I felt he wanted that from me in order to fully parse out his ideas, to explore if this would really fly, and I think my perspective was useful from that standpoint. He did have definite, clear ideas, and would sometimes leave in something that I challenged. On the one hand, his ultimate goal was that it be put forth in a way that people could understand and accept; he didn't want it perceived to be so radical that people couldn't relate or wouldn't read it. Yet on the other hand, being a bit of a rabble-rouser, he wanted it to be a bit radical because he felt that business as usual was not working. Rinpoche really believed that empowering people at the poorest level of society would result in change and be the most beneficial, so that when money is spent, there is genuine benefit to the local population, not just to a select few. Personally, it was an incredible honor for me to work with him so closely, and spectacular to witness, because he was such a force.

KHAYDROUP ZANGMO
Pasadena, California

◆ MEMORIES OF SHAMAR RINPOCHE

My first memory of Shamar Rinpoche is when I was in New Delhi, India visiting the Karmapa International Buddhist Institute. It was November of 1990, on the very first day KIBI opened for classes. My husband Ed and I arrived just before noon to see a friend from Boulder, Colorado who was enrolled. She said, "Shamar Rinpoche is here. Would you like to see him?" Without a second thought, we eagerly replied, "Yes!" Word came back almost immediately, "He will see you now."

We were led to a tiny office where Rinpoche was seated behind a very large desk, and we sat in two chairs right in front of the desk. He looked at us inquisitively.

We had had no time to gather our thoughts and he was waiting. Suddenly I blurted out, "We want to do a three-year retreat with Gendun Rinpoche." What I saw next was extraordinary. Rinpoche's eyes rolled up into his head for a long moment, suddenly snapped back, and he said, "Yes, I will write you a letter. Come tomorrow and pick it up. You should go to France now. Don't waste time." In a state of utter shock at this abrupt turn of events—that effectively transformed a heartfelt wish into an imminent reality, I stammered, "We're here for the first time, can we do some pilgrimage first?" He said, "Yes, it is good to gather blessings before going into a three-year retreat, but do not waste time!"

By then my mind was racing. I was thinking to myself that visas would be a big problem for us going from India to France, so I said out loud, "What about our visas?" Rinpoche looked at me and said, "You won't have any trouble with your visas." Remembering all the difficulties my daughter had getting her three-year visa to study in France, again I said, "But my daughter … ." Rinpoche looked straight at me and said in a firm voice, "This I know very well, you will not have a problem with your visas."

Then he said, "You should come to Rumtek. I will go there in a couple of days, and you should come too." We did follow Rinpoche to Rumtek, and then went on to Darjeeling and Bodh Gaya, receiving an abundance of kind hospitality and blessings from all manner of wise persons and sacred places along the way. By mid-December we were in Bodh Gaya, where we met two Swiss students of Gendun Rinpoche. They gave us vital details for the upcoming retreat. They said, "If you are genuinely interested in retreat with Gendun Rinpoche, you must leave India for Europe in one week. He is about to give a month-long teaching to 100 students who have been preparing several years for the next three-year retreat—and he will not give it again just for you." Shamar Rinpoche's urging us not to waste time echoed in my head. We did leave for Switzerland, arriving just days before Christmas. One of our Swiss friends had invited us to her home so she could accompany us by train to France and to Gendun Rinpoche. Arriving the day before New Year's Eve, we presented Shamar Rinpoche's letter to Gendun Rinpoche. Much later I heard from Gendun Rinpoche's secretary that Gendun Rinpoche felt he had no choice but to accept us into the retreat at the eleventh hour, with little to no preparation, because of that letter!

Shamar Rinpoche was also right about our visas. In spite of having only passports and no other documents normally required by French bureaucrats, in all the years we were in France, we never had a problem with our visas!

◆ SHAMAR RINPOCHE'S LEGACY

I first met Shamar Rinpoche at Dhagpo Kagyu Ling in France in 1979; it was his first visit to the Karmapa's European seat and everyone was nervous—because there are rinpoches, wonderful teachers and so on, and then you have the Rinpoches—the beyond the common measure Masters, such as the Gyalwa Karmapa and Kunzig Shamar Rinpoche. In those early days, we had the first visit of Karmapa in 1977, and two years later, Shamar Rinpoche. I didn't know what to expect, but I thought it would be similar to Karmapa's visit—the visit of a Dharma King. Not a worldly king, but the experience of nobility that comes from full and complete spiritual achievement. I was nervous and excited—I was merely twenty-two, and holding the incense because I was supposed to open the car door and lead the way to the house.

Gendun Rinpoche was ordinarily relaxed with us because we were young, and so he cut us a lot of slack, reeling us in gently. But that day I could see he was nervous, especially after he scolded me, saying, "We're not here for a joke." Okay, that is serious! The car suddenly arrived, the door opened and Rinpoche literally popped out of the car! I was the first one he saw since I was holding the incense to greet him, and he immediately started chatting to me in Tibetan, "Oh, Geshe, how are you, nice to see you, where's your room?" and so on. I was so surprised, I didn't know what to say or think. Gendun Rinpoche quickly whisked him away to the house—and that was my first contact with Shamar Rinpoche.

This has been the tone of my relationship with Rinpoche since then, very deep yet very light. I was often his chauffeur and attendant when he visited France, so I had a lot of private time with him, and the close contact created a very deep bond. Rinpoche has always been there; before Gendun Rinpoche passed away he told us, "Once I am gone, Shamar Rinpoche will help you with your practice; you should ask him and work with him." This was before Gyalwa Karmapa Thaye Dorje was fully empowered. It always felt natural to be with Rinpoche. He visited the monasteries and the retreat centers in France regularly; in retreat he gave us all of the instructions and transmissions of the lineage. He always challenged us—always.

We were Westerners, Europeans mostly, being brought up in a very classical Tibetan environment, where everything was in Tibetan; we had to learn Tibetan, recite in Tibetan—we had to become Tibetan. We wore robes, shaved our heads, and became ordained monks or nuns, the whole nine yards. At first it was challenging, but after a while it was comfortable. Like everything, once you get used to it, it belongs to you, and you own it. The self, your ego, is very happy to have a brand new nest—the "Tibetan thing." We learned the rituals, the mudras, we used Tibetan and Sanskrit words that other people didn't know; you know, we enjoyed the benefit of the hard work—but then Rinpoche was always there to keep us in

"Do you get it?"
Tsony translating for
Shamar Rinpoche.

check and make sure that we maintained our sanity. One of his mottos was, "Not too much tradition," warning us not to excessively grasp at the tradition—tradition is meant to be like a vase, designed to display the flowers of Dharma, offering a nice support to a beautiful flower arrangement. No tradition at all would be like creating your own thing or inventing something new, throwing away the Buddha and all his teachings along with 2500 years of hard work of millions of men and women. Rinpoche always made sure that we understood not to cling too tightly to tradition, but not to be careless either.

Then, if we fast-forward 30 years to 2007, we have what I think of as the "Big Bang." Many of the teachers who were to become the North American Bodhi Path Dharma teachers met that spring with Rinpoche in Virginia, and Rinpoche pretty much dusted us out—he aired out our minds. It was a brand new start, and we were asked to reconsider what we'd been doing for 30 years, and to throw away old habits; it was actually kind of brutal. It wasn't simply getting rid of the dead wood; he had us deeply examine the way we saw things—the way we thought, how we considered the path and our spiritual lives and commitments and all of that. Rinpoche was like a tree surgeon, pruning the dead parts, cutting out what didn't work, while keeping the vital parts and encouraging us to cultivate what was important. I think Rinpoche had been spending years assessing the most appropriate expression of the Buddhadharma for us—in our time and place.

In the last few months of Rinpoche's life, he happily organized his library in Natural Bridge; we built many Ikea bookshelves—Rinpoche handily wielded the electric screwdriver. He had his big table and his comfy armchair, and he really loved this library; he was delighted! The shelves covered three walls, floor to ceiling, and Rinpoche sorted through all his books, selecting what he wanted for his library. The books he didn't need he asked us to burn, and we were like, "What? How can we burn Dharma books?" But Rinpoche was clear, "Burn this, this, and this." He said, "So many books! Too many books to read in one lifetime." You know how Rinpoche loved to tease. He said, "Yes, some of the great Tibetan masters were in their monasteries, and had no TV or internet back then and they were bored! So they wrote books, hundreds of them, because they were bored to death, writing books, writing books, writing books. Nobody can read all these books."

This was so "Rinpoche," revealing the fine line between showing respect on the one hand, and seeing the excesses of tradition on the other. This discernment requires full knowledge of the tradition; to "think outside the box," first you have to know the box. You can't think outside the box if you don't know what the box is. Rinpoche could make these selections and not be irreverent, and he could actually be pragmatic about these books and teachers because he had a very thorough and complete knowledge of the subject—and not only details of philosophy. He loved politics, for instance; he had a strong understanding of public policy and society—he even wrote his book *Creating a Transparent Democracy*. He is also the only Tibetan teacher I have ever heard quote Machiavelli and Shakespeare. He loved science and world history; you could ask him anything.

At the monastery in France, he was our primary reference when we were trying to get the most genuine teachings on the liturgy—the chants and music. We could have asked the chant master at the monastery in Sikkim, but Shamar Rinpoche told us; "Not necessary. The chant master in Sikkim and the monks that came from Bhutan have changed things a little bit; the melody has changed slightly. In Tsurphu in Tibet, the melody was like this," and he sang it! When we were constructing the temple and planning its decoration, Rinpoche asked the master painter Drejong Norbu to come train a team of young artists to paint, but it was Shamar Rinpoche who was our reference for the iconographic style. Rinpoche was the Master whose knowledge was encyclopedic; he was the reference, a Renaissance man. Rinpoche received this knowledge "in" the box, but he could equally think outside the box. For more than 30 years Rinpoche observed, traveled, and talked with all sorts of people—Buddhist and non-Buddhist—in order to thoroughly understand the people of our time.

After Rinpoche passed away, many of us went to Nepal and saw firsthand how vast his activity had been, when so many of the different groups of people that he had worked with, who had no idea about the other groups, were together in one place. We were amazed, and wondered, "How can we keep all this together?" Well, I don't think anybody can keep this together like he did, though what is clear is that each group has received enough guidance and instruction to keep itself together—while knowing we are connected through Rinpoche's activity. It's like a body, a living organism. The lungs do their job, but have no idea who's running the heart. The heart is doing its business but doesn't try to manage the liver—yet it works, because there is interdependence. This interconnectedness works because each element of the group does its own work and doesn't worry about the others' business.

We experienced this in Nepal, seeing so many different people that had a very specific connection with Rinpoche. This connection is like a universe; he conducted an orchestra comprised of all these universes—he was the conductor of a multiverse! We don't need to wonder who can do this now, who can replace Rinpoche. Nobody can do it. But the different elements function, and they'll function harmoniously as long as each element does what they were taught and guided to do, and we maintain a strong feeling of brother/sisterhood; we are all part of this universe—the Shamar Rinpoche Universe. We're here in North America, and others are from Bodhi Paths in Asia, Europe, and Latin America; we may feel that we're different, yet we're part of the same universe, working interdependently and synergistically. The slogan, "Think globally, act locally" works perfectly in this context. We think globally as Bodhi Path, but we act locally. There's no need to be overly concerned with what's happening in Bodhi Path Hong Kong or Bodhi Path Budapest or Bodhi Path Valencia or wherever, because we can feel confident that the people there are trying to do what we're trying to do here. They may not be doing the exact same thing, but it's what Rinpoche told them to do—because it was appropriate and fitting for their own specific place and time.

This is where we are now; all aspiring and wishing for Rinpoche's new manifestation, like waiting for the sun to rise again—we're looking forward to meeting the new reincarnation (Tib. *yangsi*). Yangsi means a new opportunity, a new shuffle, a new beginning. Many of us who are older are counting the years, wondering if we can hold on long enough to be part of the Shamarpa's new activity. In the meantime, we have to sustain what we've been given, to keep it alive and thriving; not only the physical Dharma centers, but our personal practice as well—using the advice we received from Rinpoche. Many of us had the significant opportunity to meet Rinpoche personally, and were given personal guidance; we should follow this and stick with it. Even people new to Bodhi Path can continue to follow Rinpoche's spiritual guidance, because his guidance and curriculum remains. For those of us who have received personal instructions, we know what we have to do; we have our instructions, but we have to accomplish them. Each of us who met Rinpoche over the years, publicly or privately, should try to remember what was pointed out in these discussions with him—which perhaps at the time didn't even make sense. These are seeds that were planted in the soil of our mind, which will ripen when the conditions are gathered.

The first Sunday after Rinpoche died, many people came to meditate at our center in Natural Bridge, and someone wisely said, "In a way, Rinpoche's death has sealed and perfected his work. It's necessary that his presence would cease, so that we take charge of what he put in place for us." His death is shocking, and we don't want this inspiring figure to disappear from our lives—we want him to stay forever. For us to continue to grow though, the time comes that what has helped us grow up has disappeared; it's the natural cycle. The constant cycle of life and death—death nurtures life, and gives new possibility. Like the Tibetan word for reincarnation, yangsi—the new shuffle, even though we may, quite romantically, wish that the teacher who inspired our spiritual life will remain forever.

Once, in a discussion I had with Shamar Rinpoche about the 16th Karmapa, he told me: "He was a man from another time; he wouldn't understand today's world." Likewise, a transition will happen between the 14th and the 15th Shamarpa. There is teamwork, with good timing, between the Shamarpas and the Karmapas, so that one passes away when the other is of age and can find the reincarnation of the yangsi, and this is what's going to happen. The different organizations that are under Shamar Rinpoche's authority, or were inspired by Rinpoche, such as the worldwide Bodhi Path community, the Diamond Way Centers, and the European Federation of Karma Kagyu Centers, have jointly sent a letter of request to the 17th Karmapa Thaye Dorje supplicating and entrusting him with the sole authority to search for the reincarnation of the 15th Shamarpa, using traditional means. Karmapa has kindly accepted this request, and has pledged to find and educate the 15th Shamarpa.

Meanwhile, we have our own responsibilities and tasks. I'll keep doing what Rinpoche personally asked me to do, which is pretty simple—take care of the center here in Natural Bridge, Virginia, and regularly teach at the DC center; I will also travel to Europe once a year to visit and teach old friends. My job is neither administrating nor fundraising; there are others to do that. Wisdom Foundation is in charge of keeping the assets together and functioning, and they do a fine job; it's not my business. Of course, if they need my support I will respond, but I won't be minding their business. There are also the assistants who were appointed by Shamar Rinpoche to coordinate all of the Bodhi Path groups, so that there is a seamless flow when various rinpoches and teachers visit the centers, and to deal with many other matters of organization. They are doing a fine job too. The center coordinators, who have also been appointed or elected, are doing their work—all of this works as a healthy organism.

Of course, we grieve that Rinpoche is gone—it's a shock and there's a big hole; it's like a sinkhole in the Bodhi Path … whoosh, where did the ground go? This happens when we lose somebody we love; we always go through this, and the length of it depends on how we process it. We're shocked, angry, depressed, and so we try to negotiate—these are the stages of grief we all go through. But there's a lot of work waiting for us. Don't negate that you are going through the stages of grief—it's important to fully embrace them—but keep moving, don't linger. Come back to the advice Rinpoche gave you, either personally or as a group. Come back to the practice and do it. It's all about doing it. Being a Buddhist means that you put into practice what the Buddha taught. There are many ways to do this, of course, many gates, but it's still about doing it. And now we've come to a time when we are all, somehow, in charge. It's not the same as when Rinpoche was in charge: we're all in charge now—no one is in charge of the overall Bodhi Path, but each of us is in charge of what we have to do. It could simply be our practice; be in charge of this. We're not lost. If you don't remember what your task is, sit and think about it. Maybe ask for Rinpoche's blessing, like, "Can you give me a re-run?" Then, whatever you remember, even if it's not everything, but something you were told, or it was indicated for you to do, grab the beginning of that thread and keep going.

It's important for people to have a place where they have a friendly community that can assist them and help when they're going through difficulties—a space to talk and share and find constructive comfort and help; a place that holds you while you decide to change as you transform yourself, and also provides methods for transformation. This is the message Rinpoche wanted to give. Bodhi Path is a place that is open and welcoming, a place that is friendly. I asked him once how he would define Bodhi Path, and he came up with this great PR line—normal people talking about normal things to normal people. That's his idea: no fuss, with a big heart. Not complicated, but offering skillful, well-calibrated methods that can be applied in a non-religious context, which means "not" what we often associate with religion; there's no obligation to adopt a belief package. This encourages people to feel comfortable at Bodhi Path.

Another of Rinpoche's mottos is "Don't be machine-minded." Be flexible. The name of the 2nd Shamarpa was Khacho Wangpo, which means "mighty celestial dancer." This evokes the image of being able to dance in space—of formlessness, and of cultivating the wisdom necessary to be fluid while interacting with the world, neither grasping nor rejecting—but having a backbone. In *Creating a Transparent Democracy*, Rinpoche shares his advice for being citizens of this world. How do we manage to implement bodhicitta, the heart of the Buddha's teaching, in this context? We can't disassociate the reality we're in from the path, the meditation, and the practices we do. This is what Rinpoche was indicating in this book; he emphasizd being flexible and not stubbornly fixing on things; not being machine-minded, yet having a backbone. Rinpoche gave us a perfect guidebook in *The Path to Awakening*, along with a practical application for social engagement in *Creating a Transparent Democracy*, while providing additional practical advice on meditation and cultivating wisdom with *Boundless Awakening*. What you have in these three books is the essence of what the Buddha taught. These books are the result of thirty years of Rinpoche refining his experience; combining his knowledge of the Buddha's teachings with his experience of our society—specifically the mind, qualities, and limitations of the people of our time, in order to distill the most appropriate wisdom nectar. *The Path to Awakening* is a treasure trove of resources and inspiration, and offers many inspiring techniques and reflections for us to implement, at our own pace. This is how we should work with this book, by reading it again and again.

Rinpoche had a clear vision about the path and the curriculum. He said repeatedly that there isn't one path that is supreme in and of itself among all of the Buddha's teachings—but there are definitely methods that are more appropriate to a certain environment. Given the framework of the times and circumstances, these methods are most likely to be fruitful. This is what the Bodhi Path curriculum is all about; it provides such a backbone. It's quite precise, yet offers many possibilities. When you come to a Bodhi Path and meditate, and you've done that for a while, an elder practitioner or teacher will discuss with you what you've discovered, in order to help you gain more confidence and clarity in your practice. There's a sense of progression; you'll feel you're on a graduated path and accompanied on the path in a friendly environment. This starts with each of us individually; it starts with you. The general warmth and color of the community reflects all the individuals interacting in harmonious synergy.

Rinpoche's funeral was a profound experience of being together, going through this incredible journey and connecting with everyone, getting a glimpse of how vast and limitless Rinpoche's activity really was. When the political obstacles were cleared and Rinpoche's mortal remains (Tib. *kudung*) were finally allowed to come to Nepal, it was announced that his kudung would circumambulate the Swayambhunath stupa. A few of us went there early and waited … waited, and waited, and waited. We got there at 10:00 am, and waited until 8:00 pm. During that time, I noticed a Nepali family next to us, a young mother with children; one of them was a little girl who was really cute—she actually reminded me of Chris who lives in Natural Bridge. I said to the others, "Look, there's a mini-Chris." She was cheekily climbing the statues, and I took some pictures of her. Then, a few days later, we had the good fortune to receive Gyalwa Karmapa's blessing at Sharminub Monastery, where all the funeral ceremonies took place; on the staircase leading up to the shrine room there was a long line of locals on one side, and Westerners on the other. As we waited, I saw this same little girl directly across the staircase! "Hey, that's mini-Chris!" I recognized her mother too. Imagine the odds of me coming to Nepal, and of them waiting for Rinpoche at Swayambhu; and then just a few days later being together again on another staircase at the same exact time, including the fact that the Westerners were allowed to go ahead, while the local line, thousands of them, had to wait longer. This type of thing kept happening. I already knew about many aspects of Rinpoche's activity, but seeing how devoted the Nepali and Newari populations are to him was eye-opening. I'd heard he'd given an empowerment in Kathmandu a few years ago and 120,000 people had attended, and now I saw for myself the throngs of people. I personally reconnected with people I hadn't seen in 30 years. The experience wasn't just about the ritual cremation itself, but we were all also making wishes to meet again in the future, wishing that what had brought us together in this life will happen again, and wishing to be part of that activity.

There's plenty of speculation about Shamar Rinpoche's reincarnation and what might happen. By reflecting on the history of the different reincarnations, we can learn a great deal about the activity of a bodhisattva, especially the generations following the 10th Shamarpa. Due to murky political reasons, four generations of

Shamarpas were not authorized to be publicly enthroned or socially recognized as the custodians of the Red Crown—however, this didn't prevent the manifestation of the bodhisattva activity. In one life he was a physician and in another he was a hermit; fortunate beings could still meet them and benefit from their blessings. Before the yangsi of Gendun Rinpoche was presented, there were similar speculations about what his future might be. Would he be born Tibetan or not, would he have a classic monastic or a Western education? Well, in fact, he is a French teenager who goes to high school and is learning the Dharma. Shamar Rinpoche told me, "Bodhisattvas should be free to do whatever they perceive most appropriate to serve sentient beings. They shouldn't be trapped by a church; if they want to be a lawyer because that's the way to help, then let them be lawyers. If they want to be surgeons or doctors, or whatever, that's what they should be." The church needs the organization—bodhisattvas don't. The church needs inspiring leaders to teach people Dharma, it's true; but the bodhisattva doesn't absolutely need the church, even though sometimes the bodhisattva may need to teach within a structure in order to help in a structured way. Rinpoche warned us about too much tradition, and that unfortunately bodhisattvas are sometimes trapped by institutions.

Quite surely there will be an official reincarnation of Shamarpa chosen by the Gyalwa Karmapa. Shamarpa will be in charge of Bodhi Path and many things, but we shouldn't restrict the manifestation of an enlightened person to be this socially recognized, emblematic figure. He could also express his care for beings as a guy or girl in Rockbridge County, anointed by the blessing of Rinpoche, compassionately displaying bodhisattva activity in a totally anonymous way. One never knows where the manifestation of a bodhisattva may appear. Social status doesn't matter as long as the job gets done. That is the bodhisattva's own responsibility, just as we're individually in charge of our own bodhisattva activity. We can't expect other people to do it for us or instead of us. When our compassion, discernment, and skill merge in the experience of unity, we will be similar to Rinpoche. We won't worry about fame or gain, and we'll maintain a respectful and genuine relationship with people to help them open up, have confidence, and request instructions. That's why bodhisattvas are sometimes politically correct and sometimes not; it depends on what's needed. Therefore, be flexible—there is no single and absolute way. This will be the result of our practice of the curriculum brought to its full fruition, and quite frankly, I'm amazed by the skillfulness of the Bodhi Path curriculum. It offers a very complete list of topics to study, plus meditation with a sense of a progression; yet it is also very open, with many options and possible combinations. It's very flexible. To me, it reflects Rinpoche's mind, as well as reality.

In the early '80s, Rinpoche was at Dhagpo while at the same time his half-brother Chogyal was also in France; Chogyal had been diagnosed with tuberculosis. In Europe, when you have TB you're considered contagious and have to be quarantined, so Chogyal was sent to a sanatorium connected to a retirement home. It was mostly old people and Chogyal was quite young then. He was alone there and bored to death, so whenever possible Rinpoche or Jigmela would visit him. One Sunday in mid-summer, Rinpoche was in France and wanted to see his brother, and Jigmela did too, so we went. We drove to the sanatorium and visited, and on the way back, as it was extremely hot, Rinpoche said he needed to cool off. He actually said, "I need to cool the temperature of my body down." There were no

air conditioners in cars then in France, and Rinpoche was clear that he wanted to swim. We were driving through a small town, and Rinpoche kept asking me to find a place to buy him a bathing suit. I explained that because it was Sunday nothing was open, but Rinpoche insisted that we, or more specifically I, could find one. "I need to swim!" I was trying to be polite, but I knew that everything was closed and there was no way. We came to a small gas station outside of Périgueux, the main little town in the Dordogne area. Rinpoche said, "Stop! We can buy a bathing suit here." I replied something like, "Rinpoche, it's a gas station, they don't have clothes. They only have maps, tools, and candy." But he said, "Stop here, stop here," so of course we did—with me thinking along the lines of, "Whatever."

We stopped and went into the gas station, and it was tiny; there was a desk, some maps, inner tubes, spark plugs, oil; just a few things. The mechanic asked if he could help us. Rinpoche came in behind me just as I was saying, "Well, we're looking for a bathing suit for the gentleman here," and I imagine I was probably rolling my eyes. The guy looked at me incredulously and said, "We're a gas station, we don't sell anything like that." I said, "I know, but he really wants one so I had to ask." He reiterated, "No, I'm sorry, we don't have one," when suddenly we heard his wife from behind a curtain at the back of the shop, saying, "Why don't you sell him one of the bathing suits we bought at the market this morning?" Sunday mornings there are farmers' markets in the countryside, and sometimes people sell clothes there. The wife suggested that they sell one of those to us, and the husband agreed, "Sure, why not. Do you want to see it?" "Yes!" Rinpoche said, while he kind of elbowed me. The guy went back into his kitchen and came back with two bathing suits. Rinpoche looked them over, "Yes, this one will fit me. It's really nice, thank you! I'll take this one." Then he looked at the other one and said, "Geshe, you want one?" just wanting to finish me with absolute humiliation. "No Rinpoche, I'm not in the mood for swimming." Aargh.

The guy sold it to us at cost, and we were on our way! Rinpoche was happy with his bathing suit, but now we had to find a place to swim. There's a public indoor pool in Périgueux, so we went there, but it was closed on Sunday. My patience was thinning, and I suggested we go back home; Jigme Rinpoche seemed ready to go back also, but kindly offered, "Well, if you want, I know a student who lives nearby, perhaps we could go to his house and you could take a shower to cool off?" But Shamar Rinpoche insisted, "No, I must swim," asking questions like, "Can we have the pool opened? Who's in charge? Who has the key?" Me: "Noooo, that isn't the way it works. No, definitely not … that's not going to happen!" when suddenly I had a vague memory of seeing a sign once when I was driving on the outskirts of town advertising an outdoor swimming pool. I wasn't sure I could remember where it was, but I told Rinpoche that we could try that. "Let's go!" So we drove around, and eventually found the pool, and it was open! There were lots of people swimming and jumping. Jigmela and I stayed by the car waiting for Rinpoche, who went through the gate, changed into his new bathing suit, and then splash! He swam while we watched him through the fence. When he came back to the car he was thoroughly refreshed and happy, "That was the best water I've ever been in, and the best swimming. It was wonderful!"

One wrinkle in that afternoon, which became increasingly stressful, was that Shamar Rinpoche was scheduled to give a lecture near Dhagpo at the end of the day. Traveling with Rinpoche there was often a time factor, and in fact he was often late. So when we first arrived in Périgueux, we were almost late already, and we had definitely derailed the schedule with all the swimming business. There were many people attending the program, and as Jigme Rinpoche was in charge of Dhagpo, it was his responsibility, so he was naturally concerned. When we finally arrived back in town at the lecture hall, the organizer was furious. Some people had already left and the guy was fuming, asking me why we were so late—I told him it was a traffic jam; I didn't even tell him about Rinpoche swimming because I think the guy would have exploded. People had already left, but some stayed, so Rinpoche came in and started teaching really basic teachings—for maybe twenty minutes. Then he said, "Thank you very much for coming," and was gone. That was the last straw for the organizer—he was pissed!

When you think about it, you can see this experience in several different ways, depending on the vantage point. Jigme Rinpoche was concerned because the event was organized, and he was central to the organization. My viewpoint was about wanting Rinpoche to understand the constraints of this world; such as, we're in France, and Sunday means closed, and it's impossible. Then the organizer guy had some issues, that's my own interpretation, of "I'm the important organizer," or maybe even using Rinpoche's teaching to promote himself. Rinpoche was slicing through all this on different levels. Also, there's another level—relating to water—which I noticed after I read stories about the 16th Karmapa visiting an area in Tibet where they had suffered a long drought. When people asked him for some prayers, he asked for a bathtub and took a bath—and a spring developed under the bathtub! In another story, Karmapa gave his mala to the locals and they buried it, and a spring appeared; so there could be a hidden aspect. I suspect Rinpoche was actually expressing something that we all felt: it was hot and there was a lot of suffering—for the crops, the farmers, and for beings in general. In my interpretation, Rinpoche cooling off in the water and refreshing himself, in his wisdom and being connected to all beings, meant that through him there was a cooling; and maybe even something about the water energy that needed to be stirred up. You never know, but Rinpoche wasn't being a diva, saying like, "If I can't swim, I won't do anything!" With Rinpoche, it was interesting to see him do or say things that from our perspective seemed extremely ordinary or even extremely aggravating. We might even think that as a spiritual being, he shouldn't be attached to his personal comfort or ego or whatever—and we miss the point entirely.

Another time I drove Rinpoche to the southwest of France, and in the morning he woke up with an earache—he was in a lot of pain. Rinpoche wanted to see an ear doctor, but I didn't know the area, and again, of course, it was Sunday. I said, "Rinpoche, we won't find an ear doctor on Sunday, we can go to the emergency room," but Rinpoche was clear, "No, no, we need to find an ear doctor who can unplug and clean it." I looked in the phone book—this was before cell phones and Google. I tried calling all the doctors in the book, until finally someone answered. The doctor was about to go out for a walk with his family and said we were lucky we caught him. When I explained that there was a gentleman with acute ear pain, he agreed to meet us at his clinic, and he cleaned out Rinpoche's ear, which had severe blockage. In the process a connection developed between the doctor and Rinpoche, and afterward Rinpoche was thrilled, exclaiming that his hearing was better than it had been in years!

So again, the seemingly impossible thing happened—the unreasonable compromise with reality within the sphere of what I thought was possible. Rinpoche was always exploding limits; creating means and solutions I didn't imagine because I limited the scope of possibilities in my mind. I think Rinpoche lived, and I guess all enlightened people do, without preconceived ideas of what should be done. He didn't wake up in the morning trying to figure out what kind of trick he was going to pull to teach a lesson; it was causes and conditions. He exemplified the teachings of Nagarjuna: because everything is impermanent and because everything is empty, then everything is possible. "Don't be so machine-minded." Be flexible, allow things to arise, don't prevent them. That's a great lesson and the specific means are unimportant. Whether he found a bathing suit or not, I mean, he could have just skinny-dipped in the river in Périgueux!!! I could have said, "I'll pull over and you can go in the water. Swim in the Vézère in your undies, or go naked—we won't peek." But my mind was too occupied with, "No, we can't find a bathing suit today." And even after we found one, I couldn't accept that we had, I was so pissed. Rinpoche was like a fish in a pond—just moving, just swimming, with everything being possible, right and left, up and down. He was never careless; he was extremely precise, and he was never a diva.

A friend of mine told me about an experience she had during a summer teaching at Dhagpo. The teachings were in a massive tent, and it was so hellishly hot that people actually fainted—the organizers were spraying water on the roof of the tent to try to cool it down inside. Anyway, Rinpoche was teaching and there were hundreds of people at the program, and at some point Rinpoche interrupted the teaching: "Can you take the sides off this tent; it's really hot and very uncomfortable." My friend told me that her inner reaction was, "What a diva, why don't you man up? It's really hot; we suffer, you suffer; keep doing your job." She admitted she actually thought these things. Meanwhile, the teaching was stopped and everyone got up and disassembled the tent cables and it was a big operation, but when it was finished and Rinpoche started teaching again, everybody felt the breeze. He had been thinking of everyone's comfort, of course; he was perfectly able to "man up," as we've seen on many occasions—such as sitting on a throne for fifteen hours giving blessings to thousands of people. He was always, always thinking of others.

In my experience, being in close proximity to Rinpoche amplified awareness, and sometimes it was painful. One time he wanted to go out and I was driving. Rinpoche said he was hungry and wanted to eat, and he chose a very expensive, classy restaurant in town. We sat down and the waiter approached, and Rinpoche said, "May I have a spoon, please?" and proceeded to pull a yogurt out of his pocket that he had brought from the kitchen at Dhagpo! I didn't have the gumption to go along with this, so I quickly ordered the cheapest thing on the menu, an omelet. I only had a little money; that was a time in my life when I was living on almost nothing, and all the money I had was in my pocket. Rinpoche got the spoon, started eating, and was finished before my omelet arrived. "Let's go." So I spent my money on food I didn't even eat, and besides that, I wasn't hungry because I'd eaten just before we went out!

Next thing I knew, Rinpoche was running really fast and hard through town, with me running behind, until just as suddenly he stopped and said, "We can't run so much, the earth will fall apart." Who knows what he was doing when he did that? We continued walking through town—it was about 8 p.m. and the shops had closed at 5. We walked by a butcher shop where they sold liver pâté, foie gras, etc., and Rinpoche said, "This poor guy is selling his karma," when suddenly he started knocking on the door of the shop! I was behind him, thinking, "Oh boy, now the cops will come. Rinpoche will be put in the pokey; who will teach tomorrow?" I was chagrined by Rinpoche's behavior somehow. He knocked on the door, and I was hoping there was nobody there, but the shop had an apartment attached. A light came on and a door opened, and out came the butcher to open the front door. "What do you want?" Rinpoche strode right in and walked around the whole shop, "Om mani padme hung, om mani padme hung, om mani padme hung…" and then walked right out! I was left alone with the owner, who insisted, "What do you want?" Rinpoche was gone and I wanted to follow him, but I also felt like I had to justify why we were there—otherwise the guy might think that these guys in the maroon robes were weird, and then the center would get a bad reputation, yadda, yadda, yadda. I fibbed, "Oh, we're not from around here, but we heard wonderful things about your pâtés," while I was frantically looking at the shelves to find the cheapest thing. I bought something and that was the end of my money—plus I was a vegetarian! I left and chased Rinpoche down the street again. I had no idea what was happening, only what I rationalized in my mind. I still don't really know.

There is another friend of mine who now lives at Dhagpo, Shedroup, who had spent several years in India living with the sadhus—he even became a Hindi-speaking sadhu himself. He was back in France, though, and was visiting a friend who lived near Dhagpo. He was driving on the main road not far from the center one day when he saw a man he thought was a Tibetan monk, which he recognized because of his time in India. The monk was hitchhiking, holding his robe up above his ankles. Surprised, my friend stopped to pick him up; once in the car, the monk said, "Please take me to paradise." My friend was totally confused, but the monk repeated, "Keep going this way, drive me to paradise." So they were driving and talking, with the monk insisting he wanted to go to "paradise." Well, a couple of miles down the road they came to a campground, a kind of trailer park, called the Paradise, where they have a restaurant. It turns out the monk was Rinpoche, who just wanted to have a steak!

It seems that Rinpoche had "escaped" from Dhagpo. At that time there was an old lama who has since died, Dzimpon-la—a personal attendant of Karmapa—who had been sent to attend to Jigme Rinpoche. Dzimpon-la was an ornery old Tibetan who had his own idea about what Rinpoche should eat. Rinpoche preferred lean, grilled steak, but the attendant would serve him fatty momos and those kinds of things. Even though it was Rinpoche, Dzimpon-la just said, "Sure, sure," but did it his own way, always serving fatty foods, which Rinpoche couldn't digest—they made him sick. So he escaped—he snuck out, walked down the hill, got on the main road, and hitchhiked with his robes on! My friend picked him up, and Rinpoche said the only thing he knew, "It's called Paradise, bring me to Paradise." When they arrived at the Paradise, Rinpoche said to my friend, "You should come and see me, I'm giving some teachings you might be interested in." And my friend went and listened to Rinpoche, and ended up becoming a monk. He subsequently did two three-year retreats, and now he's one of the Dhagpo lamas!

On September 8 or 9, 2001, Rinpoche and I were in France together. Rinpoche was transiting between Asia and America, and we were in Paris having dinner with a few of Rinpoche's disciples and students. Rinpoche was leaving the next morning for America, so we decided to drive him to the airport and see him off. He had tickets to go to Washington, DC, and mentioned he had business in New York and would fly there from DC in a day or two. We saw him off, said goodbye, happy trails and all that, and went merrily on our way. When I heard the news about what happened in New York I was shocked! "What? But Rinpoche is on a plane to New York!" We tried to contact him, calling all the people we knew there, but we couldn't connect because the entire city was totally overwhelmed; we had to rely solely on the news reports. Afterward, Rinpoche told me that he landed at LaGuardia Airport, which is how he was able to get into the city that morning, coming in from LaGuardia up north, down through the Bronx. He landed at 8:30 am on September 11, just moments before the planes crashed into the towers. We were extremely worried, but in retrospect, maybe Rinpoche went there on purpose, and in his bodhisattva activity provided some relief for all who died and their families. Was it a mere coincidence that Rinpoche arrived at that moment?

At first, the death of Rinpoche felt like a devastating fire. After some time spent contemplating this hard fact, I could see, past my very human initial reaction of despair, that Dharma of reality shows impermanence at hand in every heartbeat. It was difficult to not see this as merely a death, a final point marking the loss of what was. As I kept contemplating, I began to notice seeds sprouting and connecting with each other in my mind; all the words and signs that Rinpoche planted in my mind since our first encounter in 1979. Most of them didn't make sense back then; some of them had vanished from my memory. Now, they resurface and draw a clear pattern of intentions and actions to be carried on. This is Rinpoche's legacy to me. Like a mind-treasury, buried to come back at the appropriate time to show me the way and provide me with a clear road map to follow. I am amazed and grateful beyond measure. Sadness is replaced now by joyful energy and tenderness.

It makes me think of the naturally occurring fires in Yosemite National Park. Firefighters let them burn because Sequoia trees depend on fire to reproduce. Their seed cones need heat to open and release the seeds, while the fire clears the surroundings to facilitate their germination. Smaller trees will burn, while the giant sequoias still stand. They've passed through fire for eons and they will continue to do so "as long as space endures."

Sarva Mangalam

EDUARDO HERRERA
Mexico City, Mexico

July 31, 2014
Kathmandu

◆ ALL KNOWING SHAMARPA

Knowing the indestructible nature of ultimate samaya
Out of Love you manifested strength amid the fearsome many

Knowing the painful nature of conditioned existence
Out of Compassion you brought us all to the Path to Awakening

Knowing the true meaning of impermanence
Out of Joy you delighted our lives with your presence
And finally.... with your last teaching

Knowing the true nature of reality
Out of Equanimity you pointed
To friends and foes alike the essence of what is unborn

All knowing Amitabha
Heir to the throne of Dharmakaya
Shramana[1] of the Kamtsang cave
May this outcast and ignorant wanderer be once again
summoned to your reign of limitless compassion.

Version Espanol

◆ SHAMARPA QUE TODO LO CONOCE

Conociendo la naturaleza indestructible del samaya absoluto
Por amor, tú manifestaste fuerza entre los temerosos.

Conociendo las dolorosa naturaleza ilusoria de la existencia condicionada
Por compasión, tú nos mostraste a todos un Camino al Despertar.

Conociendo el verdadero significado de la impermanencia
Por gozo, nos deleitaiste con tu presencia y finalmente ... con tu última enseñanza

Conociendo la verdadera naturaleza de toda realidad
Por ecuanimidad nos mostraste
a enemigos y amigos por igual la naturaleza de lo que nunca ha nacido.

Amitabha que todo lo conoce
Heredero del trono Dharmakaya
Shramana[2] de la cueva Kamtsang
Que este ignorante y desterrado vagabundo pueda una vez más ser convocado a tu
reino de compasión.

1. *Shramana*: Name that ascetics who would not conform to the Vedic tradition (Hindu) received during the time of the Buddha.

2. *Shramana*: El nombre que los ascetas recibieron en los tiempos del Buda histórico que no conformaban con la tradición védica (Hinduista).

Karma Trinlay Rinpoche
Paris, France

◆ STATEMENT FROM THE ANNUAL MEETING IN VIRGINIA, AUGUST 2014

We've been gathered together by Shamar Rinpoche, and what connects us is the love and affection we have for Rinpoche. Now that he is not physically with us, we may feel like orphans, or feel that we don't know what to do, or that we're at risk in some way. I want to reassure you that we are not orphans; Rinpoche has looked out for us and foreseen the future, and we can look at things like Rinpoche did—thinking globally. Think about the purpose and the impact of what Rinpoche has started—it is the legacy of the Buddha that we are trying to carry, the legacy of the realized masters. Rinpoche has his spiritual heir, the 17th Karmapa; his own brother, Jigme Rinpoche, who has shared everything with him; and a multitude of students who studied with him. We needn't feel afraid or worried at all. Rinpoche always wanted us to be mature, to think for ourselves, and not to have to always rely on someone else. Not the person, nor the words, but on the meaning; not the superficial meaning—the ultimate meaning. Everything Rinpoche created was meant to live beyond us, and we have everything we need to carry Rinpoche's legacy forward, to reach his goals. We are a global institution. We carry this, and we can expand; it's not about promoting a person, it is promoting a movement. We are all shadows, here for a short time, but we have a chance to benefit from the Buddha's teachings. The best way we can do that is by making Bodhi Path a solid institution of transmission of the Dharma. It's not about finding a person to replace Rinpoche; it's about his message and what he did; his legacy, continuing the teaching of the Dharma, and making it available to all.

Everyone who attended the 2014 Annual Program was invited to write one line about Rinpoche. Many did, and these lines were fashioned into this poem.

◆ In Honor of Shamar Rinpoche

Manifester of the rainbow light,
Your voice is the whisper of wind in the trees.
The warmth of the sun, your smile.
A cloud floats with bright clear light across blue sky and melts into
its own clarity.
Understand the nature of change—dispel the delusion of perception
and conception. This is Dewachen!

Able to obliterate any concept in a single moment,
Painting with clouds and rainbows,
A bird in the sky sees everything and leaves no trace.
Unbound! Unsurpassed! Unforgettable!

Om Bhagawan Ho!
My Guru, my glorious Guru!
Rinpoche, I bow with deep gratitude for your many blessings.
May we take your sudden disappearance, the ultimate teaching of
impermanence, to heart!
I wish I'd asked you to stay.

Your mind, my mind; may there be no separation—limitlessly vast,
spacious, and clear.
Great blessing, gentle bliss;
Right here, right now.
Unbound. Unparalleled. Unborn.

Thank you, Rinpoche, for the methods, strength, and compassion to practice.
Sharing your loving essence,
Precious jewel of great joy,
Thinking of compassion I will stand right behind you.

You gave us our teachers, who helped us understand you were the supreme teacher,
Thank you for everything Shamarpa, including the wonderful blessings!
Through your blessings my heart became a fully opened lotus.
Who'd have thought the harmonica could be such a potent tool of the Dharma?

I see your smiling face everyday.
In a heartbeat, your Buddha smile was on my lips,
Smiling, his eyes, my eyes, meeting …
A warm handshake with a genuine smile.

Give love! Share love! Just relax!
With a snap of your fingers you rescued us from a meaningless life,
You sat before us on a simple cushion and said: "Look at your mind."
A revolutionary mahamudra master with the presence of a warm, giant cat;
I prayed to the light and to goodness for direction.
Rinpoche answered ... by being Rinpoche!

My heart, my heart;
How precious was seeing you in Mexico and receiving your teachings
and blessings,
Looking up to you on the balcony from the garden downstairs;
The independence of me is my destiny.

Everything you said or did was an offer to learn. Thank you Rinpoche!
Although your physical presence was not known to me,
your radiant energy continues to be.
A new chapter in my life has opened, filled with countless treasures
to be discovered.
We have known each other for many lifetimes,
We will know each other for many more!

Freedom is the best!
In an instant!
Love, joy and peace are available when the mind stops—they are not emotions.
Joyful activity! Delightful presence!
Thank you for your talks about children, talking to children,
and being with my children.

We miss you, until your return;
By the power vested in all of us, may we experience mahamudra
with ultimate ease.
Exhausted by concepts is not enlightenment—think it through until the end.
You showed me my mind—what a non-concept!

Thank you. Merits gathered under the sun always reflect the sun's brilliance;
So full of everything we could ever need.
Pure joy, like a donut peach,
Anywhere. Anytime.

Thank you for founding Bodhi Path.
Rinpoche, you are blessing us through the Bodhi Path sangha!
The Eagle has landed,
All we have now are memories in this collective dream.
Okay, I'll behave myself!

◆ MY BELOVED TEACHER SHAMAR RINPOCHE

I consider myself one of the very few lucky human beings to be born into a Buddhist family. I grew up in a household permeated with a strong influence of Dharma. Our family's connection with Shamar Rinpoche dates back to the 1980s. My grandmother on my father's side, Mrs. Shiu Wong Chi Yu, a devout Mahayana Buddhist most of her life, met Shamar Rinpoche in her later years when he visited Hong Kong in the early '80s. Because of the language barrier, she and Rinpoche never communicated efficiently, but nonetheless she placed unwavering faith and devotion upon the young master—so much so, that upon her death she dedicated over half of her bountiful estate to Rinpoche to support his Dharma activity.

In 1983 my father, Kahing Shiu, had the opportunity to follow Shamar Rinpoche's lead in an "exploratory tour" of Tibetan Buddhism in Kathmandu, together with a small group of Hong Kong followers. My father quickly became a close, staunch follower of Rinpoche. Because of this auspicious connection, I had the great blessing of meeting Rinpoche at the early age of six years old. My mother, sisters, aunts, uncles, and cousins all had the great opportunity to follow Rinpoche's teachings.

Growing up, Rinpoche would often stay at our home when he came to Hong Kong. Many times, prior to his arrival, my mother would notice unusual, auspicious signs. The first time he stayed with us, a rainbow appeared in our living room prior to his arrival, even though the weather was dry. The second time he stayed with us, my mother noticed a very large, exotic, and beautiful moth perched outside our house for days before our guru arrived.

I was 28 years old when Shamar Rinpoche appointed me as one of the directors of the Hong Kong Bodhi Path Center. Thus, I began working closely with my guru, and got to know him on a much more personal level. He was not only my teacher, but my adviser and my serious boss, too. He was also like a father, giving me sound advice every time I needed it; even when I didn't want to hear it, he would still bestow advice upon me. Rinpoche's advice for me on personal matters, as well as about work, was always very direct and straightforward, just like taking medicine. Take the pill, it will cure you, you don't need to know how it works, just take it! I had doubts in the beginning, but every time I took his advice, regardless of the reason, my "sickness" would come to light in the most spontaneous manner and dissipate into the air, leaving me healthier and wiser. For example, once I was asked to lend money to a certain person whom I had every reason to trust. Rinpoche, however, insisted that an IOU be drafted for this transaction, despite my unusually close relationship. I tried to convince Rinpoche that no such action was needed since my friend would surely return the money as soon as his finances got sorted out. Despite all logical appearances, Rinpoche insisted on an IOU I followed his advice, and the reaction I received was most shocking. The moment of truth came

to light; this trusted person responded to my request with rage and blame. From then on I realized how naively attached I had been to this person.

Gampopa said that one should observe, analyze, and examine a teacher thoroughly before one can totally trust him as a root guru. I can say that I have thoroughly done my "due diligence," long ago concluding that Shamar Rinpoche is indeed genuinely compassionate and wise. His motives and actions had not an ounce of self-interest or ego-clinging. He was always very down to earth, and never promoted himself in any way or demonstrated self-importance. Every single word and every deed of Shamarpa's was in accordance with the Buddhist principles of compassion, even when he was scolding or criticizing you. He did so in the same manner as parents would their child—without anger or blame.

Rinpoche's compassion was not only felt by those close to him, but also extended to all visible beings and those invisible to our ordinary, unrealized eyes. I remember just weeks after the Indian Ocean tsunami in 2004, Rinpoche asked my family and me to join him on a trip to Phuket, Thailand. One evening after dinner, Rinpoche asked us to retire to our rooms and leave him alone on the beach. The next morning at breakfast, we asked Rinpoche if he had a relaxing time on the beach. It turned out that he had stayed on the beach for hours to pray for the victims of the tsunami. In the beginning we had thought Rinpoche simply wanted to rest and relax in Phuket; little did we know he deliberately flew all the way to this island to pray for those unfortunate victims.

Once Rinpoche was brooding for hours in his chair, sitting motionless and frowning. I asked what troubled him to such prolonged silence. He took out a piece of paper and scribbled down an intricate design of a conveyor belt with an electric shock system on two sides, with blindfolded cows lining up one after another. He said with this invention, farm animals such as cows, pigs, and chickens would not be frightened or feel pain upon being slaughtered. I think in another life, Rinpoche must have been some kind of engineer! He then went on to say that the world will not stop eating meat, but the least we can do is to minimize animal suffering. His approach to compassion was very realistic and practical.

Oftentimes when I walked behind Rinpoche, I would notice his unusually broad shoulders for a man of his height; his calves grew stout over the years, carrying all that heavy weight, and I imagined that his shoulders grew that wide in order to bear all kinds of responsibilities. He took the entire Karma Kagyu lineage onto himself, fighting an uphill battle almost all alone, and I could not help but feel sorry for him. Whenever I observed his back I would think about his life, his journey, what he did to preserve the lineage, and a mixture of grief and appreciation would surge up inside me. Of course, Rinpoche himself would never feel grief; he was always so full of courage and positivity. His only minor regret would be that if he had not been tied up with the Karmapa controversy, his life could have been used in a much more productive and constructive way to benefit sentient beings. For example, he may have liked to become a politician of a country, being able to exert more power to benefit sentient beings than he could as the Red Hat Lama of Tibet.

Rinpoche was not a person who preferred the comfort of his own chair to tackling the mountainous tasks in front of him. Nor was he a person who only tended to the personal business under his own nose and ignored those unrelated to his affairs. Far from that, his compassion for mankind extended across the globe. He was always in touch with what was going on in the world. CNN and BBC were part of his daily routine. Once he called me, joyously telling me about his triumphant petition to release a Muslim woman who was sentenced to death by a Muslim court for marrying a Christian man. At other times, he would tell me about what Robert Mugabe was doing in Africa, how he was a tyrant to his people, and that he hoped he wouldn't be re-elected. For Rinpoche, justice was equally as important as compassion.

It is said that compassion can be described in terms as simple as knowing another person or being. My guru certainly knew me inside out, as if I were transparent. He seemed to know everyone's heart and mind. I lied to him once and only once. Although it was an unimportant white lie, he responded with a piercing glare, telling me that he knew I was lying, and that I should never do it again. On several occasions he pointed out to me that I had a short temper, and that I should be aware of it instead of letting it ruin me. He went on to explain that it was not in my nature to be angry, as he understood that my short temper was a result of reasons I was not aware of. He took the time and patience to point out and correct my way of thinking and some of the wrong views I held. Some were outdated concepts passed down from old Chinese traditions, and others from modern-day capitalism. Rinpoche reiterated to me over and over again that marriage (or having a certain type of boyfriend) is not important at all because everything is impermanent. Freedom of mind, on the other hand, is much more important and valuable.

Rinpoche understood my subliminal mind despite my attempts to hide my true feelings behind words and acts. He communicated with my soul and understood my true motivations; he knew me exactly the way I am. To be seen and accepted completely as you are—that is truly the most compassionate gesture I could ever ask for. Not only did he know me as I am, he wisely and compassionately guided me at the same time. If I were to be "liberated" tomorrow, I would have lived a fulfilled life, having been able to follow such an incredible, indescribable master.

Travelling with Rinpoche from here to there over many years, we always joked and laughed on the journey; he never took the time to teach me traditional Dharma, as one would expect from a Buddhist teacher. I only listened to his Dharma teachings when he was teaching a large group audience. I have come to realize that every moment spent with Rinpoche was actually in itself the Dharma teaching. Every action and reaction, every thought of his was a lesson on compassion. His entire existence is the existence of compassion, hence the Dharma.

MARGA RET
Santa Barbara, California

June 11, 2014

◆ FOR THE 14TH KUNZIG SHAMAR RINPOCHE

Sweetest Friend …
Why did you leave so suddenly
without a backward glance?

No time to say goodbye
to watch the sun rise one more time …

Never again will I search for something
unaware that I already have it
or ask questions not believing that I
have the answer …

You will watch for us in early light,
in evening shadows of high mountain valleys,
in lowland lotus ponds
where cranes and wild birds gather.

There we will find you,
teasing with that fine touch,
the great gift you bring as you
stride the stars among the curving arms of the milky universe
and slowly take in galaxies and kalpas of lifetimes long past
to keep that balance of joy and beauty
that is only yours to give away.

◆ THE WONDERS AND WAYS OF MY/OUR PERFECT TEACHER

There are countless situations I recall with Shamar Rinpoche: his gestures, expressions, way of saying things, or giving an answer in a certain way. Rinpoche means so much to me. *Spiritual father*, as His Holiness Karmapa phrased it, is also truly the most fitting for me when I think of Rinpoche. From the many memories I have, there is one story I would like to share, as it stands out to me, and shows Rinpoche's power over the elements so clearly.

I was in Rinpoche's office here in Renchen-Ulm, Germany, trying to fix the wireless cable. Rinpoche knew that I was in there because he had asked me to help fix the cable, but he was in the next room and the door was closed. The weather was neither good nor bad that day, but all of a sudden a strong wind started, with a lot of rain. I was kneeling on the floor fussing with the wires. As the wind got stronger and stronger it caught my attention, and I was worried that things on the balcony would start flying around. Nevertheless, I kept trying to fix the cable problem, which was not simple. Then Rinpoche came out of the other room, went straight to the balcony window, and opened it. With a powerful wave of his arm and hand, he said, "Stop it!" Within seconds the wind stopped and the rain was only drizzling. I was so astonished that I looked at Rinpoche and said with a laugh, not really believing what I'd just experienced: "Rinpoche, they listen to you!" Rinpoche looked at me and replied, "Yes, they do!"

This is only one little story showing Rinpoche's power. I feel so lucky and grateful to have experienced this situation, along with many more, and for having known Shamar Rinpoche. Soon it will be one year since Rinpoche passed, but I still miss him so much. I will be grateful forever! May my memories of Rinpoche stay clear and fresh throughout my life and may he come back soon to soothe our longing, and for the welfare of all sentient beings. Please be with us—always!

From all my heart with love and devotion.

CAROL GERHARDT
Natural Bridge, Virginia

◆ MIRACULOUS MOMENTS

My husband Jay Landman and I live about a half-mile across the ridge from the Natural Bridge Bodhi Path Center. We have had the great good fortune to spend a lot of time with Rinpoche over the last twenty-five years. During that time we have experienced many interesting and "unusual" incidents first hand. I'd like to share two of them.

The first story has to do with a song near and dear to the hearts of all of us here at the Bodhi Path in Natural Bridge, *Country Roads*. It's hard to know where to start this story, but I guess a good place would be many years ago when Jay and I asked Rinpoche what we could do for him. He told us, "Pull your life situation in Chicago together over the next five years, then open a center for me." Once we'd digested this, we thought we could do that on some property we owned in Wisconsin. We made some initial steps in that direction, and ran into a few obstacles—minor, but still … . So we thought, well, we could sell the Wisconsin property and buy land somewhere else.

Rinpoche concurred and we asked him for guidance as to where we should look. His reply was succinct, "Green." That was it; his entire direction for the property that was to become his seat in the US was "green." Well, that eliminated the western third of the country, so we knew we'd be looking in the Midwest or on the East Coast. Jay and I added a few more constraints such as: the land should be within a reasonable distance of an international airport; it should also be a little warmer than Chicago, because we knew we'd be spending the rest of our lives there, and old folks like warmer weather. And oh yes, having lived in the flat Midwest our whole lives, we wanted some hills. So we started looking around the mountains south of Pennsylvania and eventually ended up in Rockbridge County, Virginia, where we are now.

We found the property in 1993, a time when Rinpoche was very busy in Asia, so he was not able to see it for himself. Of course, we conferred with him before we bought it, but he never saw it in person until months after we closed on the sale.

Some years later, after we had built Rinpoche's house, we were sitting with him on his porch when the John Denver song "Country Roads" came on the radio. Rinpoche started singing along. I was really surprised because this was back when his English was, well, a heck of a lot better than our Tibetan, but still limited. I was amazed he not only knew the song, but every single word of the song. I remarked on this and he replied, "When I was a little boy in Rumtek, there was this hippie who wandered through. He left us an eight track tape of this person singing." Obviously, "this person singing" was John Denver.

My eyes got huge and I whispered, "Rinpoche, you know *these* are the Blue Ridge Mountains. You are *in* the Shenandoah Valley. I mean these are *all the places in that song!*" His eyes twinkled and he just smiled.

Fast forward several years for the second story. The stupa consecration at Bodhi Path Natural Bridge was coming up alarmingly fast. It was planned for June 17, 2001. This was a date our local building committee had learned only six weeks prior, in an unexpected, innocent, hair-raising fax. "Would the dates of June 12 to 26 be convenient for Beru Khyentse Rinpoche's visit to consecrate the stupa?"

"Yikes!! What stupa? Our stupa? Is this a joke? Did Shamarpa forget to tell us something?" Apparently!

At that time, the stupa was about half way built—the concrete had been poured through the rectangular lower section, up to the bumpa, which is the round part. The rest was, shall we say, in the works. This means that it was stalled while construction of the tricky round forms for the next stage of the concrete pour was being contemplated.

Hence, the hasty blur of activity. Our local building team—Sanford, Peter, Jeff, Harold and Jay—blasted into action to make sure there was indeed a stupa to consecrate come June 17. Sherab Gyaltsen Rinpoche arrived to oversee the crucial spiritual side: the making and filling of the core of the stupa with hundreds of clay tsa-tsas and thousands of prayer cylinders, beautifully wrapped in five-colored threads. All these were lovingly made by many very busy volunteers.

But alas, there was a wrinkle: the Bodhi Path stupa was to be a quite rare and unusually powerful double mandala stupa. This was new information which necessitated a huge step backward in the already pressure-filled construction process.

To install the mandalas, the already completed concrete core needed to be cut open and the contents removed. Then the two mandalas were gently placed inside, along with more *tsa-tsas*, prayers, incense, and flower petals. Finally, to empower the double mandala stupa, extremely long, rare rituals needed to be performed.

A few weeks before June 17, Shamar Rinpoche arrived and the prayer rituals began. On a hot, dusty summer afternoon, several days before the consecration, Shamar Rinpoche, Sherab Gyaltsen Rinpoche, Khenpo Palden, and Lungrig were down at the site conducting the ritual. I was also there, photographing it. The lamas were behind the stupa facing east. Despite the heat, sun, and dust, they were totally absorbed in their prayers. I was clicking away when I suddenly noticed what was boiling over the mountains behind them: black, ugly clouds. Really BLACK, ugly clouds! As they rolled toward our small group, I began to fret. I didn't want to interrupt the lamas, but there was some very serious weather coming.

My anxiety must have alerted Shamarpa, who looked at me quizzically. I discreetly pointed behind him to the sky. He looked over his shoulder, and then turned back to the ritual. A few seconds later he slowly turned his head, looked up at the sky, and blew toward the clouds. One soft, nearly silent whoosh; then he turned back to the prayers.

The dark clouds kept coming, and in a very short time the sky all around us was inky—but a few of the clouds parted and went around us. This left a tiny, sunny speck of land where the lamas were able to finish their puja.

Jay was in town at that time buying groceries and supplies. He walked outside to his car and was startled by the dark sky, and then he looked toward home and saw one unusual dot of sun way off to the southwest—over Bodhi Path, of course.

For years I thought I was the only one on site to witness this, but recently David Sensabaugh, the wonderful man who has worked on the property for over 20 years, mentioned the incident. He was up on the hill above the stupa and was astonished at what he saw: A puff of breath from the master and the clouds moved around us—pretty amazing.

And oh yes … the consecration happened on time a few days later. It was perfect.

Miracles and "unusual" occurrences were always interesting and fairly common with Rinpoche, but he forever downplayed them and led us to understand they weren't the point. What was infinitely more special happened when we spent longer periods of time with him. I've never been able to adequately describe this, but I gradually came to realize that when I was with Rinpoche I began to experience mind. Being around him gave me a sense of the spaciousness of mind not bound by the confines of my skull; mind that is not boxed-in or limited. Mind that is vast. Being around Rinpoche showed me that all things are possible in that space. We don't have to be confined to the conventional view that we've come to think of as "real." There is a much bigger, roomier, more alive and awake reality.

When we were in Kathmandu for Rinpoche's funeral, I was thinking about how differently Rinpoche manifested in the US, compared to other places. (That of course is only my perception, but I think it's accurate.) From the beginning, when he was here in Virginia he was very casual and relaxed. I knew he manifested differently elsewhere, but I thought that since he was the one teaching us how to treat him, and since he was so relaxed and comfortable here, my assumption was, that was how he wanted to be treated everywhere. I mean, we would have treated him any way he wanted us to, so if he wanted it casual here, that must be how he wanted it everywhere, right?

Gradually, though, I came to understand that a great bodhisattva will manifest in a way in which the people around him can relate. When we were in Asia I clearly saw this, because the facet of Rinpoche's manifestation that I would have said twenty years ago was definitely him, was really only how he was *right here, right now* with all of us. He was fully capable and comfortable manifesting differently, as diverse people and circumstances required. At Rinpoche's cremation in Kathmandu I thought that if we could just take film-sized slivers from the minds of everyone gathered there and splice them together, we might come closer to understanding the totality of the vast being that was the 14th Shamarpa. But, probably not. He was far beyond description.

JEFF SHUMATE
Lexington, Virginia

◆ I live here in Rockbridge County; regarding the stupa, there are many amazing stories, I think. The stupa construction here in Natural Bridge started in the late 1990s, and at each phase of construction, when the Rinpoches—and there were several, not only Shamar Rinpoche, for instance Sherab Gyaltsen Rinpoche was here several times for the consecration of each phase—I think actually from the earliest phase of construction on through, a black snake would come here during the ceremony, during the puja. And it got to the point where we all thought, "Well, where is it now?" during the next phase. At one point two snakes came along, and several of us asked Rinpoche about it. He said it had something to do with the naga energies they had summoned up, or dealt with, during the puja. It was very interesting to watch the snakes come along and just sort of hang out for the puja.

Right before the dedication of the stupa, the weather was not good; it was raining a lot, and cloudy. A few days before the consecration, we were trying to complete a certain part of the construction in time for the dedication, and I remember thinking, "Well, this is going to be interesting, because it's raining and the weather's pretty iffy." That's one of the times I actually saw Rinpoche come out of his house and start blowing away the clouds. It allowed us to work at the stupa; it was pretty dark and cloudy all around, but we were able to complete the work. When I left the property and headed toward town, as soon as I got out on the hardtop it was raining—it was really raining. I remember heading toward town and looking back over my shoulder and seeing this column of light around this area, it was just open … and that's Rinpoche.

One of the other things I think was pretty amazing and beautiful was the day of the stupa dedication. There were three Rinpoches—Shamar Rinpoche, Sherab Gyaltsen Rinpoche, and Beru Khyentse Rinpoche. It was a long day, there was a lot to get together, and it was also quite hot. As soon as they started reciting prayers and mantras, and the horns and the music were going—really within a minute or two of when it started—a red-tailed hawk flew in and started circling Rinpoche's house, and just kept circling. Then shortly after that, a second one came too and they both just circled over Rinpoche's house for what seemed to be five or ten minutes. They kept circling for most of the opening part of the puja, and then they flew out—right over the stupa. That was pretty amazing.

Rinpoche's greatest impact on me has probably been inspiring a dedication to the Dharma, inspiring a dedication to practice. Buddhism and sitting meditation had been a long-standing practice of mine, but as soon as I met Shamar Rinpoche and Khenpo Chodrak, it just seemed like, okay, yeah, sure. It has never ceased to amaze me that my guru found me, here in sleepy little Lexington. It blows my mind. And I am extraordinarily grateful for that karma.

HANS L.
Hong Kong

◆ SHAMAR RINPOCHE'S BODHI PATH CENTER IN HONG KONG

Some years ago Shamar Rinpoche told us that the time was ripe to set up a new Dharma center in Hong Kong. This was very exciting for us and was consequently discussed extensively within the local circle of Rinpoche's disciples. It was not, however, at all easy to come to a consensus regarding the most suitable location, the required size of the premises, and the financing in general. Eventually some in the group started to wonder whether these seemingly endless discussions would ever come to a positive conclusion.

On the other hand, Shamar Rinpoche remained extremely confident, telling us that the new Dharma center would be established under his auspices soon. But still the arguments within the group became louder and louder, at times even unreasonable. Despite Rinpoche's obvious confidence, the planning had become completely mired in arguments, and no quick solution appeared possible.

Shamar Rinpoche left Hong Kong, and returned the following year. Although no tangible progress had been achieved on our side, Rinpoche surprised everybody with his announcement that all obstacles regarding the setting up of his new center in Hong Kong had been removed. All who were there that day were utterly stunned and remained speechless.

Then, just a few days later, two of Rinpoche's generous disciples disclosed that they had bought a piece of property that they wished to donate to Shamar Rinpoche for a center. They surprised everyone by saying that the place was being renovated to accommodate the center and would be completed soon. Upon hearing this good news we were all very happy, and considered the problem solved. We assumed that this miraculous event had happened due to Rinpoche's "secret" involvement, and therefore none of us even thought to inform Rinpoche or to ask his approval.

We did not understand, until much later, that this "miracle" actually presented a problem for Rinpoche, after we learned that he had had a vision and instantly knew that the selected property was not suitable to be used for a Dharma center.

Shamar Rinpoche skillfully persuaded the donors and all the other supporters to stop the soon-to-be-completed project, and instead to continue what had been a rather futile search for a new Dharma center.

During that visit it happened that we drove repeatedly with Rinpoche from Pokfulam to Central district. One day as we passed the first high buildings along the waterfront road, Shamar Rinpoche suddenly interrupted a short moment of silence, turned and looked intensely towards the center of Kennedy Town, and said to my wife Nelly that this place would be a very good location for the new Dharma center.

We informed Rinpoche's local supporters about this incident, but nobody was particularly happy. Some argued that Kennedy Town was a run-down area, where no decent person would ever travel to learn and practice the Dharma. Others argued that Kennedy Town's transport system was totally inadequate, offering absolutely no convenience. Upon hearing this, Rinpoche explained that he had just travelled the distance from America to Hong Kong to help us to find the right location for our new center. However, some local "experts" still continued to argue with Rinpoche, pointing out that property values in Kennedy Town were expected to fall drastically in the future, and predicted that any investment in such an inferior environment would surely end in total financial disaster. Some even became very excited and concluded that it was high time to change Rinpoche's mind. They rented a small, comfortable bus and took Rinpoche for a sightseeing tour of Hong Kong. They showed him many beautiful places with convenient locations where the new Dharma center "should," from their point of view, be built. The bus circled around the city the whole day from morning to evening. Unfortunately though, Rinpoche politely rejected all the locations and buildings that were recommended.

The next day, we accompanied Rinpoche to an appointment in the Central district, and as we passed by Kennedy Town he suddenly stretched out his hand toward the center of town and said, "The new Dharma center should be set up two or three blocks from here, in front of a mountain." Nelly and I were shocked. We had hoped that this controversial subject would be put on ice for the time being as no acceptable solution had been found. But of course my wife took up the challenge and started to search for empty premises in Kennedy Town, walking up and down the streets and talking to shopkeepers. She finally found a place on the first floor of 46A Belcher's Street. When Rinpoche entered the premises the first time he was smiling broadly, and he instantly confirmed this place as his new Dharma center. We later found out that the property had previously been owned by a Japanese Buddhist organization that had used it as their center for many years before it became too small for them. It was a truly blessed place, as the Japanese Buddhists' main practice had been the Chenrezig Puja.

Rinpoche bought the property, and everyone was happy. The new Dharma center grew rapidly and flourished for many years. Many new disciples took refuge there. Eventually an underground station was built in the neighborhood, so traveling became extremely convenient. Only when the center became too small for the group did Shamar Rinpoche decide to relocate it. The premises in Kennedy Town were eventually sold at a large profit, all of which Rinpoche donated to the welfare and benefit of sentient beings.

JULIA TENZIN
Montreal, Quebec

◆ THE DANCING SNAKE

In the spring of 2006, I arrived at Shamar Rinpoche's Bodhi Path residence and center in Natural Bridge, Virginia. It is a wonderful place, lushly green at that time of the year, with dogwoods and other trees and bushes blossoming. One morning in April, everyone else had left with some business to tend to, so Shamar Rinpoche decided to go for a walk and I accompanied him. We walked to the pond at the bottom of the hill. There were wooden benches and a table beneath the trees on the edge of the pond. Rinpoche took a seat at the table, and started whistling an old Tibetan tune. Sitting nearby and listening, I looked at the beauty of the land.

After some time we walked onto the wooden bridge. The dark water held a special attraction, and so we just stood and watched the movements on and beneath the surface as Rinpoche took up whistling the Tibetan song again, a tune of melancholic nonchalance. Suddenly, there was an unusual movement in the water. We did not recognize it as a living being at first; we just saw something slim like a blade of grass or a thin root, golden yellow in color. There seemed to be no head, either, just maybe a plant moving in the water. Then, suddenly, we realized it was a miniature snake that appeared to be dancing with its tiny body to the rhythm of the melodious tune. Rinpoche noticed it at the very same moment and pointed it out to me. The small snake was turning left and right, left and right in the water, and its body took on the shape of a vertical wave.

As soon as Rinpoche noticed the creature's dance, he exclaimed a joyful shout of surprise, and right then, the snake stopped the movements, temporarily sinking back into the darker and deeper layers of the pond. As soon as Rinpoche took up his whistling though, it continued its water dance. Things continued this way for a while; as soon as the song would end, the yellow snake relaxed and sank to the bottom of the dark water, and when Rinpoche started whistling, it would rhythmically move to the surface. I think I even saw it take a breath from time to time, but I can't be sure. The longer we watched, the greater Rinpoche's delight grew. He expressed his amazement at the rarity and wonder of such an experience. He told me then and many times afterwards that I was a "machine-minded" person who had to be told when to rejoice, as I wasn't able to recognize something wonderful on my own. Rinpoche deeply regretted that he hadn't brought anything with which he could film the snake's dance. After a while, the rain set in, and we walked back.

Some years later I met Rinpoche in Kalimpong, West Bengal, and once again he reminisced about the dancing snake. Leaning on a chair in his living room, he whistled the same Tibetan tune and imitated the movements of the snake with his hand. Then he stood there for a while, apparently savoring the memories of that April morning. I'm not sure, but I think I received another reminder to abandon "machine-mindedness" that day.

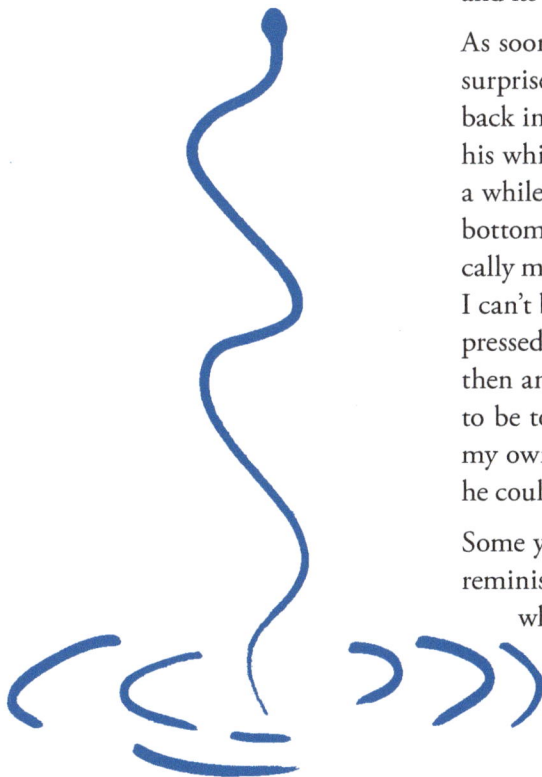

JOHN ZIPP
Natural Bridge, Virginia

◆ The first year we came up to Virginia, I brought a group of people—I think there were seven of us total—from Charleston, South Carolina. I started a group down there; it's actually a Diamond Way group, but I brought all the people up here to Virginia, and most of them took refuge from Shamarpa, ironically enough. And it was a great time, but this is the story.

So as we're driving up here and we're about ten minutes from the exit to pull off, we see a rainbow in the road, and it's actually coming down; it looks like it's touching the road. I turn to my friend—we're in a two-car caravan, five of us in one car and two in another car behind us—and I was like, "Umm, I think that rainbow is touching the ground," and my friend was like, "Nooo, it couldn't be." Well, we got closer and closer, and then we actually went into the rainbow—so for about thirty seconds we were surrounded by rainbow light, literally, like in the Buddhist meditations where they say "imagine rainbow light," well, we were in rainbow light! We looked around, and we're in a minivan and the rainbow light is all around us, and I looked at my friend's truck behind us, and he was in rainbow light! It was about—I talked to my friend afterwards—it was about twenty or thirty seconds, and then we came out of it. It was amazing—not only that it was a rainbow on our first time to Natural Bridge, and the rainbow touched the ground, but also that we were in rainbow light. I talked to my friend in the truck behind us after we got out, and he was shocked, he was like, "Yeah, did you see the rainbow? I was looking ahead at your car; you were all in the rainbow!" So, it's very auspicious I would say, very unusual. I've seen rainbows before, but never heard of this before, one touching the ground and actually being in a rainbow. So, yeah, cool blessing I guess. That's my story.

LORRIE V. COINER
Charlottesville,
Virginia

Peach glow—sun's echo
Bakes the stupa's hush
Hue finally ripened
For plucking with my brush.

Blue globe—in window
Full as mantra's moon;
The gift for my teacher
I'll give it to him soon.

Liquid rainbow drips
Icicle's melt
Mahamudra's lesson
Not understood but felt.

◆ I am the resident teacher of the Bodhi Path center in Santa Barbara, California. One story I'd like to share dovetails with something that Rinpoche once told us about flat peaches. It seems a flat peach is, I don't know, maybe a new thing, but rather than being round like an apple, it is a more squashed, flatter shape. Occasionally, during teachings, Rinpoche would refer to these flat peaches being the result of bodhisattva wishing prayers—that it was really the wishing prayers of the bodhisattvas that had brought forth those flat peaches so that people could eat peaches with dignity, without the peach juice running down their faces. After Rinpoche passed, I shared this story at the Santa Barbara Bodhi Path Center, and the next day one of the members was at the grocery store and decided to buy a flat peach. She got to the register, and the person at the register said, "You know what, I offer this peach to you; you don't need to pay for it." Just out of the blue. And she said, in her 55 years, she had never been given anything for free at a grocery store. It was an immediate blessing!

Shamar Rinpoche was very unique, in my experience. In his courage, and also in his willingness to always seek out new, better, efficient ways to reach sentient beings; Rinpoche was fearless about trying new things. He was a maverick, and among Tibetan Buddhist masters, someone who was not held back by tradition or self-image; rather he was deeply committed to the bodhisattva aspiration of doing whatever was necessary to plant the Dharma firmly in the world, and to create access for sentient beings. What I appreciate a lot about Rinpoche, and what I will miss, is his real depth of vision. I experienced him always being about ten or fifteen years ahead of the curve; he lived in a reality that most people will see unfold years from now. That was already his daily reality, where he took his cues from, and I think he was courageous and a great gift; very unique in that way. He really tried to push the envelope in order for the West to have a Dharma that can be sustained and flourish, according to our mentality, and according to the value systems and culture that we have.

Shamar Rinpoche was a maverick in his approach to Dharma in that he didn't let rituals and rites stand in the way of meaning, and he didn't let words stand in the way of meaning. I think that Rinpoche, first and foremost, was a very profound practitioner. And always, in my experience, he made sure that he "walked his talk." I think that the world of Dharma in the Tibetan culture—as with many other spiritual traditions in their culture—has become, quite naturally, a bit of a world of smoke and mirrors; where quite simply, for the purpose of perpetuating its influence and perpetuating its traditions, the real meaning may be lost. I think Rinpoche—even though he was steeped in tradition—always maintained his freshness. He was willing to really rest in the freedom of the mind, which is the tradition of the Buddha. The tradition of the Buddha is the natural freeness of the awakened mind, not the Buddhist tradition, even though that is the way we currently pass on the legacy of the Buddha. Rinpoche was able to discern between the two. And in fact, the transmission of the freeness of the mind, at the time of the Buddha, was very revolutionary; a revolutionary discovery and a revolutionary transmission. In that way, I'd say Rinpoche was a rebel because he always pointed to the aspiration of not getting trapped—by the trappings of religion and the trappings of tradition—at the cost of realizing the freshness of Buddha mind in its true nature.

Rinpoche didn't, I don't think, have an easy life, this life. He had to contend with a lot of adversity, partly due to the historical changes that happened for the Tibetan people, partly due to the challenges that the lineage went through in coming to the West. So I think he had a unique position, because he spent a lot of time dealing with adversity and really having to stand on his internal principles. That's something I admired in him, and it has also been an inspiration, where I took courage for my own practice. I think he often had to stand on what he knew to be true internally, even if externally it wasn't exactly clear or sure what the outcome would be. That in itself is a very strong teaching; in many religious schools or spiritual traditions, people like to go with the mainstream simply for a sense of belonging. Not everyone is in the Dharma for the result of awakening; many people like to be part of the community, to have a sense of belonging. To give that up for the sake of something that you really know profoundly to be true can be a very lonely path, and I think parts of Rinpoche's life had that characteristic, where he really stood on principle—even at the cost of being popular—and he was ostracized.

In my experience, Rinpoche made clearly informed choices about how he taught in the West and in Asia, realizing there were different cultural needs between Westerners and Asians. At the same time there is a globalization; I experience young people from Europe and Asia and the Americas coming together, building friendships, and exchanging more and more—so I think we are on the verge of a more global culture as a human race, and I think Dharma will also find new incarnations in which to serve this globalization. Even though at this time we might see very strong differences, I think among the younger generations, the teens and the millennials, we can already see a more unified desire for an awakened life that is aligned with Rinpoche's intentions for the Bodhi Path. I can see Bodhi Path might be something that already addresses this emerging global youth culture—maybe even more than it is addressing the very different needs between Asia and the West that are still part of the generations of the '60s and '70s.

Rinpoche's mind was in this world, not of this world. He was always in a free state. There are a lot of teachers, because of the temptation to build something for oneself—a name, a reputation, influence, and income—who may lose sight of the real meaning of the Dharma, which is to become enlightened; to be forever liberated from conditioned existence. I think what made Rinpoche's teaching special was that his mind rested in that aspiration, and even though he invested time and effort in furthering the lineage and beginning to create infrastructure and so on, the real essence is liberation and the bodhisattva aspiration to reach enlightenment for the benefit of all beings. I think when we connect with that, the blessing we get will come from that place. It will not just be about being more successful in this world; it will be in fact about liberating our minds, forever, from the trappings of conditioned existence.

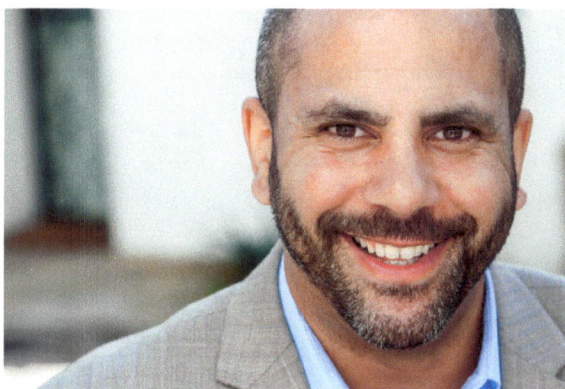

Rinpoche's understanding of Dharma was very deeply rooted in practice and his relationship with masters of the past, and understanding that the real meaning of Dharma practice is not success in this life; the real meaning of Dharma practice is liberation from conditioned existence—the attainment of the state of Buddha. I think the ease with which he was able to release attachments, from one moment to the next, and the way he was always able to respond to a situation without a lot of preconceived ideas, was his testament to that. Rinpoche had deep, deep love and compassion for sentient beings, and that was in part his guiding motivation to not let himself be caught by the trappings of power—of influence, wealth, and status. I think we saw this more here in the states than in other places, where he still needed to play the role of the Dharma king. What I know of him here is his love and affinity for this simpler way of relating to people, really being able to share his love for the Dharma, and being able to work compassionately for the benefit of beings with simplicity. I know this meant a great deal to him, and in fact made him feel at home here.

I have been through the loss of a spiritual master before, when Gendun Rinpoche, who led the monastery where I was trained, passed away. Based on my experience, it really depends on the presence of mind of the disciples, practitioners, and the students whether or not Rinpoche's mind will be present. From his perspective, I think the physical form we saw of Rinpoche is only a very small part of who he is. This was the 14th incarnation of the Shamarpas; their spiritual activity is something that has been around for centuries, and will continue to be so—if the students continue to take inspiration, remember the teachings, and apply the teachings. I am confident, in fact, that if his students remember what they learned, and follow the instructions they've received, the spiritual influence of Shamar Rinpoche will continue to be present in this world in a very powerful way, because he is a very powerful teacher. I don't think we are as dependent on the physical form, maybe, as we may believe at this time. Our relationship to these multi-generational spiritual teachers is fairly new in the West, and we don't quite know what to make of it; but because of my experience when Gendun Rinpoche passed away, I feel confident the spiritual guidance coming from Shamar Rinpoche's presence can continue to be a guiding light in the minds of his students. Then, of course, the reincarnation will be found.

One of the strong suits of this branch of the Kagyu lineage is profound spiritual practice and retreat practice. I think in the West it's taken a while for us to understand the importance of a relationship with the general public; the importance of publications, the importance of making content available in the form of products that people can access in their own homes. I think this was something that was not immediately obvious to a lineage that is so steeped in retreat practice and used to passing the Dharma on in seclusion in remote areas of Tibet. And so I think it took a while for the majority of the Tibetan masters to catch on, to understand the importance of the media and the importance of creating different media outlets and different media products that people can utilize to learn and practice the Dharma. Rinpoche only recently began his activity of publishing, and I don't know how it will unfold after my generation of teachers passes; but what I can say is we have received a lot of teachings from him, and those seeds are still ripening. I believe there are projects that Rinpoche had started that will be finished and published, and that we have many teachings that we can transcribe and publish going forward in order to preserve Shamar Rinpoche's legacy. I know there is a book on mahamudra almost ready for publication, and a book about Rinpoche's life story; and also other masters who have studied and learned from him will contribute to bringing these teachings out. We can all benefit from these precise teachings that make up the richness and heritage of the Kagyu lineage; and Rinpoche, because of his experience and depth of understanding, was able to offer a unique perspective, and also unique interpretations of those teachings. We can look again and again at the mountain from different directions, and as long as we remember Rinpoche's blessing and the Karmapa's blessing are like the sun that brightens our view on that mountain, then we will benefit from many different perspectives as different teachers elucidate these teachings.

I deeply wish all the students of the Buddha have a wonderful experience discovering the teaching and the meaning of the teachings for themselves. I, and my colleagues, have found tremendous value in studying these teachings and receiving the blessing of the Kagyu lineage, and we hope those teachings will spread in the ten directions and liberate beings until samsara has come to an end.

TAMARA RADENKOVIC
Belgrade, Serbia

◆ TIMELESS

I had the opportunity to meet Shamar Rinpoche on several occasions—listening to him while being part of a large crowd, as well as sipping tea while discussing organizational matters to be done for Bodhi Path.

My first impression was, and remains: I am grateful and so lucky to have met such an extraordinary being, who shows us by his example the qualities we strive to attain on the Path he laid out for us.

His warmth, manner of speech, sense of humor, vivid examples, and suggestions will remain part of my memory of him.

He is not here with us in physical form, but never have I doubted his continuous presence with us all. His guidance remains as present as the sky above.

HUEI-LING WORTHY
Bethesda, Maryland

◆ My Cherished Memories of Shamar Rinpoche

I first met Rinpoche on Sunday evening, August 1, 1982. I remember the precise date because he made such an impression on me then, and an impact ever since. Rinpoche was giving a Marpa empowerment at the Dharmadhatu (today, Shambhala) Center in Manhattan, and I was visiting there with my friend Cindy Lo from Hong Kong.

I had read many Chinese Mahayana Buddhist books since my high school days, but I had never thought about taking refuge or practicing Buddhism. In the late 1970s, I read several books by Chogyam Trungpa Rinpoche, which was the extent of my exposure to Tibetan Buddhism.

In the year or so before we met Rinpoche in New York, Cindy Lo had become very interested in Tibetan Buddhism, and while we were touring Manhattan, she spotted a poster in a Chinese temple announcing Rinpoche's program. She was powerfully drawn to the Chinese poster, even though she had never heard of this teacher before. I protested that I couldn't go that night because I had plans with my family. She demanded that I go with her; I gave in and accompanied her to the empowerment given by a high lama named Shamar Rinpoche.

The evening was fun for me, because I had never met a Tibetan lama before, and this esteemed lama was as beautiful and dignified as a Buddha statue. The ceremony was very foreign to me, but very interesting. More than 200 people attended that evening's empowerment. They seemed to know what was going on, so I just followed them without understanding the rites. At one point we were given a sip of strong alcohol, Rinpoche giggling on his throne when he saw the expression on people's faces. Later he explained that alcohol is often used for this empowerment and we were sipping brandy.

My friend Cindy made an immediate connection with Rinpoche and wanted to take refuge as soon as possible. She ultimately did so a month later in Hong Kong. Like Cindy, I too had the strange feeling of wanting to take refuge after I saw Rinpoche in Manhattan. I knew from a friend that Rinpoche did not regularly come to America, so I went up to Woodstock, NY, where I took refuge from Khenpo Karthar Rinpoche, because I knew that this center belonged to the Karma Kagyu Lineage of Tibetan Buddhism. Six months after first encountering Rinpoche, Cindy called me from Hong Kong and insisted that I fly there quickly to meet him personally. Even though I protested that I had work obligations and could not easily get leave, she wouldn't take no for an answer, telling me I should tell my boss that I had to take care of some urgent family matters in Hong Kong. Again, I obeyed her command.

In February of 1983, I traveled to the Hong Kong center and met Rinpoche for the second time. Cindy and I had a private audience with him. The minute I entered his room, he said, with one of his big enchanting smiles, "I remember you." I was shocked, wondering how he could possibly remember one person out of two hundred people at a gathering. Later, I learned that a highly realized person knows who has a karmic connection with him.

After chatting a bit, Rinpoche taught Cindy and me how to meditate. He also explained a short Amitabha Buddha practice, which is still my main practice today. Cindy became close to Rinpoche and traveled with him often in the 1980s. She kindly sent me cassette tapes (this was before the Internet and the digital world existed) to report on the trips she took with him, so I know about some of Rinpoche's activities from those years. That was how I kept up with news about him.

In the late 1980s, Rinpoche went to the Toronto center several times, and I had the chance to meet him there. Also, because a very close French disciple—Michel Le Goc—was stationed in Washington, DC where I have lived since 1974, Rinpoche started to visit DC periodically and would stay at our house. After Jay and Carol bought the land for the Natural Bridge Bodhi Path center in 1994, Rinpoche came to Washington, DC and the Virginia center almost every year until his death in 2014. In 1999, before he left Washington, he told me and other DC disciples who had been meeting in my home that we would have a center. He actually saw our center in a vision and tried to direct us to look for a place in the area of Potomac, Maryland, a DC suburb that he had never visited. At the end of 2001, Rinpoche bought the Potomac property, which established our DC center.

In a similar way, Rinpoche also foresaw the closing of our center in Potomac. When someone asked him about attachment the first night he met people at our center, he said, to illustrate his point, that it would be okay with him if he lost the Potomac center someday, but for 13 years we enjoyed the DC Bodhi Path center in Potomac. Rinpoche visited at least once a year, and sometimes several times a year. Then, a few months before his death, he decided to sell the DC center; the transaction closed before he died. During the early years, Rinpoche planned to remodel the building; he dreamed of creating a small shop and establishing an international Buddhist study center there, saying he wanted lamas from different schools of Buddhism to teach at the center. For example, he hoped to invite some good meditation teachers to teach the Burmese style of meditation. He tried every possible way to help his disciples advance their practice. Unfortunately, due to lack of funds, causes and conditions, this plan never materialized.

Rinpoche always tried to teach us the core values of Buddhism. I remember when the DC Bodhi Path was first established, we decorated the center very simply. I asked him if we should buy Tibetan flags to hang and use silk brocade to cover his chair. He said, "No need," explaining that we were here to learn Buddhism and not to worry about Tibetan culture. As everyone knows, Rinpoche's teaching style was direct, simple, and yet very clear. In 1987, during the first dinner Rinpoche had in our house, in the middle of dinner, my then 18-year-old son Brian abruptly asked him, "Please explain Buddhism in one word." I nearly fell off my chair when I heard this question, because at that time Rinpoche barely knew me well enough to call me by my name. How could my son ask such a challenging question the very first time he met him? However, after a few seconds' silence, Rinpoche replied:

"Mind." I think that answer convinced Brian that Buddhism merited serious exploration. After that he read lots of my Buddhist books, and took refuge from Rinpoche in 1993, and has devoutly practiced Buddhism ever since.

Regarding my own practice, Rinpoche knew my main interest is the Amitabha practice. One year I told him I was worried that following him so closely might cause me not to go to the Pure Land after my death, but to come back as his disciple again. He said it's better to go to the Pure Land first and then come back to help.

We all know Rinpoche had a very powerful personality. One small incident showed me, though, that he really had a very soft, tender heart—like a mother's. Back in the 1990s, when my husband Ed and I visited the Natural Bridge Bodhi Path Center, we would stay at what today is called "Rinpoche's house." Since Rinpoche liked Chinese food, I often cooked dinner for him. Late one cold afternoon, while I was preparing food and standing in my bare feet on the stone floor in the kitchen, Rinpoche entered the kitchen and told me, "Huei-ling, your feet must be cold. Go put something on." At that moment, I felt like my mother was talking to me. I was very moved!

Another incident that touched my heart occurred in 2008, when Rinpoche gave us permission to plant a tree near the stupa at the Natural Bridge Bodhi Path Center—I wanted to spread my recently deceased sister's ashes around the tree. On that day, first he did the Red Chenrezig Puja for her in the house, and then came outside to plant the tree with us. When my brother-in-law spilled some of my sister's ashes outside the hole for the tree, Rinpoche naturally, without thinking, bent down and pushed the ashes into the hole with his bare hand. This spontaneous selfless manner and kind action really touched my family members who were present. We also experienced how a bodhisattva shows compassion for all sentient beings, regardless of their personal connection to him. He treated my sister, who had met him only once, like all other beings.

Rinpoche was very funny, and he also made fun of himself. One hot day, a few of us accompanied Rinpoche on a walk in Great Falls Park along the Potomac River. Wearing an orange T-shirt, he walked ahead of us. Suddenly he turned his head back and remarked, "Oh! When people see me, they must think a big pumpkin is coming!" Sometimes Rinpoche could be very childlike, which I interpreted to be a manifestation of his purity. Once he liked a dinner I cooked for him so much that he overate. The next morning he teased me that I was forbidden to cook for him again.

It is impossible for me to recount all my memories of Rinpoche for the 31 years I followed him. I hope that what I have recorded here is not only meaningful for me, but also sheds some light on who he truly was. For me, the most impressive thing about him was his ability to touch thousands of people so deeply. Only a true Maha-Bodhisattva can do this. For 31 years I witnessed his tremendous drive, courage, energy, dedication, compassion, and wisdom in conducting bodhisattva activities and helping sentient beings. My profound regret is that although I followed Rinpoche for many years and tried to work on myself, I have not gotten far enough along in my practice. He must have been frustrated with me.

Oh, my guru! Forgive me, and continue to help and inspire me in your nirvana for me to become a bodhisattva like you. This is my sincere wish.

JAY LANDMAN
Natural Bridge, Virginia

◆ REMEMBERING RINPOCHE

High lamas, teachers, students, and friends from around the world have already paid tribute to Rinpoche's many extraordinary qualities far more eloquently than I can. I heartily agree with their sentiments. In addition, because my wife Carol and I were fortunate enough to know and work for Shamar Rinpoche for 25 years, we often saw him in informal settings. Below are a few glimpses of the Rinpoche we knew:

Rinpoche loved to relax in casual clothing. He loved his Bodhi Path T-shirts. We loved an old one he wore that said, "Too Blessed to be Stressed."

Rinpoche loved *thukpa* (Tibetan noodle soup) for breakfast.

Rinpoche had a special method for preparing rice, and another one for a perfect cup of tea. His attendants learned both, yet he was more than happy to fix his own.

Rinpoche loved Brazilian restaurants. Mmmmmmm—all those different meats and a sip of red wine. Carol and I are quite sure we hold the world's record for vegetarians eating at steak houses.

Rinpoche loved to travel anonymously. He loved to drive, and loved road trips, especially in roomy cars.

Rinpoche could direct a driver to the best restaurant in any new town in which he found himself. And yes, this was long before Yelp or Trip Advisor.

No matter where he was, Rinpoche unexpectedly ran into people who had some connection with him. It was always a surprise to us, but was it really a coincidence?

Rinpoche loved flowers, especially the ones he could see while sitting in his favorite chair on his back porch.

Rinpoche loved birds, bird feeders, and talking to birds. We once saw him calmly walk up to a frightened little bird that had flown into his house, slowly reach out for it, gently cup it in his hands, and quietly walk out the kitchen door to release it. Calm, quiet, no fuss, and … freedom.

Rinpoche used a squirt gun on the squirrels ravaging his bird feeders. He tried this on some greedy blackbirds, too, with minimal success.

Our dogs loved Rinpoche. Somehow they always knew when he arrived from afar, and went immediately to his house to greet him. He always blessed them.

I once had the "opportunity" to lift Rinpoche up to the top of the stupa in the bucket of our tractor. He was fearless. I was a wreck. (Imagine the karma of dumping your teacher on his head!)

Rinpoche was gracious about posing for pictures.

Rinpoche loved Western movies, classic Bollywood movies, and historical movies.

Rinpoche loved international news and was surprised at how little of it we got here in the US.

Rinpoche got up early in the morning and was up late at night, as worldwide concerns across many time zones required his attention. He was on the phone a lot and snoozed when he could.

The first time we met Rinpoche in Delhi, he surprised us on the evening of our flight back home by arriving at a restaurant to say goodbye. He could not have known—in a conventional sense—where we would be, because we decided where to eat only after we had left KIBI.

During a visit to Wisconsin in the early 1990s, Rinpoche got some distressing news. During the five hour drive back to Chicago, Rinpoche and three other lamas did the Mahakala puja all the way home in the car. I imagine this was quite surprising to the tollbooth operators: The car rolled up, the window went down, and the tolls were paid—all to the sound of mantras in the background.

Rinpoche was famous for his divination *mo*s. We seldom asked for one, but when we did, we always found it accurate and helpful, if not precisely what we wanted to hear. Carol once asked if she should have eye surgery to correct her extreme near-sightedness. This was several years before Lasik surgery was perfected. To her immense disappointment, he said no, but added that it would be okay to ask again in the future. Several years later, she did ask again and he said, "Fine, go ahead." In the intervening two years, the technology had vastly improved and her surgery was a complete success.

Rinpoche was often nearby to help alleviate suffering when extreme catastrophes occurred. He was in Manhattan on the morning of 9/11, Miami for Hurricane Wilma, and Thailand for the tsunami.

In 2005, Geetu was staying at our house in Virginia while we were in Chicago. She was awakened early one morning by coyotes howling very close to our house. She told Rinpoche and he immediately did prayers to ward off any negative implications. Later that same day Carol called Rinpoche to tell him I suddenly needed brain surgery. Rinpoche immediately flew to Chicago to help. He greatly relieved our anxiety by telling us everything would be fine. He also advised the surgeon.

Even though it was far from his early experience, Rinpoche embraced new technology—from computers to smart phones to iPads. Carol once joked that a future thangka would show him with 1000 arms, each holding a cell phone or laptop. He did not laugh.

Rinpoche loved to learn. He studied everything from ancient Tibetan texts to the piano, flute, and harmonica. He laughed while learning English with books like *Yes, Minister* and *The Sayings of Harry Truman*. He always asked the precise meaning of new words, while those around him scrambled to articulate exact definitions.

Rinpoche made up words and phrases to illustrate his points: Pushy, crowdy karma. Machine-minded. Rid away.

Rinpoche was spontaneous. Plans changed and changed again. Spending time with him was the antidote to machine-mindedness.

Rinpoche loved to draw, illustrating his ideas with drawings and plans.

Rinpoche had a great singing voice.

Rinpoche loved hosting parties at his house. He always had music playing and encouraged everyone to dance. One time, just one time, he danced himself for a few seconds.

Rinpoche loved the singing at the Annual Teaching farewell party. He especially enjoyed the rewritten songs—familiar tunes with new dharma lyrics. One in particular, Dewachen, to the tune of the Banana Boat song, with Tsony leading the back-up dancers, tickled him immensely.

Rinpoche had a very sensitive nose.

Rinpoche loved the fall, and the few winters he was able to spend in Virginia. One time he made a snow angel outside his back porch.

Rinpoche made time to practice Mahakala daily, no matter where he was or what he was doing.

Rinpoche was a master at setting up situations where we, his students, could understand an important point without being explicitly told. Often this was in brief and informal situations—the 30-second master class.

Rinpoche explained Mahamudra once while sitting at an overlook on the Blue Ridge Parkway. "What you need for meditation is open space. It's like this," he said gesturing to the infinite view.

Like everyone who knew him, we miss Rinpoche a lot and long for a swift return. We'd love to see him sitting in his Adirondack chair on his back porch again. We'd love to sit there with him again.

SHARON GAMSBY
Martha's Vineyard, Massachusetts

◆ When I walked through the door of the original Martha's Vineyard Bodhi Path Buddhist Center in September of 1999, I'd already taken refuge with another teacher from a different lineage. I'd never heard of this teacher, Shamar Rinpoche, who'd decided to open a Buddhist Center on the island, but I was thrilled that a center was opening, and I went the very first night. What ensued over the next seventeen years has enriched my life and fueled my commitment to waking up. From the beginning, Lama Yeshe Drolma, our resident teacher at the MVBP center, provided the perfect bridge to understanding the potential relationship I could develop with a teacher such as Shamar Rinpoche. She advised me that it was up to me, that one's own open-mindedness was the key. I remember her saying something like, "If you see him as a 'nice guy,' you'll receive the blessing of a nice guy, if you see him as a 'knowledgeable teacher,' you'll get the blessing of a knowledgeable teacher, but if you perceive him as a 'realized master'...." This illuminated the possibilities and pointed me toward developing an open mind. By walking over that bridge, I gained a clarified perception of Shamar Rinpoche which developed into absolute, without a doubt, confidence and trust. I received many gifts from Rinpoche in return. I think that over the years I've grown into certain aspects of myself that he seemed to have confidence in, ways in which he seemed to trust me. This for me is the amazing alchemy of Buddhist practice: that first confidence can plant such a rich seed, and then the fruit of the practice can begin to purify one's mind, so that both outer and inner perception can move towards maturity. Obviously, I have much more to learn, but I don't minimize the effects that knowing a teacher like Shamar Rinpoche can reveal; a quickening of karma, as well as a golden invitation of encouragement to develop oneself in a positive direction.

I noticed early on that when Rinpoche was nearby, my awareness of my thoughts magnified markedly—it was easier for me to see my petty grievances, my irritation and anger; perhaps this was highlighted by my belief that he could see what was happening in my mind, and therefore heightened my vigilance. Self-awareness is an inside job, I know, but when Rinpoche was around, I paid more attention to the subtleties. On the other hand, I felt that I could be myself, and felt genuinely at ease around him. Rinpoche seemed to prefer a relaxed atmosphere; he didn't, in my experience, want too much formality. I noticed over the years that Rinpoche loved to have the "youngs" around him (I was already beyond that category). I think he loved the laughter and lightness, as well as educated people who could eagerly discuss things with him; he also liked to tease and joke. Rinpoche embodied going with the flow; not always, of course, but he did not seem adverse to silliness. Many times I observed him take part with a youthful exuberance; he loved music, and would gamely participate in playful activities if asked. He was also amazingly quick to catch on to new things. I remember being on a sailboat with him when the captain showed him how to tie a bowline knot. After watching only once, Rinpoche tied it with ease. Hand him a harmonica; he would play a song.

Have a plumbing problem, there he was in the basement, banging on a pipe (and clearing it!). We all have stories like these. He loved drawing; sketching things we were discussing, like building plans, animals. He even drew a picture of Padmasambhava last winter, when I somewhat squirmily admitted that I find images of Padmasambhava kind of creepy.

I think Rinpoche also enjoyed the rare moments he was left alone. One summer I arrived at the house on MV and found him by himself. All his attendants had gone off on an errand, it was lunchtime, and Rinpoche was cooking himself some soup. I think it was a Bhutanese recipe; there were fiddlehead ferns and "old cheese" in it, as well as plenty of chili. I couldn't refuse when he offered me a bowl, and he was clearly tickled to be cooking.

In the fifteen years I knew him here in the US, amazing, dedicated helpers usually traveled with him, supporting his activity. From the earliest days, Jay and Carol were there to make things happen, and his personal attendants took care of myriad other tasks: cooking, laundry, driving, secretarial tasks, etc. Lungrig and Neeraj were with him from young ages; Rinpoche was also a bit like their father, and oh my, Delphine—she did so much during the last years. Geetu, Lama Jampa, Tsering Ngodrup, among others, all tirelessly setting Rinpoche's needs first, happy to be of service to him—which could not have been easy—and to the Dharma. The Bodhi Path teachers are tirelessly dedicated as well; chosen by him and trusted to impart his vision, and to help bring the Dharma here to North America, their confidence resonates outward. Rinpoche gave so much, every single minute it seemed. There was always someone asking for his guidance, his blessing, his support. He was a supreme Bodhisattva, traveling around the planet continuously, endlessly doing everything for beings here in this world and other realms beyond my imagination. When I bring Rinpoche to mind, he is here. Still here. The confidence and trust remains.

◆ AT SHARMINUB

Again and again, as I sit on the cushion
I recall your eyes on the banner suspended above us
While we waited below as your kudung's final kora circled around Swayambhu
We staked out our place, we jockeyed and jostled

Thousands and thousands and thousands of us
Marigold petals strewn near our feet
We chatted and chatted and chatted below
While your lifeless body forged its way up the hill
We waited and waited and waited some more

Devoted, reverent, amazed, shocked, and awed
While three stories above us "The Eagle" soared
Your meditative absorption and compassion unwavering
As your lifeless body inched toward the final fire

Finally, the first faint Tibetan horns wafted ahead
As the sun sank down below Kathmandu
Weirdly jubilant, we sang "Country Roads"
Supplicating, and calling you home

It got darker and darker, that day on the hill
Still your absorption above and around us shone
We, your devoted students, were giddy and laughing—
and joking below your constant gaze

Finally, finally the procession was coming
Colorful, loud, a sight to be seen
Any moment your lifeless body was coming
We prayed intently, our focus united
The moment had come, you had finally arrived

Time leapt ahead as your casket, your paladin, raced up the hill,
rounding the corner we'd stood on all day
But the crowd pushed us backwards in a tornado of power
High emotion, anger flashing, your body flew by in a blur!
We pushed through the crowds to get down the hill
in the dark and the rain, in the dark and the rain.

—Sharon Gamsby

ERIK CURREN
Staunton, Virginia

◆ A CONFIDENCE GAME

*What happened when Shamar Rinpoche asked me
to write a book about the Karmapa controversy:*

In 2002, I told Shamar Rinpoche I hoped to do a three-year retreat. At the time, he was visiting the Bodhi Path Center just outside Washington, DC, where I was a member. Rinpoche was supportive, and even invited me to do the retreat under his personal direction at the Bodhi Path Natural Bridge center in the Shenandoah Valley of Virginia. He said that after the retreat I'd develop great confidence in Dharma.

Confidence—who doesn't want that? Of course, Rinpoche didn't mean assertiveness or more certainty in one's own ability, exactly, though those could be results of gaining confidence in Dharma. I think he meant that I would develop more faith or stronger belief in Buddhist teaching. Either way, it sounded good to me. I hoped that believing more in Buddhism would help me to live a more examined and meaningful life.

During my time in Natural Bridge, I did the prostrations, meditation, and chanting that are traditional in a Dharma retreat. But the main training I received from Rinpoche was less orthodox.

A few months after I arrived in Natural Bridge, after I began to assist him with some English-language writing projects, Rinpoche asked me to write a book. The topic was the controversy over the identity of the current Karmapa Lama that began after the death of the 16th Karmapa in the 1980s. Shamar Rinpoche took more than an academic interest in the subject because he himself was a leading player in the contention, supporting Trinley Thaye Dorje as candidate for 17th Karmapa over another boy, Ogyen Trinley Dorje, who had been chosen by other leading lamas in the Karmapa's own school, and endorsed by the Dalai Lama.

I accepted the challenge, and at the end of my retreat in 2006, I published the results of this work, *Buddha's Not Smiling*. Rinpoche himself came up with the title. Though he didn't insist that I use it, I thought it was perfect.

Over the course of a couple of years during my retreat, Rinpoche guided my research and spent many afternoons with me, sitting at a table downstairs in the library at the Natural Bridge center, translating documents *viva voce* and telling stories, while I typed them into my Dell laptop for later use. Rinpoche also gave me lots of homework, which included a reading list with hundreds of items, as well as dozens of personal contacts in the Himalayas and beyond, in order for me to get more information.

It should be noted that in writing this book, Rinpoche didn't steer me away from sources that were critical of him. Quite the opposite! He directed me to read the major books and articles from the "other side," and then to deal with their main arguments, point by point. The fact that he would ask me to read material which was sometimes very critical of his own role, accusing him of various kinds of corruption, certainly raised my confidence in Shamar Rinpoche. I thought he must have felt he had nothing to fear from these criticisms.

Admittedly, when I encountered the arguments from Rinpoche's opponents, written in some cases by experienced journalists from Britain, along with well-known American supporters of the Dalai Lama, I couldn't help but find their points convincing. These writers had so much authority on their side—so much publicity in the Western news media, so many university professors of Buddhism. The "other side" also had three full-length books just on the Karmapa controversy alone, each professionally edited and put out by recognizable publishers. One was written by a British newspaper journalist, another by an Australian novelist. By contrast, Rinpoche's "side" had a handful of self-published tracts in English, which were not professionally marketed or endorsed.

This imbalance in authority—one side so institutionalized, the other side more homemade—challenged my confidence in Rinpoche's position, and by extension, in Tibetan Buddhism as he taught it. I'm all for the underdog, but as a writer with a background teaching English composition at the college level and working in public relations agencies on the West Coast and in Washington, DC, I couldn't get over the difference in the quality of communications on each side. Let's just say that by conventional standards, from my point of view at the time, the other side was much more convincing than Rinpoche's side was.

I brought my doubts to Rinpoche, downstairs in the library at the Natural Bridge center, quoting and citing arguments made by his critics, including the most scathing charges about Rinpoche's own actions. His responses were sometimes more vehement than others, but he always responded; he never put me off. And he seemed to be able to answer every important criticism of him, even often turning them around on his critics—helping to restore some of my confidence. But no matter who was right, as a Western Dharma student, I was honestly starting to tire of the whole subject, which consisted of myriad tales of Byzantine court intrigues, greed, and thuggery by lamas, tulkus, and rinpoches who were not only supposed to believe in karma, but who set themselves up as teachers with multiple lifetimes of experience. Near the end of my research into this confusing morass, my confidence really began to lag. As I wrote up my conclusions, I started to wonder just what I'd gotten myself into.

When I began to share drafts of my manuscript with Rinpoche and the American volunteers he'd asked to help with the project, we had some tense discussions. As my name was going to be on the book, I didn't want it to be just a PR puff piece for Rinpoche's side. I insisted that the book make a well-supported argument that would stand up to standards for credible journalism. More discussions with Rinpoche ensued. More clarifications followed, some of them impatient. In response, I did more research and made revisions. In the long run, I'm glad I stuck to my guns and didn't write anything I couldn't support with good evidence.

When Rinpoche was satisfied with my telling of the story and I could stand behind all the argument's claims, we sent the manuscript to the publisher. Since it was published in the United States in 2006, *Buddha's Not Smiling* has been translated into several languages and published in Europe and Asia. Right up until his death last year, whenever I'd see him on one of his trips to Virginia, Rinpoche was kind enough to share stories with me about how the book had been helpful in his work on the controversy.

Whatever the book has done for anyone else, I can say it's helped me gain confidence. Perhaps that was what Rinpoche planned all along. I wonder if, like Marpa making Milarepa build towers and tear them down again, Shamar Rinpoche was some kind of benevolent mastermind, all-seeing in his plans for assigning just the right work to help devotees make the spiritual progress they needed. In researching this book Rinpoche tasked me to write, I had to read more criticisms of my chosen Buddhist teacher than any student should ever have to hear. Then, "I enjoyed" the rare chance to confront this teacher with my doubts. I wasn't always especially respectful, but for the most part, my teacher was patient. I got answers back that were at least pretty good. The answers were often startling, causing me to question my own assumptions about religion, politics, and how we know whether or not things are true.

At the end of the day what was clarified for me is my confidence in Shamar Rinpoche. The Buddhist philosophy of the Middle Way cautions us that even though we know our visible world is an illusion, we shouldn't become jaded and cynical about it, withdrawing into a nihilism that will do nothing to get us out of that illusion and relieve our suffering. I learned from Rinpoche that it takes skillful means by a teacher to inspire a student to do the hard work to deal with his or her own illusions.

CÉSAR AUGUSTO SEAS
Pasadena, California

◆ THE FULLY-LOADED LAMA

How do I begin to describe the Shamarpa? I leave this question as it is, so it may resonate within our being. I know we can all relate to this question. How do you describe Shamar Rinpoche?

I discovered Bodhi Path Pasadena in 2005, and began a lifelong friendship and commitment to studying and implementing the Buddha's precious teachings. I quickly took refuge—only a few months later—with Dilyag Sabchu Rinpoche. Early the following year I met the Red Hat Lama, Kunzig Shamar Rinpoche. I was in awe and on somewhat shaky ground, while Rinpoche seemed amused by my appearance and inquired where I was from.

I told him I was from Peru, and he proceeded to ask me if I had heard that they had just discovered the smallest man in the world there. He seemed very interested

and genuine. I was hooked. Throughout the following years I attended almost all of Rinpoche's visits to California, and also traveled to Natural Bridge for his annual teachings. I remember having such a warm feeling in my heart when he began to recognize me and remember my name. Silly confirmation, perhaps, of not wanting to be left behind by this great Bodhisattva.

My local resident Dharma teacher, Khaydroup, said to me once, "Don't worry, he remembers everyone." Later on there was no question of this. My meetings with Rinpoche were always a joy. Sometimes brief, sometimes extended. I always felt that Rinpoche was completely authentic. No nonsense. He would ask about my practice and even gave a "thumbs up" when I shared the completion of *ngondro*.

A few memories I have about encounters with Rinpoche: first, Rinpoche didn't seem to like us prostrating to him when we were in his presence (a form of bowing that one performs, laying one's body completely on the floor in reverence). I tried to always remember his dislike, yet I sincerely wished to pay my respects to my teacher, a Dharma King. I worked with this by bringing it to the path. I remember one time after seeing him and not prostrating, I didn't feel good, and I promised myself never to let a moment that I could prostrate to my Guru go by. The next time I saw Rinpoche, in Menlo Park, I remembered this promise as I waited in line to approach him and traditionally offer him a scarf. But again, my mind was so busy, yes, no, yes, no? I resolved to do only one long prostration while visualizing limitless prostrations within that one, using the bodhisattva ideal of big, big, view. So as I approached Rinpoche, I did one long prostration, and as I rose up expecting to hear his admonishment for doing this, I was met with the most brilliant smile and warmth. He seemed to have seen what was in my mind and heart. I know he did. He could see everything.

Another time when I met him I shared that I had attended a teaching by a Dzogchen Master. I told Rinpoche that I had received an Ati Yoga instruction, and had been doing this along with the practices he had given us. Rinpoche said that it was good to get the blessing, but that I should not mix. He seemed very determined to get this across to me. I said I would follow his advice. Towards the end of the event, as the remaining people approached him, I was nearby having a conversation with Lama Jampa. At the conclusion, I bid farewell to Lama Jampa and moved to the exit. As I walked past Rinpoche's seat, he reached out and grabbed my hand, while he was in conversation with a person offering a scarf. He pulled me close, looked at me and said, "Do not seek esoteric teachings." I can still feel his grasp of my hand. I said, "Okay Rinpoche," and headed home. This event displayed to me how much Rinpoche cared about me, about us. I felt great love and devotion. I will miss my precious teacher very much. But I feel well equipped for the journey ahead. Cheers to the fully-loaded Lama, Shamarpa Khyenno! Love & devotion, Cesar

Poster for Shamar Rinpoche's first program in Chicago, December 1989

◆ I first met Shamar Rinpoche in December 1989 in Chicago. Jay Landman and Carol Gerhardt invited me to a program that they were hosting for a Buddhist teacher they had recently met, being held at the Dharmadhatu center in Chicago. I'd just returned home for the holidays from my first semester in college; I was hanging around town and so I went to one of the public teachings. Afterwards Rinpoche was giving brief audiences, and I went to meet him. This was my first face-to-face encounter with the man who would alter the course of my life.

Jay and Carol were at the interview, and Suzan Garner was too; before I went in, Suzan gave me a little context. The example she gave was the story of the blind men describing an elephant—each one describing the elephant according to the part they could perceive. "Well," she said, "this man can see the whole elephant." I don't remember much detail from that meeting; I mainly recall sitting on the floor, asking a few questions, and having a nice conversation. Honestly, I really didn't know what to ask or say. I was 18 years old.

Fast-forwarding a couple of years to 1991, I had become disenchanted with college and decided to take a year off to study abroad. I was drawn to global regions that had contemplative traditions, and ultimately I decided on Nepal. Despite the seeming happenstance of my choice, once I got to Nepal I instantly became absorbed in studying all things Buddhist—living with a Buddhist family, traveling to Buddhist holy places, meeting with Buddhist teachers, and spending hours talking with seasoned practitioners.

Then, as I was reaching the end of my studies in Nepal, I received a letter from Jay and Carol, who were in New Delhi with Shamar Rinpoche at KIBI (Karmapa International Buddhist Institute). Rinpoche was coming to Kathmandu, and they had mentioned to him that I was there. At first he didn't react, but, as Carol tells it, when they mentioned that I had met him in Chicago a couple of years earlier, "His eyes rolled back, like a kind of mental Rolodex, and he said, 'Have him come meet me when I arrive.'"

I had been preparing for my final project, a month-long solo pilgrimage to the Yolmo valley, where I hoped to learn about the tradition of *beyul*s, the sacred valleys said to hold special power. I intended to experience the valley's famous meditation caves once inhabited by Milarepa and Padmasambhava. (Little did I know at the time that Yolmo was the birthplace of the 8th Shamarpa!) So that I could see Rinpoche before I left the city, I was given the address of his brother's house in Kathmandu, and I went there to see him.

We exchanged memories of having met two years earlier—then I sat next to him while person after person came to meet with him. I actually hung out there for most of the day. There were people from all around the world. One of them was a very young, maybe 18-year-old, Gyaltrul Rinpoche, who offered me a ride home since it was dark by then and there were packs of dogs roaming the streets. I remember Gyaltrul Rinpoche drove me home in a little car that had a keypad you could dial to play "La Cucaracha" and "Dixie" on the horn.

During our visit, I told Rinpoche about the project I was about to begin. I had no idea then that there is a connection between the Shamarpas and Yolmo. I explained to Rinpoche that I was planning to travel around the valley, meditate in some caves, and tell their story from a combination of first-hand experience, references in famous texts, and local folklore. When I asked him, "What should I do there?" Rinpoche said, "You should do the Manjushri practice." I said, "Manjush … what?" And so he gave me a spontaneous teaching on the Manjushri practice.

Mind you, I was not even a Buddhist at this point. Rinpoche drew me the seed syllable, wrote out the mantra—I still have that—and encouraged me to do the practice. And then he added, "Afterwards, when you come back, you should come and be my guest at KIBI."

"Absolutely!"

I embarked on my independent study project, but not before announcing to my parents that I wasn't returning for the next semester of college. My experience in Yolmo was amazing, but that is a whole separate story. My parents then came to meet me in Nepal, partially to just visit, and partially to check in on me... maybe to make sure I wasn't going to disappear into the Himalayas. I arrived at KIBI in January of 1992 and studied there for 3 months, and Rinpoche was in and out of KIBI during that time.

At a certain point I said to myself, "You just spent months in Nepal studying Buddhism everywhere you went, you meditated in caves in the Himalayas, and you spent three months studying at an institute of higher Buddhist learning. Hmm, I think you're a Buddhist." So I asked Rinpoche if he would give me refuge vows, and he said "Sure, sure," but it didn't happen right away. Over the next few weeks I kept trying to pin him down. I'd ask again, "Rinpoche, can you give me refuge vows?" and he'd say, "Yes, absolutely. We should do them in the main hall." Still nothing happened. Finally I said "Rinpoche, I'm leaving tomorrow and, uh, I'd really like to do this … ," and then he said, "Okay, let's go." He took me downstairs and gave me my refuge vows, just the two of us in front of the grand Buddha and shrine of the main hall at KIBI. The next day I was on my way back to Chicago by way of Europe—and the rest is history!

That same summer Shamar Rinpoche came to Viola, Wisconsin, along with Jigme Rinpoche, Khenpo Chodrak, Tsultrim Namgyal (Khenpo's brother, who had been an attendant of the Sixteenth Karmapa), Lama Tashi, Hannah Nydahl, and Jay and Carol. My family has a farm there that at that time we owned with Jay and Carol, who were looking for a place to open up a Buddhist center for Rinpoche. They were planning on creating the center on their half of the Wisconsin farm. Rinpoche had come to check it out, perform some pujas and blessings, and determine possible locations for the buildings. It was a great chance for me to see him again so soon after being with him in Nepal and at KIBI—I was all excited! Here I was, fresh from the Himalayas—if the center opened up here it would be right in my backyard! Of course the center wound up being in Virginia instead, but at the time everyone was in Wisconsin, poring over plans and topographic maps of the area, trying to determine the best places to build.

Shamar Rinpoche, Matt, and his mother Diane. Viola, Wisconsin, 1992

My parents were there too, still trying to figure this whole thing out, I think. One night, everyone was reviewing plans in the central room of the farmhouse, and my parents were sitting by themselves in the adjacent living room. Rinpoche quietly got up from the table and went into the other room to sit and talk to them. I don't really know what they were talking about but eventually Rinpoche said "Matthew, please come here," and he had me sit down next to him across from my parents.

I should go back in the story for a second. In KIBI, back in March, around the time Rinpoche gave me the vows, he repeatedly asked me if I was coming back to KIBI in the fall, and I kept saying, "No, actually, Rinpoche, I'm mid-way through college in the US and I should finish my studies there. I'm very interested in studying more Dharma, but I don't think I can come back to KIBI right now." I thought I'd made it very clear to him, and figured he'd have remembered that conversation. But here we were in Viola, Wisconsin, sitting in front of my parents, and the first thing Rinpoche says to me in front of them is, "So Matthew, are you coming back to KIBI?" "No Rinpoche," I replied, "remember, we had this conversation? No, I'm not. I'm going to stay and finish my college here." And he was like, "Oh, okay."

At the time, I remember being a bit crestfallen that Rinpoche didn't remember our previous conversations. As a new disciple first getting to know a teacher, and wanting to be close to them, you wonder, "Gosh, does he remember anything about me? Does he remember the things we talked about?" How little I understood! It was years later that I realized this was Shamar Rinpoche's skillful means in action. My parents actually had tremendous concerns about me going on retreat or becoming a monk; the Buddhist path was a bit of a mystery to them, and they felt somewhat threatened by it and fearful they would lose me, their only child. Part of the reason they had come to visit me in Kathmandu the previous December was to make sure I wasn't getting brainwashed and going off to join some crazy cult, wondering if my head was still screwed on straight.

What Rinpoche did with a simple question in our living room in Viola was to create a situation where my parents could witness me saying no to him. It is precisely what they needed to see at that moment. And I think it actually did a tremendous amount in terms of quelling their concerns—they recognized I still had personal agency and I wasn't blindly following a guru and doing everything he told me. I began to understand that the wisdom of Rinpoche's words and actions is not always immediately apparent.

Throughout my 25-year relationship with Rinpoche, the first thing he would ask me during each of our our visits was, "How are your parents?" And after I got married, it was, "How is your wife?" It was always the first thing. I think Rinpoche understood my commitments to the secular world, and the various pulls I faced as I integrated the Dharma into my daily life, career, and family—without ever framing that as an obstacle. He frequently reminded me that regardless of the conditions in which I found myself, the opportunity to recognize my mind's true nature was there (even as we waited for a table in a crowded DC restaurant).

Rinpoche was an authentic teacher in the purest sense—not bound by convention, but rather by a commitment to help us realize the true Dharma by whatever means were most appropriate to the conditions of the moment. My experience of him as his disciple was that he showed an unsurpassed sensitivity to my condition—to my personal veils, to the challenges I faced in balancing my commitments, to my blind spots—and showed immense compassion and patience as I endeavored to learn what it is he had to teach me. In homage to this great master, I have given everything I could to serve his vision and activity, and will continue to do so for as long as I am able.

Karma Mönlam

◆ To start with, in the beginning I didn't know what a Rinpoche was, let alone a Shamar Rinpoche. In 2011, my friend recommended that I meditate; actually she had recommended that I meditate throughout all of 2010 and part of 2009 too, but I avoided paying attention to her advice. Then, in the winter of 2011, I decided, "Okay, I've never wanted to be religious, but if I had to pick one, it would be Buddhism. I'll just go to this meditation thing once." That's how I thought of it.

I went, and Dharma Teacher Rachel Parrish was teaching on the Eight Worldly Concerns, and I thought, "Oh, this makes sense." I went back the following week, and Lama Jampa was giving Refuge Vows, and again I thought, "Oh, this makes sense." I went from then on. I especially liked the 35 Buddhas practice; for some reason I really liked saying the names of the buddhas. At some point, I mentioned to the center coordinator that I liked learning languages, and that I wanted to study more. His response was, "We always need translators; you should talk to Shamar Rinpoche about it."

This was all new and I didn't really know, other than from a few Google searches, who Rinpoche was. Then Rachel suggested the same thing about talking to Rinpoche, and I was able to meet with him when I went to Virginia that year. So I went. Shamar Rinpoche was very majestic; he had a lot of gravity and at the same time was approachable and funny, and it seemed like whenever the students got too pious or religious, you know, sitting up very tensely or something, he would tell a joke, and the whole room would just relax.

I was strongly drawn to his presence, and felt very safe when he was teaching. Then, I went to meet with him up at his house, and I was so scared. I was thinking, "I'm going to ask Shamar Rinpoche if I should study Tibetan to see if he thinks that would be beneficial." I went in and sat on the edge of the chair at his table, and was kind of shy, and he said, "Oh, sit comfortably!" I tried to relax, and from that point forward I felt open to whatever might come up, with his blessing. When I asked him about studying Tibetan, he said "Oh yes, very good, very good." Later I asked him about studying art, working on books, and other possible subjects, and he was very positive about that, also; I was always encouraged by his support of my studies. People have different capacities, and it seemed like he supported and really pushed people into different possibilities.

I feel very fortunate and privileged to have known Rinpoche, and it's a privilege to miss him; to have this loss means I was able to meet him in this life, which is amazing. But what I miss right now is when I would go to him with some question, whether it was in a group or personally, and he would roll his eyes back in his head and say, "Very good." I miss Rinpoche's vote of confidence, and his encouragement.

Amanda D.
Christiansburg, Virginia

◆ I attend the Natural Bridge, Virginia Bodhi Path center. I was listening to someone talking earlier about how he met Rinpoche and thinking about my own version of that story. It's amazing how different our stories are; yet the net result is the same. In my version, I was rudderless, in the sense that I didn't have a plan to study Buddhism, I didn't have a path; I was young, 21 or 22 years old, had left college, and really didn't have a sense of what I wanted to do. I met Rinpoche at the restaurant where I worked. It was one of those very quick situations—I was told, "Here's this Buddhist master, and you really should go and meet him." I thought, "That's cool." I didn't think anything of it, and so I went outside and I was kind of struck dumb just being around him. I've always been a big skeptic and pretty cynical, so it was an experience I was not used to—the way he smiled, it just felt really good being near him. He noticed the necklace I had on, a simple silver Aztec medallion, and he asked, "What is this necklace? What does it mean?" I said it didn't mean anything, it was just a little Aztec sun, and he had a smile on his face, and I had all these thoughts in me like, "Who is this guy? Why would he comment on that?" It made me very curious.

I started going to the center in Natural Bridge when it was still in Rinpoche's house. Suddenly there was a program coming up, and he was giving refuge, and I said, "I'm going to do this." I'd had a world religion course in college, but knew very little about Buddhism, so it was totally uncharacteristic of me; I tend to overthink everything, but I was compelled to do this. I didn't know what to expect from the ceremony. It was very comical, actually, because there was a social aspect, and everyone else seemed to know what was going on but me. I went up to Rinpoche and he was just chuckling. I think what struck me was that he had this profound presence, and in one sense it was so serious and so important—and I felt that—but he was so light-hearted, warm and compassionate. I took the plunge for no other reason than that I had met him, and the way he made me feel, and again, it was so uncharacteristic. It just happened, it wasn't even something that I knew I

was seeking. That's what I think about sometimes, how a chance occurrence resulted in this wonderful relationship, and how amazing that such a profound being was right here in my little hometown in the middle of nowhere. That has stayed with me, how lucky I am, the amount of gratitude about how fortunate that was; how it really changed everything for me in the best ways possible.

From then on, studying Buddhism was all I wanted to do. I attended every teaching program that was going on, and for a while I was helping with the center organizing. I immersed myself as much as possible. What was interesting was that after taking that uncharacteristic initial leap of faith, Buddhism seemed to make so much logical sense. It's funny; I'm not quite sure what happened to me, because I'm not a leap of faith kind of girl. I don't believe in blind faith, and the encouragement not to rely on blind faith in Buddhism appealed to me—that confidence is gained from experience, reflection, and study. This path is a very good fit for me, sort of like I had always been a Buddhist, but just didn't have the term for it. Strange and interesting, how I came to it, like a bizarre hook. They talk about the hook that a teacher will have and to me it's a very good argument that there was some prior connection. I was just completely hooked.

Presently I work as a nurse. What I received from Shamar Rinpoche permeates all I do, because everything is through that lens now. Especially with nursing, there is so much acute suffering. I think that my connection with the Dharma has helped me be calm and present for others, whether it's holding someone's hand, being open, or listening to them. Many of my patients are at the end of their lives, or I am with families making decisions about end-of-life care for their loved ones. Nursing is a very direct way that I can help other beings, that I can feel that connection. Dharma is certainly not something that I engage with a patient about, unless they say, "I'm Buddhist, and I want to talk about this." However, it's always with me; Rinpoche's teachings, the experiences I've had in meditation, and the moments of clarity I've been fortunate to have in a teaching. I'm able to talk to a patient in a way that allows them to feel that what they're going through is a natural process, and I just try to be still, calm, and accepting. It gives a framework so that when I talk to patients and their families there's objectivity, a broader understanding about the inter-connectedness of things and how things are constantly changing. Impermanence. It's a very in-your-face experience of impermanence.

It's a good feeling to know that this has worked, that the Dharma has worked so well for me, and now I have a chance to help others. In one sense it has made my peers at work more open-minded to other paths, and that's all from an action of Rinpoche's, from that one chance meeting. It's so incredible when you think of all the connections and lives that are able to impact me and that I am able to impact, and it all comes back to a chance meeting in a restaurant. Oh, and oddly enough, the last place I saw Rinpoche was at that same restaurant—a totally chance meeting in April of this year. I was in town for one day on a rare visit, eating dinner with friends, when in walks Shamar Rinpoche! I was like "Oh my goodness! What are you doing here?" He just happened in for the evening; in retrospect it's so fitting. An amazing circle!

Hilary H.
Lexington, Virginia

◆ My name is Hilary, and I am a regular here at Bodhi Path Natural Bridge. I came to Bodhi Path based on very little information. I wandered up into the garden during a teaching; I had heard from someone in town that something was going on at the center, and I was new, and I like to wander around in the woods where it's beautiful. I met a man in casual clothing. It was 2005, and we were still using Rinpoche's house. It didn't take long to realize "this man" was not the gardener.

I came into the teaching not really knowing much; there was everything that I thought I knew about Buddhism according to the textbooks in Religion 101 courses in school, so I had a very rudimentary understanding of Buddhism. Yet I had never experienced such joy as when I heard Rinpoche reciting in Tibetan. Spontaneous joy. I had the words in front of me along with the English translation. At first I couldn't always get my head around it, like, "Am I okay with this?" and "What is my experience of this?" It felt very important to me, but at the same time I didn't really know what it was. It was a process of, "Oh, okay with this, okay, okay … ." After a while there was no judgment necessary, and it was an absolutely extraordinary time.

I think it was the next time I was there somebody asked me, "Will you take refuge?" I didn't know what that meant. Someone started to explain, and I said, "You know what, I really don't know what this is, but if it means that based on what I hear and what I am feeling that I will continue to seek and understand—then I'm all in!" And I have pretty much been here ever since. Actually, I was just here for a few months, my folks retired here, and then I went to graduate school; I left but I came back in 2010, right around the time that Tsony came to stay. It has been very active, all kinds of activity, and I got to see Rinpoche in the garden again. In my last conversation with Rinpoche, I actually got to tell him, "Rinpoche, I love you, and I love that I heard these teachings from you. I love that I am part of your family, and that I will always be part of your family."

Rinpoche encouraged me to practice. Even though there are aspects of this Buddha, Dharma, Sangha that I struggle with a tad, he said, "You stay, you practice." The essence of his teaching was practice, but true to one's nature, true to each one's ability to be there and ability to hear; I get that now. Listen and be instructed and be supported and have confidence in the teachings. I have that confidence now more than ever. He is still totally with me. I often watch Rinpoche's last teaching on impermanence, which I have on my phone. To have his voice to listen to on that particular teaching, well … it's a good one!

On the day of the cremation ceremony in Kathmandu, there were a few of us here, and in support of that, we had a very devotional day of making flower offerings, stringing them together and hanging them over our Buddha here in the meditation hall. It was fabulous actually, and like the flowers, we were all sort of threaded together. Marigolds, dahlias, Rose of Sharon. Since I met Rinpoche in a garden, it was a little perfect. A moment of complete devotion.

RUDY O. KARSCH
Vesuvius, Virginia

◆ THOUGHTS OF SHAMAR RINPOCHE

On June 11, 2014 the ground under my feet suddenly opened up into a sinkhole of despair and my world shattered, swallowing my joy. Word reached us at Dhagpo Kundreul Ling, where I was visiting at the time, that Shamar Rinpoche had suddenly and unexpectedly died earlier that morning. My beloved teacher and friend was gone. Never again in this life would I meet with him to share laughter or stretch our minds by contemplating samsara's many paradoxes—one of those paradoxes being how unlikely it was for an unremarkable person like me, living on a remote mountain in the Blue Ridge, to meet and be befriended by such a remarkable and famous a person as the 14th Shamarpa, and to have him accept me as his student. None of this could have happened had I not, decades before, bought property in that wild place where Rinpoche established his US headquarters near Natural Bridge, Virginia, only a half-hour drive from my home. Go figure, what are the odds that we should meet?

Before meeting Shamar Rinpoche, I had been a student and practitioner of Mahayana Buddhism for 30 years. Taking inspiration from Milarepa's life story, my ultimate goal was to find a remote and peaceful place to retire into a long-term solitary retreat. After years of construction and preparation, I finally moved full-time into my mountain fastness. All went well for a while, but after a year I began to feel that my practice was becoming stale and that maybe I should once again look for a teacher. Within days of having that thought, a postcard mysteriously appeared in my mailbox informing me that Shamar Rinpoche would visit his Natural Bridge Center to teach on mahamudra. I decided to attend, which turned out to be a life-altering decision.

His Holiness Shamar Rinpoche is one of the most unique individuals I have ever met. I felt an instant connection with him. He possessed all the wonderful qualities one hopes for in a spiritual guide, but for me, the most striking were his desire to know those he met and his uncanny understanding of people. It seemed that he could read minds, as if he understood my questions before I even asked. It was like he knew my innermost thoughts, my history, my faults and shortcomings; yet he always remained nonjudgmental, infinitely patient, generous, and empathetic. He always asked how he could help, and his suggestions and advice were always perfectly right on.

When I met Rinpoche, I told him that my career was in science, and that scientists are skeptics by nature and training. We want to see proof before we accept any claims. As a meditator and student of Buddhism for several decades, I was aware that Tibetan Buddhism claimed to know methods that, when properly applied, lead quickly to enlightenment by providing experiences which fundamentally transform consciousness. What would he recommend I do so I could have those same experiences and resolve my doubts? He was kind to me and gave me a specific "to-do" list. I devoted time and effort to carrying out his instructions and definitely benefited from the results. He must have been pleased with my progress because he invited me into his company. On his later visits to Virginia, we often met together on informal occasions, when we would casually chat about Dharma topics or matters of interest to Rinpoche, usually questions about science. I got to know, love, and admire the man himself as well as the titled one—His Holiness, who is the lineage holder of the Karma Kagyu wisdom. I like to think that through all of the varied dimensions of our relationship, we became friends as well as teacher and student. Rinpoche was endlessly curious and vastly intelligent, but he was never hidebound or dogmatic—only infinitely patient, compassionate, and generous. I always saw him find the best way to deal with difficult situations and take the appropriate actions, which never failed to give the best result.

I was very grateful for Rinpoche's help and valued our time together. I constantly hoped I could find ways to help him in return. What could I do to repay his kindness, and support the dissemination of the Dharma? I tried to think of a suitable way. When Professor Harry Pemberton went to the Karmapa's school in Kalimpong to instruct the monks there in the thoughts of Socrates and Western philosophy, I had the idea that it might be useful if the monks also gained some grasp of the Western sciences' view of reality, especially in emergent findings in cosmology and quantum physics. Rinpoche knew that many Buddhist cosmological concepts are similar to those emergent discoveries; he understood how this knowledge might be of value to the monks and support the madhyamaka view. He encouraged me to draw up a curriculum and try it out on him. Understanding the relevance of Buddhist philosophy to modern physics might serve to reinforce the monks' confidence in the Buddha's teachings, and to demonstrate how the Dharma is still fresh and relevant even twenty-five centuries later.

This idea fermented over the next two years, during which Rinpoche asked me several times, "How is it coming?" We tried to find time together, but Rinpoche's busy schedule precluded any meeting. Meanwhile, I composed and rejected several outlines for the class. Where do you begin explaining science to someone who has none of the knowledge that we in the West take for granted, such as knowledge of protons, neutrons, and electrons; Newton's laws; fields/action at a distance; chemical bonding and so forth? None of these concepts are part of a monk's education. Rinpoche himself came up with the way to begin. He asked me to explain black holes to him. Here was a way to enter the discussion using a current topic of interest. Two days before he left for Europe, we finally met in his living room and I had my chance to present the material I had in mind for the course. Those two days were the last time we would be together. That is the remembrance I would like to share with you because that memory of our last time together is so precious to me. His immediate grasp of the many complex topics presented shows what a remarkable mind he had.

Cosmology is the science that explains the origin and evolution of the universe and all of its contents. I felt that an overview of cosmology would give Rinpoche some context for understanding conventional space and time, how black holes form, and how everything else comes to be. Understanding the vastness and beauty of our universe could produce a sense of awe and wonder and act as a counterbalance

for human pride and egocentrism. In his teachings, Rinpoche often referred to sentient beings living in nearby galaxies. I decided the best way to begin was to show him a series of images from the Hubble Space Telescope (HST). We started with views within our solar system; then moved outward to our Milky Way galaxy and its structures, nebulas, dust clouds, star nurseries, and supernovas. Along the way, we discussed the speed of light and distance, using light's speed as a way to express distance, ranging from light minutes for the distance to the sun, light years to nearby stars, thousands of light years to span our galaxy, and millions of light years to nearby galactic neighbors like Andromeda and our local group of galaxies, to billions of light years for the entire universe. I showed him images of the various types of galaxies, spirals and globular clusters, and images of galaxies colliding. Finally, we looked at the deep field image sometimes referred to as 10,000 galaxies. NASA produced this image by aiming the HST at a tiny area of the darkest part of the sky and opening the camera's shutter for ten days to gather light. What came out when the data was processed stunned the scientific community! What seems to be empty space is in fact teeming with galaxies of stars, unimaginably far away in unimaginable numbers; trillions of stars in billions of galaxies.

At this point, Rinpoche asked if I thought sentient beings exist on other worlds. We now had a basis for understanding the vast scope of the universe with its billions of galaxies of stars. I explained the Drake equation to him. In this conjecture, a hierarchy of probabilities is stated, starting with planets forming around other stars, then a habitable environment capable of sustaining life, sentience developing, and finally the potential presence of receptive minds. Even if the odds of any one of these occurrences are a million to one, because there are so many stars and planets in our universe, it is a certainty that other sentient beings must exist out there somewhere. Rinpoche was very pleased to hear that. By practicing compassion, we benefit innumerable beings, not only limited to this earth. Speaking about the power of our intentions led to a discussion of action at a distance, the four forces found by science (gravity, electromagnetism, the weak force, and the strong force) and how they operate to build our material universe. We also talked about the mysterious dual nature of matter, how it can be both a wave or a particle depending on how it is observed, and that the actions of the observer affect what is observed. We talked about energy and how the experiments at CERN (the European Organization for Nuclear Research) in Switzerland are a way to look back in time to the early universe, simulating the energy densities shortly after the Big Bang, so that those conditions can be studied. We talked about how their findings verified the existence of the Higgs field. This field transformed the massless energy of the early universe into solid particles, creating mass and gravity: form from emptiness. Finally we got around to black holes, Rinpoche's original question.

I showed Rinpoche images from the HST that proved the existence of gravitational lensing: the bending of space alters the path a light ray travels. Gravitational fields actually warp space itself and thereby bend light's path. In the vicinity of a black hole, gravity is so intense that space/time folds back onto itself and the structure of space and time collapses. Because of the strength of the gravitational field that surrounds a massive black hole—perhaps representing billions of times the mass of our sun—"normal" space and time cease to exist in a sense. These phenomena have been observed at the centers of most galaxies, including our own. As the black hole is approached and the event horizon is crossed, light can no longer escape; time slows down and stops. As matter and energy fall into the black hole, they are irretrievably lost from our reality. Moreover, the information and history associated with it also vanish.

The Buddha spoke of relative and ultimate reality, with relative reality being divided into three realms: the desire realm, the form realm, and the formless realm. We as sentient beings inhabit all three realms, but mostly consciously operate only in the desire realm due to the limitations of our sense perceptions. Science has determined basic laws and properties for the desire realm based on those perceptions. I explained to Rinpoche how those laws determine the way things manifest at a scale greater than subatomic size and are understood through Newton's laws and Einstein's theories. These phenomena of the desire realm, the Newtonian/Einsteinian reality, however, emerge via poorly understood processes from a realm of matter and energy whose characteristics are defined by discrete values or quanta. This is the realm of quantum mechanics, where an entirely unique set of laws applies. These quanta exist as an indeterminate fog of quarks and forces that are the basis from which the things we experience with our senses emerge. Current thinking is that these emergent properties are a function of information—information, unfortunately, obliterated by a black hole.

To summarize, the similarities between Buddhist and physics concepts are: three realms—desire, form, and formless; three manifestations: *nirmanakaya*, *sambhogakaya*, and *dharmakaya*; and three levels of physical reality: Newtonian/Einsteinian, quantum, and wave function reality. This is an interesting convergence of ideas, if not of nomenclature. We wanted to discuss the implications of this convergence and the effect that information lost into a black hole might represent.

By this time, however, it was getting late in the day, we had covered a lot of ground, and we were now at the threshold of what promised to be a lengthy and interesting discussion. So Rinpoche and I decided that these issues of quantum mechanics, the nature of the three realms, and what properties might be inherent in buddha-nature would set the agenda for our next meeting. Tragically, this was not to be; I will never know what Rinpoche's thoughts on these questions might have been. I went to visit him the next day to see him off and wish him well. By then he'd had some time to think about the content and substance of what we had talked about the previous day. He expressed his appreciation for the truly immense expanse of our universe and the rare event the presence of sentience represents. He reiterated and emphasized the preciousness of human life, the importance of living up to our Bodhisattva vow, and that our pure intentions of compassion do affect the information content of the universe and thereby do produce beneficial results. We can and do make a difference; our practice and good intentions matter. We should not waver in our efforts. As we parted he said that we would meet again. My feelings of loss are eased by the hope that Rinpoche's promise will soon come to pass, and we may once again experience his presence.

◆ ENCOUNTERING SHAMAR RINPOCHE

Marc and I did not grow up Buddhist, we didn't meet with Buddhism in our teens, and we did not study at a formal Buddhist institute. However, we feel connected to Shamar Rinpoche and Bodhi Path through the very unique circumstances that surround Shamar Rinpoche. There were always magical encounters with Rinpoche throughout our lives, and I have to believe they happened for a reason.

Our first encounter took place shortly after Marc met Suzan in 1999. Marc was Suzan's teaching assistant in her MBA program at UCLA. Suzan asked Marc for help with her coursework responsibilities, as she was going to miss some classes while traveling with a small group to Nepal. She also mentioned that she was a practicing Buddhist. This terminology intrigued Marc. The request for assistance with her class load quickly turned into Marc's joining Suzan's merry band, which was visiting Nepal to further pursue a contact who distributed Tibetan medicines in the US. This trip was Marc's introduction not only to the Tibetan style of Buddhism, but also to Nepal. Around this same time, Suzan and her husband Bart started a meditation center in their home in Santa Barbara, and they invited Marc and me—complete novices—to one of their early meditation retreat programs. We decided to attend the weekend teachings without really knowing what we were in for, except for some independent reading we had done about meditation. Marc drove up from Los Angeles, and I flew in from San Francisco. Funny enough, I was waiting for my flight with Marc's friend—a pilot no less—and while we were talking my plane took off without me. Fortunately, there was another flight that day, and I made it to Santa Barbara for the program.

When Marc and I arrived at Suzan and Bart's, the house was abuzz because "Shamar Rinpoche" was flying in for the program, which was totally unplanned. After Rinpoche arrived and met some of the folks, including Marc, Marc's friend Carl, Carl's girlfriend, and me, Rinpoche announced he would give refuge. We had no idea what that meant, and Bart had a slightly stunned look, needing to quickly explain refuge to us, the completely uninitiated. For whatever reason, the four of us had no hesitations and that was how our refuge vows happened.

We saw Rinpoche every so often over the next few years, while attending and helping to organize programs. Suzan would always mention when Rinpoche was coming, and she informed us that he would like it if we could come to see him when he came to Santa Barbara. We met many of the Dharma teachers whom Rinpoche was sending to the US, as well as Jigme Rinpoche, who came to visit Los Angeles. Khaydroup, Marc, and I started a Dharma group in Santa Monica that eventually evolved into the Pasadena group.

A magical encounter happened just after my dear cat, Tristan, died in 2005. I've never been one to take the death of my pets lightly. The weekend after the ordeal (we were living in Los Angeles, preparing to move to Miami), I was a walking zombie. In fact, over the weekend I had to face putting away most of Tristan's belongings and donating the rest to her vet's office for charity. Marc suggested inviting our friends Tony and Martha to see a movie, which I agreed to in spite of my distress. When we went to park for the movie, which was close to the yoga studio I ran in Santa Monica, for some reason we parked at a different garage than the one I always used for work. We saw the "March of the Penguins," which, as many know, has significance in Rinpoche's world all on its own. After the movie the four of us decided to grab a bite to eat, then we meandered over to a magazine shop before parting ways. Marc and I continued on this unusual route back to the parking garage, and as we approached the final corner, I blurted out, "Shamarpa!" Marc, who knew what a bad emotional state I was in, did not know what I was saying. We had rarely seen Rinpoche, usually only when Suzan let us know that Rinpoche was in town. This meeting was completely out of context.

But there was Rinpoche sitting with Hannah Nydahl on the patio of a crepe shop on the 3rd Street Promenade. To our knowledge, Rinpoche and Hannah were not even expected in California, but there they were, sitting at a spot directly between the movie theater and the parking lot! Among the topics we discussed, Rinpoche asked about the other couple that took refuge with us. "Tell them not to waste the refuge." Rinpoche encouraged us to visit the Natural Bridge center, and then asked if we had been in Miami during the recent hurricanes. We mentioned that we hadn't moved there yet. In actuality, we did move just weeks later and had one of the worst hurricane seasons in the history of Miami, which included Hurricane Katrina. Toward the end of our chat, Marc asked, "Rinpoche, is it true that meeting you here could have been a one-in-a-million chance, or could it only have happened this way?" Rinpoche said, "Yes."

Soon after we moved to Miami, we hosted Tsony for a weekend, and along with others who attended his teachings, we went on to form the Bodhi Path Miami group. Incidentally, Rinpoche landed in Miami for the first time shortly after that day we saw him in Santa Monica—during Hurricane Wilma! This action followed a pattern of Rinpoche arriving places during or just after disasters for the benefit of others, such as in New York City during 9/11.

In 2007, when I became one of the North American Bodhi Path assistants, our interactions with Rinpoche became more frequent. We had moved to Miami for Marc's job as a professor; I even remember opening the first bank account for the Bodhi Path Central Fund there. Occasionally we would drive to Natural Bridge, Virginia, and visit Jay and Carol; eventually we built a structure on the land, as Rinpoche had encouraged us to do since our very first visit to the retreat center. During that first drive from Miami to Natural Bridge, as Marc drove I spotted a white bird soaring through the air in a deliberate pattern, as if to greet us. When we arrived at the center we were surprised to see Rinpoche there, accompanied by Neeraj and Sylvia. As we were saying goodbye at the end of our stay, Rinpoche turned toward the windows and said, "It is going to snow," even though it was sunny out. Indeed, it snowed all the way north on our drive to Washington, DC! These days we live in Virginia, which was never planned, and Marc is a professor at a nearby university.

When I was appointed as a Bodhi Path assistant, I told myself I'd keep one folder on my computer desktop labeled "HHSR," and that one folder would be the limit of my work. I tend to overwork myself, which I need to regulate so as not to go overboard. In true Rinpoche-fashion, my engagement in Rinpoche's activities grew slowly but surely inside that one folder. It was like an entire world growing on my computer desktop. By the last two years of his life, Marc and I worked more closely and intensely with Rinpoche then we ever had with anyone.

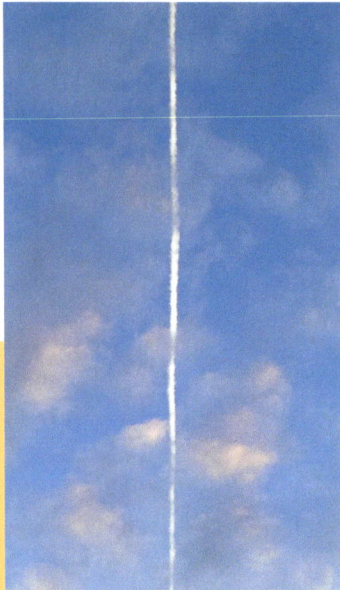

One recent profound encounter happened when Marc and I traveled to France for the opening ceremony of the Dhagpo Library. I informed Rinpoche that I would soon be leaving my position at the yoga company in Santa Monica. Rinpoche responded that I would be able to help. "Help the Kagyu lineage?" I asked. "No." "Help you, Rinpoche?" I asked. "No," he replied. "Help sentient beings."

A Haiku for SR

Came out of nowhere.
All the born is unborn now.
Left, into nowhere.

—Marc J.

Eva Greenberg
Lübeck-Travermünde, Germany

◆ Tribute to My Beloved Master, Shamar Rinpoche

Dear Shamar Rinpoche,

The first moment I met you, you opened my heart, filling it with devotion and inspiration. Throughout the years I was fortunate to see you again and again; each word, each gesture, each glance, and even your wonderful humor were an inspiration and teaching, leaving deep imprints in my mind.

A special expression of your blessing, protection, kindness, and compassion, which I was fortunate enough to experience in manifold ways, was that you gave me the most helpful support for my path, being always right by my side.

For all and everything I will never stop thanking you, with deep appreciation from the bottom of my heart.

Thinking of you and turning my mind towards you is always deeply comforting, encouraging, and clears away clouds of confusion.

I feel your presence—my connection with you is unchanged. Nevertheless, I join in the urgent request of your many followers that you return to our world swiftly!

With all my devotion, love, and gratitude.

◆ My name is Carmen, like the opera—that's what I always tell people to help them remember me. I have a wonderful story, my favorite story. I met Rinpoche seven or eight years ago in Natural Bridge. When I first met him, I could not stop touching his hand, and I kept saying, "Why do I know you?" He just sat there very politely and indulged me, he never said, "Go away, leave me alone," he just smiled at me. I remember running behind him any chance I got. We just developed a connection, and he would always remember who I was. And I would do the unthinkable: I would always touch him, I would hug him. I would just say "I have to touch you," and he would laugh.

About two years ago, I became ill, and I had to go to the hospital on Christmas Day. There is a very large and famous hospital, Johns Hopkins Hospital in Baltimore, and I live in Damascus—so it was a pretty good distance away—but this hospital is known for treating the neurological illness that I have. It was Christmas, very late, and I was in triage, and at about two or three o'clock in the morning they admitted me to my room.

I set up my little Buddha statue and my little Christmas tree on the table next to my bed. There were nurses coming in and out, and then someone came in and said, "Hi, my name is Dechen. I'm a nutritionist. We need to find ways to keep nutrients in your body," because I was having trouble chewing and swallowing. After we talked more about the medical situation, she asked me, "Are you a Buddhist? Do you practice Buddhism?" I said "Yes, I do." Dechen said "I'm Buddhist, too." I replied, "Wonderful! Every time I come to this hospital I run into a Buddhist somehow!" So we talked more, and she was getting ready to leave, but asked, "What kind of Buddhism do you practice?" I responded, "I practice a form of Tibetan Buddhism. I am part of the Kagyu lineage, and my teacher is Shamar Rinpoche." At that point, there was an extraordinary look on her face; because she had known Rinpoche when they were little children! Her brother was in the same monastery as Rinpoche. With all the difficulty happening in Tibet, she and her brother got separated; she ended up coming to the United States with her aunt, but her brother stayed in Tibet.

I called everyone I know to say, "You are not going to believe this."

It was late December and Rinpoche was not expected back at our center until some time in June. I was released from the hospital and began to feel better, so I started going back to the center in March or April. When I walked in, there was Rinpoche sitting at the table! I exclaimed, "Rinpoche, you are not going to believe this." I hugged him, and I had Dechen's card tucked away in my purse. I took it out, and said, "Look at this."

He saw the name and immediately recognized it; he got the same look on his face that Dechen had, the most joyful smile, and said, "Is she all right?" "Yes, Rinpoche, she's fine." He didn't know what had happened to her or her brother, and I said, "Her brother is fine, too," and he was elated. I gave him her contact information so that they could at least speak to each other. The only thing I'm sad about is they never got to see each other in person, but they did get to talk. I contacted Dechen, to make sure she had heard about Rinpoche's passing; she had, as had her family. Of all the stories I have about Rinpoche, this is my favorite.

Oh, and just one other thing. I used to tell Rinpoche, "I know you from another lifetime, I know it." He more or less agreed with me that we knew each other, and it was just little things that happened between us. One of his attendants, Lama Tashi, was the first person to tell me this. He said "You knew Rinpoche in another life; I know this, I know this."

And yes, I believe it in my heart, I know, because when I first saw him I said, "I know you, and I don't know why I know you." Rinpoche is always in here, always in my heart, and he is always with me.

CHRISTINE L.
Washington, DC

◆ Here is a dream image of my encounter with Shamar Rinpoche shortly after his death. Rinpoche appeared in my dream on the night of June 20, 2014. I never dream, let alone remember it! In my dream Rinpoche showed up in my house. I heard a sound and came out to meet him in the hall. He walked towards me with outstretched arms and touched my head with his hands to give me blessings. Rinpoche was wearing a loose gray and black patterned robe, and was accompanied by Lama Tashi. I went over to greet Lama Tashi, but when I looked around, Shamar Rinpoche had vanished into the distance.

This image remains vivid in my mind till today. When I shared the dream with a Dharma friend, he responded, "Thank you for sharing your thoughts and experience from your dream world. I would like to tell you what I see in what you have shared, if you like. Everything has some meaning. First, the hallway is a passage from one place to another. Second, the arms outstretched are the offering of a gift. Third, the touching would be the act of giving and receiving of the gifts. Fourth, he left, which must be his death in this life. Your dream is your life's journey. Meeting the Master, receiving the perfect teaching, and now having the tools to finish the rest of the trip home. Blessings on you."

Though I don't read much into my friend's response, it's fun to ponder. I definitely feel blessed by my connection with Rinpoche.

Harold Puneky
Lexington, Virginia

I am part of the Natural Bridge Bodhi Path Center near Lexington, Virginia, and I've been here from when the center first started, so there were lots of times that we had meditation in Rinpoche's house, in his shrine downstairs. When we came in, he was so accessible to us; it was like he was just a normal person to interact with. I can remember one time when I came in on a Sunday morning and walked into the kitchen, and Rinpoche was behind the stove cooking up some eggs. Tsering Ngodrup, the translator, who was living here, was teaching Rinpoche to cook.

He was easy to talk to—always asking questions, trying to figure out the Western mind, always asking what we thought of this, what we thought of that. I think in the early days he was looking for more ways to present the Dharma in a way we could relate to from the Western point of view, so he was constantly asking us questions to get into our minds. This was 17 or 18 years ago, before we built the meditation hall; after that, when he would come, we would leave him alone—but before that we were in his house all the time because that's where we practiced.

Whenever he would see me he would ask, "How is your practice doing?" I'd never know what to tell him, never know how to respond. I remember one time I did have an experience with a certain practice I was doing, and I thought about it and thought about it, and I finally went to talk to him about it. I'd get these preconceived ideas about what I'd think he was going to tell me about experiences like that, but he always had a way of pulling the rug out from under me that would make me think. I went to him with this one experience I'd had and he said: "Why don't you try to loosen your belt." And it just shocked me; not what I really expected him to say, you know? Just something totally off the wall. But then it made me think about how even the experiences I have are just my mind perceiving things. It made me look at how I think, how I look at things, and I realized even the little things he would do that seemed like ordinary normal things were actually a teaching. When he said that about loosening my belt, it made me think in a different way, not in a conventional way. Like I said, he'd pull the rug out from under me. It made me look at the reality of it; I was building something up in my mind, which was my own doing, my own mind making it up. Basically what he was saying was: you have to look beyond that.

And that was a really big teaching for me, because from that point I started looking at things a little bit differently. I started looking at my mind as I would do something, or say something, or react to someone—I would start to look for the motivation in my mind; I became more introspective. And I think that was probably the teaching, and it had a good effect on me. Sometimes when you look into your mind, you find out things you may not want to see, things you're afraid to find out; but it's all good, it helps you to grow.

When I was watching the videos from Rinpoche's funeral in Kathmandu, the thing that got me was the number of people from all over the world, the entire proceedings, and the respect—at that moment I realized how strong a person he was, how respected he was globally—since our experience here locally was to have such easy access to him. All we had to do was show up; he would always receive us. We would sit across from him in a relaxed way, but he was teaching us, in a very subtle setting, in a very comfortable way, in his living room, or even out in the yard or on the porch. Shamar Rinpoche had a profound effect on everyone around here, anyone who met him. I consider myself incredibly fortunate to have had him here, and to have had that kind of access to him. I know a lot of people didn't have that kind of access. It has been very precious to be here, and to have this. I think Rinpoche really enjoyed it here; he told me that he was able to do things that they wouldn't really allow him to do anywhere else. He could just be himself, and relax; we tried to make it as comfortable for him as we could.

JORDAN GANZ

◆ I've been at Shri Diwakar Vihara in India for less than a day. An exceptional opportunity to learn, mature, and share, courtesy of an exceptional teacher who encouraged just that. Shamar Rinpoche passed away three days ago, and things here are moving in full swing: phone calls, updates, airplanes, bodies. Soon, I hope, countless other practitioners will arrive on the subcontinent to pay their respect to this authentic teacher, to celebrate his kindness and remember his qualities. I'm struck by the synchronous events that bring me here during this time as well, and fondly remember a highlight of our last meeting together—advice to use during these times of great transition.

On a pleasant day in early spring, I met with Shamarpa on his back porch in Natural Bridge. He was watering flowers, and we sat down to talk. The conversation was casual, touching on a few subjects: my education and practice—going to teach the monks in India, learning more Tibetan while I was there, the future course of Buddhism in the West, the food in Lexington. During a break in the conversation, one of the numerous birds drawn by the backyard feeder perched itself on a nearby branch and stayed longer than the others. It started whistling. Rinpoche whistled back.

"Look," he said, "he's talking." A pause. It started singing again and Rinpoche returned the refrains, sometimes adding an extra verse or two; the bird responded in kind. Half joking, I asked, "What are you saying?" Rinpoche whistled at the bird again, then paused a moment. He smiled. "Relax! Enjoy yourself!" The bird whistled back and then flew away.

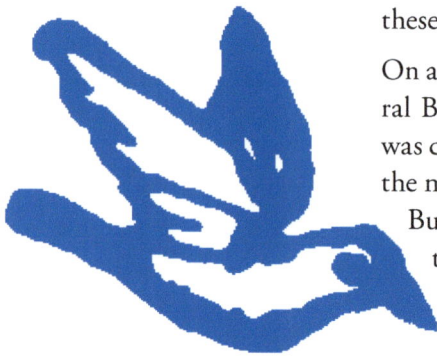

TSERING NGODUP YODSAMPA
Lexington, Massachusetts

◆ REMEMBERING THE KINDNESS OF MY TEACHER GYALWA KUNZIG SHAMARPA

"This is the Teaching of the Enlightened One."

A simple room with basic furniture, filled with misty morning light in the Himalayan foothills of Sonada, Darjeeling. Kunzig Shamarpa is sitting in the room where he receives visitors. Entering, I offer the traditional three prostrations, the gesture of respect to a high spiritual teacher from whom you seek blessings or teachings on Buddhadharma. Bowing, I hold my head down to be touched by his hand in blessing. With the light touch of his hand on the crown of my head, I feel my awareness soar into space. My critical mind is thinking, "This lama could influence your mind!" Before that thought is over, I feel my head being gently pushed down, and my forehead touches his feet, which are in the lotus posture. I realized then that he had read my mind, and that pushing my head down brought me deeper into space or the galaxy. I am dazed when Kunzig Shamarpa utters this sentence: "This is the Teaching of the Enlightened One."

I woke up from this very vivid dream early one morning in April 1983, and immediately made up my mind to accept an opportunity that had been offered to me. I had been asked to go to Germany as translator and assistant to a very humble yet highly accomplished meditation master—a unique example of a monk free from attachment to worldly concerns. Lama Tendar was selected from among many lamas to be the resident teacher of the Kamalashila Institute for Buddhist Studies and Practice. Founded by Shamarpa in the early 1980s, the Institute had such a growing Buddhist population and strong interest that its members had requested a permanent Dharma teacher. By the power of good karma and positive prayers, enhanced by equally supportive friends bonded by the same ideas and interests, I happened to get drawn into the spiritual realm of Kunzig Shamarpa, the 14th reincarnation of the Red Hat Lamas of Tibet.

The Karma Kagyu tradition of Tibetan Buddhism is 900 years old, and the Karmapa Red and Black Hat Lamas were the first among all the tulkus of the reincarnation tradition of accomplished spiritual masters of Tibetan Buddhism. Shamarpa is a revered emanation of Buddha Amitabha: Boundless Light. To be under the spiritual umbrella of Shamarpa and to have the tradition of Karma Kagyu to advance upon the spiritual path is by no means sheer coincidence, but the fruit of unwavering faith and devotion to the Three Jewels of Buddha, Dharma, and Sangha, and of the blessings of the masters of the lineage.

If I had not received this life-changing instruction in my dream the night before I was to go and meet Shamarpa in Sonada, India—where he was receiving teachings and initiations from one of the oldest and most revered Kagyu masters, Kalu

Rinpoche—I may not have benefited from the spiritual wealth grounded in my subsequent connection with Shamar Rinpoche. The transmission Rinpoche was receiving was a high initiation, and many tulkus and teachers were present. A delegation from the German Karma Kagyu group also attended, and together we planned to follow Shamar Rinpoche's instructions regarding Dharma activity for Kamalashila Institute.

This spiritual journey began on June 17, 1983 when I was picked up at the Frankfurt Airport in West Germany. Kamalashila Institute was in a small village near Bonn called Wachendorf, housed in an impressive castle. There were 14 resident members and Lama Tendar, the resident teacher. Jigme Rinpoche, the representative of Karmapa in Europe, was visiting when I arrived from Kathmandu, Nepal.

I stayed 17 years in Germany, acting as the dedicated full-time translator for lamas, khenpos, and rinpoches from all the schools of Tibetan Buddhism. In the early transmissions of Tibetan Buddhism to the West, the teachers and masters were mostly from the old world and only spoke Tibetan. Back then, other than monastics who had renounced the ordinary way of life, there were not many students who were committed to this work, yet able to withstand unfavorable economic and itinerant circumstances. I worked and studied mainly under the teachers invited by the Karma Kagyu organization, but also on certain occasions with lamas of other schools who needed a translator.

Shamarpa's kindness to me is not limited to the exposure I've had to the profoundly vast and deep Buddha-dharma; it has also protected and lifted me out of difficult times of physical illness and personal crisis. One time in particular I was critically ill and in the hospital for emergency treatment. Shamarpa was in Switzerland at that time, and I called him to tell him that I was ill. Rinpoche told me, "The lama will protect you." I felt very reassured and had no fear or worry at all. After having spoken to him, I had a significant dream, in which I was riding a very strong, gallant white horse. The horse was galloping too fast, carrying me off somewhere, when suddenly in front of me I saw Sharmar Rinpoche regally walking along, with his right hand swinging in the air at his side. In normal situations, lamas of his status don't go out alone without an attendant by their side. I was surprised and happy and was attempting to stop the horse so I could get down, thinking that it was totally disrespectful to ride a horse past your teacher. I was physically weak, the steed was strong, and the distance between my teacher and the horse was getting smaller. I used all my mental power and brought the horse to a halt, and Rinpoche, without even turning his head, spoke firmly but kindly. He said that I should tie the horse to a tree, and ordered me to sit down and be at ease on the ground in front of him. He himself sat on a bench that appeared under a tree in the middle of a nice meadow. After that dream my recovery was rapid, my mind was at peace, and I had care and love from my Dharma friends and others.

The Karma Kagyu School was going through very difficult times, and Shamarpa was facing many challenges from both outside and within the tradition over the issue of the 17th Karmapa reincarnation. I was myself going through a personal crisis of a troublesome divorce from my first wife, and my legal status in Germany was being affected. I was unhappy, even though I had the most wonderful, loving children: a daughter and a son. I didn't have any particular direction and was just waiting for the right situation to develop, when one day I received a message from a student of Shamarpa who said Rinpoche wanted to speak to me. When I called him, he was leaving for the US, but he told me to come to see him in France in two weeks when he would be returning to Dhagpo Kagyu Ling, the main European seat of Karmapa. I went to meet him, and he suggested as he had before that he would be very happy if I would go to the United States. He said he had founded his own centers in many cities—centers by the name of Bodhi Path—and that I could assist and translate for him, as well as for visiting Tibetan teachers. Bodhi Path centers were founded, directed, and guided by Shamarpa in a non-sectarian way. He had the great vision that this would bring vast benefit to those seeking the path to enlightenment.

This was exactly what I was wishing for. I had always wanted to go to the US. Many years before, I had been invited to go there as a translator, but my visa had been rejected by the US Embassy in Bonn. After this meeting with Rinpoche, the visa application and the whole process went smoothly. People I had no personal connection with contacted me at Rinpoche's suggestion, and generously assisted me with the plane tickets and financial assistance needed for the journey. Before I made the final decision, I discussed the matter with my children and their mothers, who agreed if I was happy and able to pursue my dreams, they would also be happy. It was very important for me to have that understanding with my children.

On January 17, 2000, I landed in Washington, DC and was driven to the Bodhi Path Center in Natural Bridge. It was in the middle of the woods surrounded by the Blue Ridge Mountains. I was greeted the next morning by a landscape blanketed in soft white snow; I felt it was a very welcoming sign.

During those first years in the states I traveled with Shamarpa, translating his teachings in many Bodhi Path centers across the country. Later I helped some young khenpos who were sent to these centers as teachers. Then, Rinpoche endorsed me as a Dharma teacher, and told me I have the right propensity for teaching Dharma to others. He authorized me and gave me his blessing to share my knowledge, experience, and skill in interpreting the Dharma accurately in the Western context. Since then, my bi-weekly public Dharma talks and meditation classes have steadily grown. Dharma is priceless, so I only accept voluntary donations when I teach. In this way, I feel I am offering something to others, and feel a true sense of reward.

I believe I am practicing Dharma by sharing the precious teachings with those who find it helpful. When I told Rinpoche about my experiences and their positive impact on others, he was very pleased. He suggested I now wear the attire of Kagyu Ngakpa, to represent the ancient tradition of spiritual teachers who are householders with precepts and vows.

Based on the blessings of Rinpoche, which gave me the strength and confidence to teach the Dharma, and the experiences I gained as a teacher, I became strongly inclined to pursue the vocation of chaplaincy in clinical settings. In this path, I have the privilege and direct opportunity to help in the journey of humans in their most critical and vulnerable moments of life as a spiritual friend and caregiver, and to inspire the calm presence, strength, and courage that one requires in these important moments. Since decades of Dharma study and experience do not qualify one for this setting, I completed four units of Clinical Pastoral Education training. Now I am a staff chaplain at Beth Israel Deaconess Medical Center in Boston, ministering and guiding patients and staff in the practice of meditation. Having received bodhisattva vows and studied and been inspired by the Mahayana teachings, such opportunities are prayers answered for the accumulation of virtue and positive merit.

After meeting and marrying my wife Andrea, I started to feel at home in the US. It is very insecure, in worldly terms, always being stateless as a Tibetan. Having a home and family in the US, my two older children could visit us annually during their vacations. This was such a joy and happiness for all of us to spend the summer holidays together as a family. As my wife and I wanted to have children together, we approached Rinpoche for his blessings, and he told us that there would definitely be a child in our life, and he would say prayers for us, so we should not worry. He told us Andrea would surely bear a child, and when she got pregnant we should inform him. I called him one day to share the happy news of Andrea's pregnancy, and Rinpoche told me that he was very happy, and said he had a very strong feeling that this child was special. Even though it doesn't make any difference, he was 95% sure the child would be a boy. He requested to be immediately informed when the child was born. Indeed, as Rinpoche had told us, the child was a healthy and beautiful boy. At that time Rinpoche was in Kalimpong, India, and after I told him that we had a son as he had predicted, Rinpoche said, "This boy is a tulku, a reincarnation of a bodhisattva." He said it was very auspicious; we should take very good care of the child, and in due time he would let us know more details about the reincarnation; and that the boy should be named Karma Yeshe Dorje.

When Yeshe Dorje turned 2½ years old, Rinpoche officially recognized him as the reincarnation of one of the 21 Bodhisattva masters in the Karma Kagyu tradition, from Yangpachen Monastery in Tibet. Karma Yeshe Dorje was given the official title of Goshir Karma Tenzin Choyki Nyima, the reincarnation of one of the grand abbots of Yangpachen who was endorsed by the great 5th Dalai Lama to oversee the seats of the Karmapa and Shamarpa during their physical absence in certain critical circumstances.

Yangpachen Monastery is the historical seat of the Shamarpas. From the 10th Shamarpa to the 14th Shamarpa, there was a political restriction formed by the Tibetan government that prevented the official recognition of Shamarpa tulkus.

During that time, the monastery was confiscated by the Gelugpa tradition. After the loss of Tibet to Chinese occupation, H.H. 14th Dalai Lama lifted the restriction of Shamarpa tulkus upon the request of the 16th Gyalwa Karmapa, and so the Shamar Rinpoche we all know as the 14th Shamarpa was recognized.

The great Bodhisattva Kunzig Gyalwa Shamarpa engaged in his Bodhisattva activities by reclaiming his spiritual connection to Yangpachen Monastery, and by recognizing the reincarnation of 17th Gyalwa Karmapa Thaye Dorje, in accordance with the spiritual tradition of the Karma Kagyu School in which Shamarpa tulkus are second in hierarchy. During one of our conversations regarding the Dharma in this world and the role of highly reincarnated tulkus, Shamar Rinpoche told me that their role and function is to bring the essence of the Buddha-dharma to sentient beings in this time of fast-growing population and communication. Rinpoche told me he had been able to recognize the reincarnations of a few of the high masters in his tradition, and had great hope and confidence that these tulkus would serve sentient beings as great bodhisattvas.

We discussed the upbringing of my son, and how to make sure he is properly educated in both traditions in order to bridge the East and West effectively, carrying on the blessings and system of the Karma Kagyu lineage. It is our sincere and solemn responsibility to raise our son towards that goal. With Shamarpa's blessing and inspirational prayers for all the lamas and tulkus, I have full faith that all will flourish with great glory—and there will be the great joy of meeting the 15th Shamarpa not too far in the future.

My heart, like for all those who are so deeply connected, feels the lack of the bodily presence of Shamarpa, but his spiritual presence in my life is beyond one lifetime. I feel blessed that this is an unceasing connection. It was such an honor and privilege to be among the tens of thousands of devotees in Europe and Asia who gathered from all over the world during the final ceremonies in order to pay last homage and prayers to the exhausted physical body of Rinpoche. To witness all the signs of a great Bodhisattva's passing away, such as seeing various rainbows formed beautifully across the blue skies, and especially the very auspicious dates of the Buddhist calendar coinciding with each and every stage of the funeral procedure, was very profound. These were true marks of the great being he was. For my personal comfort, I cherish the voicemail he left for me that I did not delete, and his voice calling my name and asking me to call him back keeps my special connection with him alive and fresh. It sometimes increases the pain of his passing into parinirvana, but SHAMARPA KHYENNO!!! Shamarpa Knows/Sees. I really believe so.

JACQUELINE SHIU
Hong Kong

◆ TRIBUTE TO SHAMAR RINPOCHE

I had the good fortune of growing up in Shamar Rinpoche's presence because my father started following Rinpoche when I was a toddler. There was never a moment when I felt uncomfortable with him. Every gesture was gentle—every word, every hand gesture—and nothing suggested any kind of aggression or ill will. Of course, the fact that my father was so devoted made Rinpoche very special to our family. Our relationship was gentle and casual, much like a dear uncle I would see from time to time.

Although this last lesson of impermanence has seared my heart, Rinpoche's passing has been a great blessing to me. Even the biggest of them all, the anchor of a tradition, and the mountain that everyone depended on, ceased. Then, I remember how trivial my life is; everything, every person, and every thought I hold dear, will also come to cease. It might sound depressing, but in fact understanding and remembering impermanence makes living so much easier.

Shortly after his passing, we started to hear incredible stories about people's experiences with Rinpoche. Through these accounts, together with his unspeakable blessing, I came to clearly see Rinpoche as other people have always described him. I finally understood he is the one single beacon of light in the pitch-black darkness who will guide us to salvation lifetime after lifetime, until we no longer need him. His importance is beyond concept. To me, he is an unwavering power who has sentient beings' interest at heart.

Suddenly, I felt great devotion towards Rinpoche, and great regret that I had not been more devoted when he was alive. Now this feeling of devotion is so strong and comforting, as if I finally know where home is. Reason cannot describe this feeling of devotion, as if one had just found one's biological mother. It is a type of realization! This is the huge blessing he has granted me upon his passing. I am extremely grateful that I can experience this.

Every time I heard about someone's dream of Rinpoche, I would listen with great joy because it was an affirmation that his compassion for sentient beings and his disciples would never cease, no matter what form he takes. I wished patiently that I would meet him again in my dreams, and finally I did.

My husband Eric and I were watching TV in a hotel room; the program seemed to be Tibetan local news. The news was about a man who committed serious crimes and was about to be on trial. In the next scene, we were at a square outside the courtroom where the trial was taking place. Under the cloudless sky, the square was very bright from the sunlight that shone on the white stones covering the ground and architecture. News reporters and the masses were gathered awaiting the verdict from the king. When the trial was over (the criminal was sentenced to death), people started to leave. At a distance I saw an important person, perhaps one of the judges, coming towards me in a sedan chair carried by four attendants at each corner of his seat. He called out to me happily when he saw me. I did not recognize this person with white hair and a square face until he came close enough to bump heads with me. Shamar Rinpoche would be the only person to bump heads with me like this! As soon as I recognized him I knew I was dreaming, and he had finally come to visit me! I was so happy to see him.

In the next scene, a lama brought me to Rinpoche's room, where he sat on an elevated throne situated next to the door. He was no longer the strange man with white hair, but the young 14th Shamar Rinpoche whom we all recognize. The room was cozy. There were windows on the left sidewall. It was a yellowish room with a maroon carpet. I was so happy to see him! I told Rinpoche I had missed him. He replied "But you don't miss me in the mornings." I was puzzled why he said that, but instead of asking him what he meant, I replied jokingly, "But I miss you in the afternoons!" (Don't ask me why I said this.) I went on to do prostrations immediately, as I regret not having done enough when he was alive. (His humble personality always spared us from performing gestures of worship.) At one point when I stood up from my prostrations, I saw him wearing two diamond rings on his left hand—one was a larger round diamond, the other had two smaller almond shaped diamonds. Eventually I did five prostrations instead of the intended three because my hand was somehow tangled with the mala that the lama was holding. The lama started to prostrate to Rinpoche when I finished my second prostration, and I was led to do three more prostrations with the lama.

I came closer to see Rinpoche's face as he leaned forward. He was so beautiful, with very long eyes and a pointy chin. He looked completely serene and gentle, and he wore the traditional yellow Buddhist headdress. No words were spoken but there was such comfort and familiarity being in Rinpoche's presence.

Soon I felt I was about to wake up, like a gust of wind had come to suck me out of the room. Before waking, I hastily asked Rinpoche if he had any messages for me. As I was waking up, I caught the sound of his voice, "I will be back soon." Then, I woke up to a room with soft music playing in the background, and Eric, my husband was asleep next to me. I was so grateful Rinpoche had come to visit me, I wanted to share my dream with Eric, so I turned around to wake him up. The next thing I knew I was lying in my own bed with Eric still asleep next to me (again). Then I realized the room with music was also a part of my dream. I had met Rinpoche in a dream inside a dream—just like in the movie *Inception*.

I was overjoyed to be able to say my goodbye in this dream. If our existence is a kind of mirage, then my dream is no less real than seeing Rinpoche in person.

I really look forward to meeting the next Shamarpa, to continue to follow his teaching, and to offer my assistance to him in any way possible. I know most surely that I want to live in his presence lifetime after lifetime after lifetime.

ROLANDO KLEE
Guatemala

◆ I met Rinpoche in 2008 at KIBI. But a long time before that, when I was new to Buddhism, I went along with a good friend of mine and some Mexican friends to El Salvador to a series of lectures, and coming back we were talking about Lopon Tsechu Rinpoche and how he was a living Buddha. On my way home, I made strong wishes to eventually meet a teacher that was a Buddha, because part of the lecture had talked about how great it was to have a teacher who was also a Buddha, how he could give you exactly what you needed to make advances on the path. I met Lopon Tsechu Rinpoche back in 2002, but unfortunately he passed away. Then, Hannah passed away—Hannah Nydahl—and when Hannah died I realized I had to really do something about going to find teachers, because if I didn't do anything but sit back in my country waiting for them to come, I would never meet them; I would never see them. That's why I decided to go to KIBI in 2008.

Then, I met Shamar Rinpoche, and I had a funny dream. There is a place between two mountains in Guatemala where I used to go mountain climbing, so it is a place I know well. In the dream, in the middle of these two mountains there was a kind of throne made of stone, and Rinpoche was sitting there. He gave me really funny teachings—of course nothing "real"—about how to glue plumbing pipes. That's what he was talking about! And looking back, it *was* a funny dream because in the end, the two greatest things Rinpoche told me were first of all, to loosen and get free from whatever magical views I might have; if I came to Dharma expecting something magic, I could lose track of what Dharma actually is. That was one of the first things, and I relate that to the dream. The other thing Rinpoche told me was that we might think we are special and deserve the highest teachings, and we always think we should be doing some special tantric practices … but Rinpoche always advised us all to do lojong. In the end, that's what I really need to do.

The fruit of the wish that I had when I was coming back from El Salvador in '98 was Rinpoche's teachings. He gave us enough teachings for the rest of our lives, even if he's no longer with us in his physical manifestation. As long as we keep on practicing what he advised, then we are not orphans.

Brett W. Hood
Christiansburg, Virginia

◆ I currently live in Christiansburg, but I lived in Rockbridge County, Virginia for seventeen years. I first met Rinpoche in either 1996 or '97. At that point in my life, in the mid-to-late '90s, I was definitely on a spiritual quest; I was searching very hard. I had left the religion of my youth—a form of Christianity—and every day I would pray fervently to whatever power was out there; I would list all the names that I knew. God, but I would also get down to, "Okay, I'm talking to the light, I'm talking to goodness, give me some direction, I'm searching for you." My friend Jeff Shumate and I were working on a carpentry project together, and he asked me if I'd heard of the Buddhist Center in Natural Bridge, which I hadn't at the time, and he told me there was going to be an open house. I came out; that's when I met Rinpoche. I was blown away.

It took some time to get over leftover Christian issues. It was a long time before I could prostrate, a year and a half or two years probably. Refuge was hard too, but I was able to overcome that—I would say it was because of Rinpoche's presence. But then, when I found out Rinpoche was said to be the emanation of Amitabha, the Buddha of Boundless Light, it struck a chord; like the prayer I was always offering up was answered in this way by Rinpoche.

We were very lucky here in Natural Bridge to have access to Rinpoche like we did, seeing him in small groups; it was often in very intimate, casual settings. He was also an incredible teacher—back in the early days Rinpoche taught in Tibetan and had a translator, but he could speak English, and he would talk to us afterwards. I'm assuming he didn't feel comfortable at that point trying to teach in English. But it didn't take long, even though he still had a translator with him, for him to begin teaching in English. He would turn to the translator, they would speak a little bit in Tibetan, and then the English word, and he'd be like "Yeah, that's the word I was thinking of," and he would move on.

I don't know that I can find words to do Rinpoche justice. His presence was powerful and peaceful. Opportunities would come up to have a private meeting with him, and a lot of times it would feel very daunting, like, you know, "I'm not worthy." Often I would sit in front of him, and whatever question or issue I had would just go away. I would feel like a babbling idiot. Or else it would come up, and he would say a few words about it, and I would just be like, "Duh, why'd I even ask that question?" It was always simple and straightforward. He didn't make you feel stupid, but what I'm trying to say is his answer or solution was just bright and clear.

I have two boys. My wife at the time and I met with Rinpoche and had the boys with us. We talked about what we needed to talk about; the meeting was coming to a close, and I said, "Rinpoche, may I ask, could you give a blessing to the boys?" His response was, "I did! I've done that already, but bring them here." And then he did it formally, for our benefit.

I felt bashful, shy, and unworthy around Rinpoche, but he always emitted or beamed openness and kindness to me. He wanted to cut through all of the cultural trappings of the lineage and just focus on the Dharma, particularly for us Westerners; anyway that is the take I had. He cut through my feelings of inadequacy and was always open, warm, and welcoming.

Fae Kontje-Gibbs
Martha's Vineyard, Massachusetts

◆ The first time I had an interview with Shamar Rinpoche, he listened to me for a while (I had no idea what to say to a Rinpoche or really any notion, really, of who he was… I just dove in because it was suggested that I could and I might want to… good suggestion!) and then he said "You need to practice contentment."

"Sounds nice," I thought to myself, and I didn't have a clue that it was up to me—that it had everything to do with my state of mind, not the goodies that either did or didn't come to me. Slowly, over the intervening 14 or 15 years, I've gotten clearer on how to do that, to practice contentment.

When Shamar Rinpoche died suddenly, I was sad but also very peaceful. I trusted that if he'd chosen to die at that moment, he knew what he was doing, and, as Sharon Gamsby said to me, "He wasn't attached to his physical form. He certainly wouldn't want us to be."

The night he died, I saw him in my sleep. Three or four times, I didn't exactly wake up, but I was sleepily conscious of my face being a bit pinched, folded in towards the center in a frowning way. The moment I became aware of my face, I saw Shamar Rinpoche there, smiling at me. Even remembering it, my face opens up into a smile, just as it did each time that night. When I woke up, I felt utterly blessed and gifted from the very inside out, from my feet and belly button, from behind my belly button, up. It's like Rinpoche downloaded a contentment program into my basic human computer and then activated it.

A month or so later, Rinpoche brought Thich Nhat Hanh in for reinforcements. Both of them showed up in my sleep and Shamar Rinpoche encouraged Thich Nhat Hanh to say his smile mantras to me (I've read them in books before). I woke up laughing! Funny old guys! (Actually, Rinpoche was only a year or so older than me.) Anyway, that is the long story.

The short story is that often, when I find myself creasing in to worry or anxiety or disapproval, or any kind of agitation that results in a frown, I catch it and smile instead. I don't have to figure it out. I don't have to resolve it. I just have to wake up to it, to be aware, and to choose to smile. That's it!

PETER SILS
Lexington, Virginia

◆ RINPOCHE CALLED ME ONE DAY

Rinpoche called me one day—I think it was the summer of 2005, or so—about wanting to look for a site for a Buddha pavilion near his house. The pavilion would best be built on a flat spot, so his idea was to go up into the woods on the hill next to his house to look for a place that felt right to him. Hannah Nydahl was visiting at the time, so she was enlisted in this effort as well.

We went up into the woods to look around. The undergrowth is usually pretty thick in the Virginia woods—there are lots of dead branches and thorns, as well as a thick layer of dead leaves—which makes it kind of awkward to just walk around. Rinpoche and I were up on a part of the hill that was a little bit steep, and Hannah was off in the woods, away from us. He was wearing his flip-flop sandals, footwear suitable for city life in hot countries, but completely wrong for trekking in the woods. He was about ten feet away from me when his feet went out from under him, whoosh, and he fell down right on his butt in the leaves. I ran up to him and somehow it came into my mind that this was funny, since he wasn't hurt, and I said, "It's lucky you Tibetans are short, because when you fall, you don't have far to fall!" Me—I'm a tall, rather foolish person (who had appropriate shoes), and I thought this was quite a funny (and witty!) thing to say, given the circumstances!!!

But Rinpoche didn't think so. He brushed the leaves off himself, and gave me a long-suffering look that clearly said, "And you, you are a big jerk, and I find it quite unpleasant to be in these woods with you!"

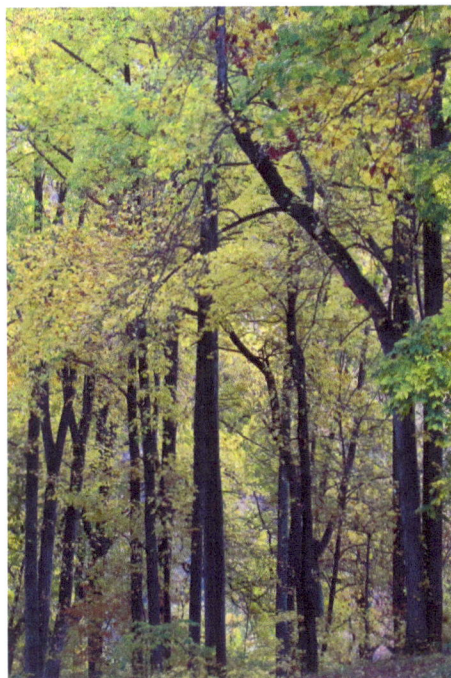

This impressed me. I remember this incident as if it happened yesterday. After that, somehow I knew that this man would tell me the truth about things.

George L. Tirado
Miami Beach, Florida

◆ I am from Miami, and I have been a member of Bodhi Path since 2011. For me, finding Bodhi Path, or Bodhi Path finding me—you never know what's what—has been a big change in my life. It's something I can't really describe, but it has been a life-changing experience. When I met the people in Miami—Marc, Chris, Nic, and Carmen—I thought they were wonderful. It was exactly what I was looking for; a group for meditation, a group that studies—studies more than anything else. I had searched out other groups, but they were not what I was looking for. Since the first day, when I went to that first meeting with Bodhi Path, I just fell in love with it, with everyone. I was so lucky and blessed when three months later they told me there was going to be a retreat in a place called Natural Bridge, in Virginia, with this super "guy" called Shamar Rinpoche. When I saw his picture, actually it scared me in the beginning. When I saw his face, it was like, "Oh my God, really?" His face was compassion. I needed to come here to Virginia, I was even dreaming about it, and was very excited to come to Natural Bridge. I didn't know what to expect about Rinpoche or my experience in Virginia, but I felt that it was my home, that everyone there was my family.

When I first saw Rinpoche in person, I froze. I just didn't know what to do, it was almost a sensation of being in front of a supernatural person. The first time he set eyes on me, I was terrified, actually. I felt like he turned some kind of scanner on me. I felt naked, like there could be no secrets with him. It was absolutely a mind-blowing experience. I wanted to hear every single word he had to say, I couldn't be distracted around him; it was hypnotic. His words made so much sense; it was incredible. When I had the chance to talk to him in person—I had all these questions—I tried to think of a smart question to ask, to be prepared, and then I asked it. He again turned his scanner on me and said "No, no, meditate, meditate." That's all he said, all the time. "No, no, no, don't worry about that, just meditate."

I left very much in peace; I wasn't upset about it not going my way or receiving the answers I was looking for. I was actually kind of released, because I didn't have to think much about anything—just drop the questions and meditate. And that's what I'm trying to do all the time. Now a year has passed. On that first retreat I took refuge with him; I could not believe that Shamarpa was the one I took refuge with—wow, that was just an amazing blessing, a really very special time in my life.

Time has passed, and I have been studying and meditating, and when I found out about his passing, it was shocking. I read it, and I needed to read it again because I thought that I had made a mistake, that it was not true, not happening. Finally, I did understand. I received a phone call at 7 a.m. from Emmy, and she told me.

I logged onto the pages and I saw all the commotion. I immediately remembered that I'd taken his picture the last instant that I saw him. He was leaving. He was in a car leaving with Chris driving. I took the picture as he was waving to me. That's when I told him, actually, that I wanted to come and do a retreat, and he told me that he would help me. Then he left, so his last words to me were "I will help you."

Wow! Amazing! And now every time I meditate I see his face right in front of me, every time I open a book to read, I see his face right there, and I have also dreamt about him a couple of times since he passed. When I saw the live stream ceremony from Kathmandu, it was amazing; I put the TV right in front of my bed. I started watching around 11 p.m., and at the beginning I was thinking, "It's late, I have to work tomorrow." But I couldn't stop; little by little I was absorbed by what was going on there, I wanted to see as much as I could, I just couldn't believe the number of people that were there, standing in those long lines for hours to pay their respects. I hadn't known that my "friend" was so important. I mean, I know he was the Shamarpa, I know he was great, but to see him here in Virginia was like you see anyone—it was informal. It was a shocking view to see all these people in Kathmandu, how they were there with their families, with their kids, doing prostrations, mountains of khatas, etc. Hours were passing by, and I could not take my eyes off the TV, and when the cremation started, I felt confused; between sadness and a certain joy. It was like, wow, he is mine forever, both through my memories and his teachings. I feel very lucky that I got to know him, that I was able to receive teachings from him, and amazingly fortunate that I took refuge with him; so in that sense I am happy and grateful.

When the smoke went up and then filled up the tent that was on top of the cremation stupa, and it spread all over, I thought, "Wow, I guess this is exactly what he was teaching," because I felt like a cycle was closed, the cycle with me and of our relationship. He is not here anymore in a human form—it is closed because it isn't about him anymore. He is not the hero of the movie of my life, although I want to think that he was, but I know that he didn't want me to think of him as a superman. When I saw all this smoke spreading around, I thought of all his teachings spreading, and how all his work will be spreading all over, and a cycle was closing. I feel, now more than ever, a sense of responsibility with his teachings, his memory, and myself—and especially with Bodhi Path. Now more than ever, I feel that it's not the end of something, but the beginning of a new time for Bodhi Path. I believe that now all the people who have had the honor and the blessing of meeting the 14th Shamarpa have the responsibility to keep on going with his vision of Bodhi Path, and I'm here for that.

◆ I had been traveling to India for my teacher H.H. Karmapa, and each year students at KIBI who recognized my love and affection for H.H. would tell me I was lucky to have another enlightened being like Karmapa in the United States. They assured me it was the same as being with "our Karmapa."

I was skeptical, but as things happen in our lineage, a friend encouraged me to go meet Shamar Rinpoche. He even offered to come along, and so we booked a flight and went to Natural Bridge, Virginia. I had no expectations other than to experience a new place and get a little Dharma to go with it. Shamarpa's teaching that year was on mind training, which I had just begun learning in a course at KIBI taught by H.H. Karmapa. I couldn't imagine that anyone could approach the depth and scope of Karmapa's teaching. Then, I met Shamarpa—the other half of H.H. The experience was so much more than I had the capacity to anticipate or fully understand. I felt he knew me right away. All that I wanted was to pour my heart out to him. His heart opened mine and I knew I had found another part of my spiritual family. Little by little, I learned how to open myself to him.

I developed a strong wish to see H.H. and Rinpoche side by side. My wish was granted the very next year when I traveled to KIBI in March for the annual teaching with H.H. The rumor was that Rinpoche was there. I spied his car a few times, but could not catch a glimpse. The last day before going home, I was sitting on the front steps of KIBI, feeling sad that I had not made enough good karma to meet Shamarpa. Then I took a chance and tried to get a last minute blessing from H.H. before I left. As I sat in the hall under the balcony of the suite that houses our beloved teachers, a door opened and H.H. stepped out. He looked at me and smiled, then entered another door and disappeared. Then, Shamarpa stepped out of the same door, smiled at me and again entered the second door. My heart leapt, and I felt that my wish had been fulfilled by their smiles alone. But then the unimaginable occurred; they both came out and together, side by side, looked down on me and gave me blessing. As if in a dream, Shamarpa came down to meet me. He offered me this remarkable opportunity, and I jumped at it. I explained that in my practice, I had experienced a heavy feeling near my heart and feared that I had done something very wrong. I feared that my heart was closed and that I would not experience love, or learn how to love, in this lifetime. He listened intently, said very little, and then gave me his blessing. Two months later, I met a man. Not just a man, but a very special being that possessed the qualities that could heal my heart and allow me to breathe for the first time. He came with me to India the next year, and Karmapa gave us the wedding blessing.

Shamarpa's blessings grow and flourish in everyone whose lives he touched. We should remain mindful of those precious times we had with him. His was truly the gift that continues to give. I wish to carry that gift throughout this life and all lives to come.

LAMA PUNTSO
Bordeaux, France

Translated by Jourdie Ross. Originally appeared on the Dhagpo Kagyu Ling Blog.

◆ NURTURING THE CONNECTION: COMMEMORATIONS OF SHAMAR RINPOCHE'S PARINIRVANA

Celebrating an anniversary is a group affair. We gather together around an event in order to nurture a shared memory. The reminder, the awareness, and the gratitude we practice individually in this way becomes collective. This is why the celebrations of the first anniversary of the parinirvana of Kunzig Shamar Rinpoche are important for all of us, Karmapa's sangha.

The departure of the manifestation of a highly realized bodhisattva like Shamarpa is a great loss for the world, for everyone. Gathering together to practice on the occasion of this anniversary is important for several reasons.

Karmapa told us several months ago, "The time of mourning has come." Commemorating a departure allows each of us to integrate the loss, and to grieve in his or her own way. But this is not the heart of the matter. The most important aspect is to generate the conditions for Shamarpa's return. We need his physical manifestation, his *tulku* (body of manifestation). Of course his activity is continual; it is much more vast than the Shamarpa we knew and wish to meet again. Nevertheless, we also need this physical support. The much-awaited manifestation of the 15th Shamar Rinpoche is also the guarantor of the continuation of the Kagyu lineage, in the same way as the Karmapa. It is their commitment as bodhisattvas for the benefit of beings to preserve the heritage of Gampopa, the lineage of Mahamudra; to preserve this jewel in its authenticity in order to make it available to as many people as possible.

For all of us, commemorating the departure of Shamarpa means generating the causes for his return, his swift return. On this occasion, at Dhagpo, we are practicing Vajrayana meditations together (Amitabha and Gyalwa Gyamtso) and particularly offering feasts (*tsok*). In addition to the blessing that these practices carry, they are the source of great merit—what Karmapa Thaye Dorje calls the life force of the mind. Furthermore, group practice of the tantras exponentially multiplies the benefit accumulated. Gendun Rinpoche often explained to us that if three of us practiced Chenrezig at the same time, but each in their own house, it was of course beneficial, but it would be vastly more so if all three got together in the same location to meditate on the detiy.

Obviously, not everyone is able to come to the Dordogne to join these celebrations. But during these two days, throughout the world where Buddhism is practiced, people inspired by the Dharma and the Kagyu lineage will gather together to assemble the causes and conditions for the return of this master teacher. One can, on this occasion, practice Chenrezig, accumulate the prayer for swift rebirth composed by Thaye Dorje, or accomplish the ritual of Amitabha, of which Shamar Rinpoche is an emanation. Each individual is welcome to offer the time that they can. Small streams make great rivers. This action will be beneficial for those who carry it out and, by the force of wishing prayers and dedication, for all beings.

When we say that the activity of highly realized bodhisattvas is inconceivable, and transcends time and space, this is not just an image. Nonetheless, this activity is subject to the openness of ordinary beings, it depends on the faith and merit accumulated by each individual. One day the Buddha and Ananda, his disciple, were walking together; they crossed paths with an old woman. Ananda asked the Buddha why he did not help her. The Buddha replied that it wouldn't do any good, as the causes for this to be possible were not present. Ananda insisted. The Buddha went towards the old woman, and turned to speak to her. She turned away. The Buddha turned to face her and spoke to her again. She turned away once more. And so on, several times. Ananda was forced to give in to the evidence; in Buddhism, there is no savior. The Buddha set forth all conceivable (and inconceivable) means to aid beings, but the path depends on each of us.

Commemorating the departure of Shamar Rinpoche is yet another opportunity for all of us to nurture the connection, to create the causes, and to bring together the conditions to once more be able to—and as quickly as possible—meet a personification of enlightened activity: the 15th Shamarpa.

ON MAHAMUDRA
BY SHAMAR RINPOCHE

Adapted from Shamar Rinpoche's forthcoming book, Boundless Wisdom.

Mahamudra is a Sanskrit word which is translated as *chakgya chenpo* (*phyag rgya chen po*) in Tibetan. *Maha* (*chenpo*) means great, in an absolute sense of being beyond compare. *Mudra* (*chakgya*) refers to buddha-nature, the wisdom of emptiness inherent in every sentient being. This *mudra* is *maha*, beyond compare. In other words, *mahamudra* expresses mind's being empty in nature, pervading every phenomenon and encompassing both samsara and nirvana. It is boundless wisdom and method inseparable from each other, the timeless clarity of mind. In Sanskrit, words and even single syllables often convey more than one meaning. *Buddha-nature* is one of several possible meanings of the word *mudra*. In the context of mahamudra, the word *mudra* takes on the meaning of the inexhaustible manifestation of absolute reality in the sense that every outer and inner phenomenon is the inseparability of appearance and emptiness. The mahamudra tradition is usually described from three perspectives: ground mudra, path mudra, and resultant mudra. In certain sutras you find other enumerations, such as the fifteen or the twenty forms of mudra, etc.; but categorizing the teachings according to ground, path, and resultant mudras fully covers every aspect of the teachings.

Ground mahamudra is the intrinsic nature of mind, and the intrinsic nature of every possible phenomenon conceived by the mind. In clarity and emptiness, the pure mind encompasses both samsara and nirvana without discrimination. Ground mahamudra is as inexpressible as it is unimaginable. Being non-conceptual, it cannot be defined, located or identified. *Path mahamudra* is the course you follow to realize beyond any doubt that every phenomenon is intrinsically empty. Emptiness here is not synonymous with the concept of hollow nothingness. A genuine understanding of emptiness cannot be attained through a habitual confused way of thinking. In the initial stages of examining the meaning of emptiness, you should keep an open mind and pay particular attention to the relevant teachings. Whatever knowledge you have acquired through the teachings should be carefully reflected upon. You should also steep yourself in reading, until a broad understanding of the subject is formed. Then you can further extend your understanding through applying *shamatha* and *vipashyana* meditations. It is only through direct personal experience in meditation that you can know beyond a doubt how emptiness is truly the intrinsic nature of everything. This entire process is called path mahamudra. *Resultant mahamudra* is none other than the realization of ground mahamudra, attained through the progressive stages of path mahamudra. When the morning haze lifts, the clear sky is perfectly visible. The clear sky is unchanging, yet as long as there is haze you don't see it. Likewise, the clarity of mind is unchanging; yet as long as delusions persist you don't see it. Once delusions are completely done away with, ground mahamudra is experienced as the unchanging clarity of the mind.

Presently, ground mahamudra is obscured. We are unable to see the true nature of mind and the true nature of every possible phenomenon conceived by the mind. In itself, however, ground mahamudra is timeless and unchanging. It is merely the perception of it that drastically changes through gradually improved understanding, until we are finally fully enlightened. In the enlightened state of mind, we will know beyond any doubt how ground mahamudra and resultant mahamudra are in fact undifferentiated. Path mahamudra refers to the process of familiarizing yourself with the nature of mind through shamatha and vipashyana meditations. Ground mahamudra, path mahamudra, and resultant mahamudra are all based in the mind and inseparable from the mind. Therefore, mahamudra is not something alien that needs to be brought home from some distant pure land—it is nothing other than the primordial purity of mind, which, in a sentient being, is called buddha-nature. It is ignorance of ground mahamudra that makes for the confused state of an ordinary sentient being. A sentient being on the advanced stages of path mahamudra is known as a bodhisattva. A sentient being who has fully realized ground mahamudra is an enlightened buddha.

Gampopa (1079-1153) presented the mahamudra teachings from three perspectives: by way of conceptual understanding; in the context of tantric practices; and as a path of direct experience. The first approach is based on the sutra teachings of the Mahayana. Through logical reflection you arrive at an intellectual understanding of mahamudra. Even though in general the term *Sutra Mahayana* has a much wider implication, in the present context, it is synonymous with logical reasoning and sutra teachings. The second path is the tantric Vajrayana. Gampopa called it the path of blessing. In this approach, you meditate on a mandala and identify yourself with a deity or a certain buddha aspect. You recite mantras and engage in yogic practices, regulating the channels of energy in the body. The third is the path of direct perception, mahamudra meditation itself. It is a practice without the support of intermediary means, resulting in a direct experience that can neither be verbally expressed nor conceptually imagined.

Another way to present this is as follows: distinctions are made as the *path of removal*, the *path of transformation*, and the *path of knowing the essence*. The path of removal is based on the intellectual understanding that the mind, in its natural state, is pure and unchanging. This natural state of mind is simply temporarily covered by adventitious stains. These obscuring mental defilements are caused by afflictions that arise out of our deluded sense that everything truly exists. In order to remove these adventitious stains, remedial means are required. In the initial stage, the object to be removed, the means of removal and the act of removal are not yet understood as illusory. They are therefore not yet understood to be non-conceptual and non-dual. The goal here is the removal of mental defilements, so that the pure mind may be seen in its natural state. A practice based on such an understanding is called the path of the *paramitas*, or the path of detachment. This is also commonly known as the *Sutra Mahayana* teachings.

The path of transformation refers to the Vajrayana, where a practitioner no longer focuses on removing mental defilements. Here, on a more advanced level of the teachings, you practice transformation. The intellectual understanding of the mind is the same as that presented in the context of the path of removal: in its natural state, the mind is pure and unchanging, and this natural state of mind is temporarily obscured by adventitious stains. Only the methods differ. The method here is a fundamental transformation of the mundane into the sublime. Thus, the body is transformed into the body of a deity. Speech is transformed into mantra. All afflictions and confusion are transformed into wisdom. Here nothing is being removed. All things, mundane as they are, are transformed into the sublime and enlightened. This human body of solid flesh and blood is transmuted into a translucent body, and is experienced as a mirage or an illusion. Understanding that this extraordinary manifestation arises out of the mind, you experience it as insubstantial and unreal, just like a dream. Appearance and emptiness are inseparable.

The path of knowing the essence is the highest level, where the practice of meditation is accomplished without having to rely on any outer support or remedial means. Neither the practice of removal nor the practice of transformation is needed to accomplish this level of meditation. Knowing the essence refers to knowing the ground, the true nature of mind. Here, on the highest of levels, a practitioner knows what the intrinsic nature of mind truly is and what the intrinsic nature of every possible phenomenon conceived by the mind truly is. In this practice the pure mind is sustained in awareness, aware of itself by observing its own true nature reflexively in a calm state. The mind is aware of its true nature in undistracted repose. This is mahamudra meditation.

To practice this path of knowing the ground, you begin by acquiring an intellectual understanding of the nature of mind. You must also be aware that the intrinsic nature of mind is not different from the intrinsic nature of every possible phenomenon conceived by the mind, that every phenomenon is an illusory experience arising out of the mind. In that sense, the mind and its experiences are undifferentiated in nature. In clarity and emptiness, the nature of mind is without identifiable attributes. The luminous mind manifests itself in inexhaustible illusory forms. Based on such an understanding of the mind and its manifestations, you experience everything in life with calm, knowing that everything that happens, good or bad, equally reflects the pure mind. This is, in fact, how an enlightened mind remains unperturbed through the turbulence of life. This is the highest and the most profound form of meditation practice that you can ever hope to know. In his *Songs of Realization*, the great mahamudra master Saraha said, "On this most exalted path of the essence, one uses the result as the method, because the beginning, the end, and what is in between are undifferentiated."

You therefore do not rely on other methods, because the fundamental nature of mind is beyond any conceptualization. This mahamudra is the quintessence of all practices, the very awareness of mind's fundamental nature. The mahamudra teachings come from the great masters Saraha and Maitripa, and are known by various terms, such as *mental non-engagement*, the *direct path*, the *quintessential approach*, *mind's luminosity*, *joining with the innate*, etc. Ever since the translator Marpa transmitted them to Tibet, these teachings have been solemnly transmitted from guru to disciple.

The sutra teachings are incorporated into the early stages as ordinary shamatha and ordinary vipashyana. With the foundation well laid, you can then enter into the supreme path of mahamudra meditation. In mahamudra meditation, the mind rests moment by moment in wakeful shamatha. The mind, directly abiding in innate emptiness and clarity, is beyond all afflictions and mental defilements. What afflictions could there be in a pure mind? What mental defilements could there be to purify? The mind in innate emptiness and clarity is beyond all conceptual thinking. What analytical skills could you use in vipashyana meditation to realize the true nature of mind? In ordinary shamatha meditation, you focus on a given support to stabilize the mind. In ordinary vipashyana meditation, you deliberately use conceptual reasoning to draw logical conclusions. These are valuable methods that belong to the Mahayana sutra teachings, also known as the *prajnaparamita* teachings. Ultimately, however, we can only rely on the true nature of mind itself to attain full realization. We have to see that every moment of the day the mind, in clarity and emptiness, actually reveals itself in absolute purity. To observe what the mind truly is moment by moment, to let the mind watch itself, gives us access to mahamudra meditation right here and now. The result of the meditation does not come from anywhere else. The true nature of mind, mind itself, has always been the result. To realize the true nature of mind through the mind is the path. To know beyond all doubts that ground mahamudra, path mahamudra, and resultant mahamudra are undifferentiated is the ultimate realization. This is the quintessence of the highest and most profound of teachings. Teachings superior to this cannot be found.

Before embarking on such an advanced form of practice, however, you should take heed of the danger that lies not in the practice itself, but in an inadequate understanding of the teachings. It is said that the immutable mind transcends all dualities, and that all things good or evil equally reflect its existence. You could easily, therefore, make the mistake of thinking that the law of karma, like everything else in life, is but an illusion and a fabrication of the mind. Thinking this way, you may believe that good and evil deeds are of little account and imagine that you are free to behave in any way you choose without suffering the consequences. Samsara, however, is very much a reality for everyone who remains ensnared in delusion. In samsara, when the causes are present, the consequences cannot be eradicated. They always come to fruition.

To support his or her students in avoiding perils on the path, a mahamudra master must have the ability to gauge the aptitude of the student. The master must be able to see whether or not the student is ready for so extraordinary a teaching. The students for their part must have complete confidence in the master to guide them safely along the path most suited to them. To ensure a correct assessment, conscientious masters are known to use clairvoyance to read the mind of a prospective student. Putting their clairvoyance to good use, adept meditators can give very helpful instructions to those in their initial stages of meditation. For the sake of clarification, let us assume that the meditation master is a buddha. As an all-knowing fully enlightened being, he or she would not have any difficulties helping others in their practice. If the meditation master were a bodhisattva on any of the ten bhumis, he or she would still not have any difficulties, because of being highly clairvoyant. If the meditation master were a meditator well advanced in practice and very close to realization, they, too, would not have any difficulties guiding others towards enlightenment, because their supernatural power of clairvoyance would be advanced enough that it would serve them adequately in helping others. However, if the meditation master had yet to reach the direct experience of realization, he or she would be less able to accurately assess the aptitude of a beginner.

The capability of different students varies. Most are suited to the gradual approach in meditation. For those who are well-suited and ready for the instantaneous mahamudra teachings, the path of knowing the essence should be taught without delay. Often in the Kagyu tradition, these teachings would be given based on the text called "Mahamudra, the Instruction Called the Four Words." For those of a less immediately high capacity, the mahamudra teachings would be gradually introduced through the ascending stages of instructions. For the gradual approach, the text used as a basis would usually be "Mahamudra, the Instruction for Uniting with Innate Wisdom." In that case, the shamatha and vipashyana teachings commonly shared by all Buddhist vehicles should first be practiced. With this foundation well laid, the students proceed with the practices specific to the mahamudra meditations; i.e., the specific shamatha and vipashyana meditations.

In the Kagyu tradition, the gradual approach of mahamudra is highly regarded. In addition to the outstanding merits of the teachings, it was blessed by the great Kagyu master Gampopa. When Gampopa gave his first teachings on gradual mahamudra, two deer came out from a nearby forest and stood by him in rapt attention. Gampopa was overjoyed. He saw it as an auspicious beginning to the gradual mahamudra teachings that would benefit countless beings, and as a sign that the teachings would prosper through future generations and bring fulfillment to countless meditators. He made the wish, as a bodhisattva, that his predictions would all come true. The compassion and blessings of a great bodhisattva ensure the fulfillment of his noble wish. Gradual mahamudra, known as the "union with innate wisdom instructions," has been flourishing ever since.

Detail, Parinirvana of the Buddha, *thangka by Nawang Zangpo.*

www.ingramcontent.com/pod-product-compliance
Lightning Source LLC
Chambersburg PA
CBHW042031090426
42811CB00016B/1802